STUDYING INDIVIDUAL DEVELOPMENT IN AN INTERINDIVIDUAL CONTEXT

A Person-Oriented Approach

Paths Through Life

A Series of Volumes edited by:
Dovid Magnusson

Magnusson • *Individual Development From an Interactive Perspective* • 1988

Stattin/Magnusson • *Pubertal Maturation in Female Development* • 1990

Gustafson/Magnusson • *Female Life Careers* • 1991

Bergman/Magnusson/El Khouri • *Studying Individual Development in an Interindividual Context* • 2003

PATHS THROUGH LIFE
Volume 4

STUDYING INDIVIDUAL DEVELOPMENT IN AN INTERINDIVIDUAL CONTEXT

A Person-Oriented Approach

LARS R. BERGMAN
DAVID MAGNUSSON
BASSAM M. EL KHOURI
Stockholm University

New York London

First Published by
Lawrence Erlbaum Associates, Inc., Publishers
10 Industrial Avenue
Mahwah, NJ 07430

Transferred to Digital Printing 2009 by Psychology Press
270 Madison Avenue, New York NY 10016
27 Church Road, Hove, East Sussex BN3 2FA

Copyright © 2003 by Lawrence Erlbaum Associates, Inc.
All rights reserved. No part of this book may be reproduced in any form, by photostat, microform, retrieval system, or any other means, without prior written permission of the publisher.

Cover design by Kathryn Houghtaling Lacey

Library of Congress Cataloging-in-Publication Data

Bergman, Lars R.
Studying individual development in an interindividual context : a person-oriented approach / Lars R. Bergman, David Magnusson, and Bassam M. El Khouri.
   p. cm. — (Paths through life ; v. 4)
Includes bibliographical references and index.
ISBN 0-8058-3129-0 (cloth : alk. paper)
ISBN 0-8058-3130-4 (pbk. : alk. paper)
1. Developmental psychology—Social aspects. I. Magnusson, David. II. El Khouri, Bassam. III. Title. IV. Series.
BF713 .B464   2002
155—dc21   2002022548
                                                                                        CIP

Publisher's Note
The publisher has gone to great lengths to ensure the quality of this reprint but points out that some imperfections in the original may be apparent.

CONTENTS

PREFACE   xi

ABOUT THE AUTHORS   xiii

Chapter 1   INTRODUCTION   1

Chapter 2   THEORETICAL FRAMEWORK   4

                1. Introduction   4
                2. A Holistic-Interactionistic Perspective   6
                3. A Modern Holistic-Interactionistic View   9
                3.1. The Role of the Holistic Perspective in Developmental Research   10
                3.1.1. Conclusion   11
                3.2. Interindividual Differences from a Holistic Perspective   11
                3.2.1. Individual Differences in the Organization of Operating Factors   12
                3.2.2. Individual Differences in Biological Timing   14
                3.3. Research Strategy Implications of a Holistic View   16
                3.4. Methodological Implications of a Holistic Perspective   17
                4. The Variable Approach   19

	4.1. Data Treatment 19
	4.2. Assumptions 20
	4.3. An Empirical Illustration 21
	4.4. Inferences to Individuals in a Variable Approach 23
	4.4.1 Conclusion 25
	5. The Person Approach 26
	5.1. Pattern Analysis 26
	5.1.1. Conclusion 27
Chapter 3	GENERAL METHODOLOGICAL CONSIDERATIONS 28
	1. Some Methodological Issues Raised by the Holistic–Interactional Research Paradigm 28
	2. Types and Typology 32
	3. The Measurement of Patterns 36
	3.1. Measurement in Standard, Variable-Oriented, Multivariate Studies in Relation to the Person Approach 36
	3.2. Patterns and Linear Transformations 37
	3.3. Multivariate Scaling for Pattern Analysis 38
	3.3.1. On the Limitations of Relative Scoring 38
	3.3.2. Quasiabsolute Scaling 41
	3.4. Measuring Change 42
	3.5. Missing Data 43
	4. An Overview of Person-Oriented Methods for Studying Individual Development 44
	4.1. Model-Based Methods 44
	4.2. Descriptive Methods 45
	4.2.1. The Cross-Sectional Perspective 46
	4.2.2. The Longitudinal Perspective 46
	4.2.3. Some Methods for Analysis of Special Aspects of Patterns 47
	4.3. The study of "Anticlasses" 50
	4.4. Variable-Oriented and Person-Oriented Methods as Complementary Approaches 50
	4.5. Some Computer Programs for Carrying Out Pattern Analyses 51
Chapter 4	CLASSIFICATION IN A PERSON-ORIENTED CONTEXT 52
	1. Introduction and Overview of the Chapter 52
	2. Similarity and Dissimilarity 54
	2.1. Measuring Proximity 55

CONTENTS vii

        3. Handling Outliers in Cluster Analysis   58
        3.1. The RESIDAN Method   59
        4. Selected Methods for Cluster Analysis:
           An Overview   60
        4.1. Hierarchical Methods   61
        4.1.1. Agglomerative Methods   62
        4.1.2. Divisive Methods   62
        4.2. Partitioning Methods   62
        4.3. Density Search Methods   63
        4.4. Some Other Methods   63
        5. Hierarchical Agglomerative Methods: Technique   63
        5.1. Algorithm   64
        5.2 Updating Dissimilarities   65
        6. Some Practical Considerations for Achieving
           a Well-Functioning Classification Using
           Cluster Analysis   67
        7. Latent Class Analysis   69
        8. Clusters, Types, and Classes   70
        9. Man as a Classifier   72

Chapter 5   ANALYZING ALL POSSIBLE PATTERNS   74

        1. Introduction to Configural Frequency Analysis   74
        2. An example of the Application of Basic Configural
           Frequency Analysis   76
        3. More About Significance Testing in CFA   79
        4. Interaction Structure Analysis Within CFA   80
        5. CFA Related to Other Methods   81
        6. A Final Look at What We Have Learned About
           the Structure in the Data in Table 5.1   82

Chapter 6   SOME METHODS FOR STUDYING PATTERN
               DEVELOPMENT   84

        1. Studying the Development of Single Individuals   84
        2. Model-Based and Descriptive Methods for Studying
           Pattern Development   85
        3. Classification-Based Methods for Studying Interindividual
           Differences in Individuals' Value Patterns Across
           Development   86
        3.1. The Direct Identification of Typical Longitudinal
           Patterns   86
        3.2. Cross-Sectional Classification Analysis Followed
           by Linking Over Time Using LICUR   88

3.2.1. The Removal of a Residue   89
3.2.2. Age-Specific Hierarchical Cluster Analyses   89
3.2.3. Relocation Cluster Analyses   90
3.2.4. Linking of Results Between Ages   90
3.3. Analyzing Sequences of Subwholes   91
3.3.1. Introduction   92
3.3.2. Outline of ISOA   92
4. Studying Pattern Development by Mapping All Possible Value Combinations   94

Chapter 7   EXAMINING THE GENERALIZABILITY OF RESULTS   96

Chapter 8   SLEIPNER, A STATISTICAL PACKAGE FOR PERSON-ORIENTED ANALYSIS   103

1. Introduction   103
1.1. Module Blocks Characterizing SLEIPNER   103
1.2. SLEIPNER, the Program   104
1.3. The Organization of the Chapter   105
2. SLEIPNER, a Workbench   105
2.1. Data Preprocessing   106
2.1.1. Data Description   106
2.1.2. Handling Missingness With Imputation   107
2.1.3. Residue Analysis   109
2.2. Classificatory Analysis   111
2.2.1. Clustering the Data   113
2.2.2. Relocating Cases in Clusters   115
2.2.3. Searching for Types and Antitypes   117
2.2.4. Using I-states as Objects of Analysis   119
2.3. Classificatory Simulation and Evaluation   121
2.3.1. Simulation Analysis   121
2.3.2. Structural Stability and Change   123
2.3.3. Individual Stability and Change   125
2.4. Special Purpose Modules in SLEIPNER   128
2.4.1. Random Samples   128
2.4.2. Artificial Data Sets   128
2.4.3. Including Classification Variables in the Data Set   128
2.4.4. Mapping the Neighborhood of a Unit   129
2.4.5. Evaluating and Comparing Partitions   129
2.4.6. Preparing a File Composed of Subindividuals   129
2.5. Concluding Remarks   132

Chapter 9	STABILITY AND CHANGE IN PATTERNS OF SCHOOL ADJUSTMENT: AN EMPIRICAL STUDY	134

    1. Introduction   134
    1.1. Theoretical Background   134
    1.2. Description of the Data Set   136
    1.2.1. Sample   136
    1.2.2. Variables   136
    1.3. Note on the Presentation of SLEIPNER Results   136
    2. Cross-Sectional Classifications of Patterns of School Adjustment Followed by Linking   138
    2.1. Introduction   138
    2.2. Preparatory Analyses   140
    2.3. Cross-Sectional Classifications   147
    2.3.1. Introduction   147
    2.3.2. Deciding the Number of Clusters   150
    2.4. Structural Stability and Change   151
    2.5. Individual Stability and Change   156
    2.5.1. Looking for Types   156
    2.5.2. Looking for Antitypes   158
    2.5.3. Exploring the remaining Cells   158
    2.6. Replicating Results on a Random Half   161
    2.6.1. Replicating the Cross-Sectional Cluster Structure   161
    2.6.2. Replicating the Cross-Sectional Classification With Regard to Individual Cluster Membership   162
    2.6.3. Replicating the Linking Over Time   164
    2.7. Testing the Results Against a Null Hypothesis of No Relationships in the Data   164
    3. Analyzing Patterns of School Adjustment Within an Age-Invariant Classification Structure   166
    3.1. Introduction   166
    3.2. Age-Invariant Cluster Structure   166
    3.3. Structural Stability and Change   166
    3.4. Individual Stability and Change   169
    3.5. Comparing ISOA States to LICUR Clusters   169
    3.6. Exploring the Remaining Cells   172
    3.7. Replicating Results on a Random Half   172
    4. Analyzing All Possible Patterns of School Adjustment and All Possible Patterns of Change   172
    4.1. Introduction   172
    4.2. CFA of Patterns of School Adjustment   173
    4.2.1. Configurations at Age 10   175

        4.2.2. Configurations at Age 13   177
    4.3. Developmental Types and Antitypes   177
    4.4. Analyzing All Patterns of Change   178
5. Summary and Discussion of Empirical Findings   180
    5.1. Summary of the Results of the Cross-Sectional Classification Analysis With Linking   180
    5.2. Structural Stability and Change   182
    5.3. Individual Stability and Change   183
    5.4. Syndromes of Bad School Adjustment   183
    5.5. Typical Patterns of Good Adjustment   186
6. Some Methodological Considerations   187

Chapter 10   DISCUSSION AND DIRECTIONS   189

1. Studying Processes   189
2. Theory-Testing and Exploration   192
3. Accurate Prediction Versus Identification of Principles and Mechanisms as the Scientific Goal in Developmental Research   193
    3.1. Understanding the Constraints of Development   195
    3.2. Searching for Types   195
4. Some Guidelines for Future Research   196

REFERENCES   199

AUTHOR INDEX   211

SUBJECT INDEX   215

PREFACE

This book is number four in the series *Paths Through Life*, edited by David Magnusson. The aim is to give a coherent introduction to the theory and method of the person approach that emanates from the holistic, interactionistic research paradigm developed by him. This paradigm is presented in detail in his 1988 book, the first in the abovementioned series. In the second and third books in the series, biological maturation and female career patterns, respectively, are studied in the framework of the holistic interactionistic paradigm and person-oriented methods are applied to some extent.

The person-oriented approach has matured considerably during the last 10 years, both theoretically and methodologically, and we have felt pressure to write a text that can serve as an introduction for the researcher who wants to carry out research in this new tradition. This short book in no way completely covers the person approach, but we hope it will be sufficient for a number of applications. For the reader who "wants more," references are given.

To obtain a broad overview of different approaches to the study of individual development that transcends disciplinary boundaries, the reader is referred to the Nobel symposium volume, *The Lifespan Development of Individuals: Behavioral, Neurobiological, and Psychological Perspectives*, published by Cambridge University Press and edited by David Magnusson. A follow-up of this book that is strongly rooted in the new developmental science, especially from the perspective of developmental psychology, is *Developmental Science and the Holistic Approach*, published by Lawrence Erlbaum Associates and edited by Lars R. Bergman, Robert Cairns, Lars-Göran Nilsson, and Lars Nystedt. A study of the two books just mentioned, together with the other books in the series *Paths Through Life*, in conjunction with studying the present volume would give the reader a good insight into the issues involved in the study of individual development from a developmental science perspective.

Lars Bergman and David Magnusson had joint responsibility for chapter 1 and chapter 10. David Magnusson wrote chapter 2. Lars Bergman wrote chapter 3 and chapters 5 through 7. Bassam El Khouri wrote chapter 4 and chapter 8. Bassam El Khouri had the main responsibility for chapter 9, with contributions from Lars Bergman.

This book has taken the efforts of many people and we especially want to thank Luki Hagen for efficient secretarial help throughout the whole process, and Cornelia Wulff for her help with the reference list and the subject index. Alexander von Eye, Magnus Sverke, András Vargha, and Margit Wångby have given us many useful comments and also tough questions that have led, we hope, to an improved presentation. In addition, many colleagues, inside and outside our department, have given us helpful comments: Ola Andersson, Christin Mellner, Eva Chinapah, Juliska Kansi, Rita Zukauskiene, and Reidar Österman.

Behind this book are many years of methodological and empirical research carried out within a number of research projects. It would not have been possible to write this book without the financial support to these research projects given by various funding agencies. Primarily involved have been the STINT foundation (main grant holder: Lars R. Bergman), the Swedish Council for the Planning and Coordination of Research (main grant holder: David Magnusson), the Swedish Council for Social Research (main grant holder: David Magnusson), the Swedish Council for Research in the Humanities and Social Sciences (main grant holder: Lars R. Bergman).

—Lars R. Bergman
—David Magnusson
—Bassam M. El Khouri
Stockholm, February 2002

ABOUT THE AUTHORS

LARS BERGMAN

Lars R. Bergman is professor of longitudinal research methodology at the Department of Psychology at Stockholm University. He currently directs the Stockholm Laboratory for Development and Adaptation, founded by David Magnusson. He holds an MA in Statistics and has been the head of the Measurement Evaluation and Development Laboratory at Statistics Sweden. His work in longitudinal research methodology is internationally recognized and he has also done considerable work relating to the study of the adjustment process. He was one of the editors of a comprehensive book on developmental science and the holistic approach, published by Lawrence Erlbaum Associates in 2000.

DAVID MAGNUSSON

David Magnusson is professor emeritus at the Department of Psychology, Stockholm University. He is an internationally highly recognized researcher who has given important contributions both with regard to theoretical issues in relation to the interactionistic research paradigm and with regard to the study of the adjustment process. He holds several honorary degrees from universities around Europe and he has been the chairman of the longitudinal network for longitudinal research in the European Science Foundation. In 1994 he organized a Nobel symposium on the life-span development of individuals, published as a book by Cambridge University Press in 1996. Together with Robert Cairns he can be considered as the founder of the new developmental science.

BASSAM EL KHOURI

Bassam M. El Khouri received his PhD from the Department of Psychology, Stockholm University. His research focuses on methods for studying classification in psychology. He also holds an MA in computer science and he is also doing research on improving computer algorithms for solving classificatory problems, partly based on computer simulation.

1
INTRODUCTION

The aim of this book is to introduce the reader to the person-oriented approach. It is hoped that the book will be complete in the sense that we present both the basic theory behind the approach, selected methods for person-oriented analysis (cross-sectional and longitudinal), a statistical package, SLEIPNER, for carrying out such analyses (including the program available on the Web), and empirical examples. Although we believe the book contains enough information to enable the careful reader to apply a person-oriented approach in her or his research, the book is by no means exhaustive. We sometimes only indicate methodological approaches other than those treated here and guide the reader to the appropriate literature.

A theoretical background to the person-oriented approach is provided in chapter 2, where its roots in the holistic, interactional paradigm are emphasized. Some basic ideas of developmental science are also presented there. A view of individual development emerges as best seen in terms of a complex dynamic system, as a process involving many interacting factors at different levels of aggregation and transcending disciplinary boundaries. After reading this chapter, it should be clear to the reader that the essence of the person-oriented approach *at the theoretical level* is the recognition of the necessity of considering the individual as far as possible as an organized whole. This theoretical perspective is usually translated *at the methodological level* into the use of person-oriented methods, designed to study individual development from the perspective of the individual as the organizing principle. Methods concentrating on patterns of information are near at hand. The idea is to treat a whole pattern of information as the indivisible unit of analysis instead of the variable, which is the usual unit of analysis. In other words, the information *Gestalt* is the focus, not the separate parts.

In chapter 3, some basic methodological issues relating to person-oriented analyses are presented. The crucial issue of how the measurements are conceptualized and collected is emphasized. It is pointed out that we concentrate on methods that use the profile of values in a set of variables as the basic unit of analysis. Different classes of methods are reviewed briefly. A special point is also made of the concept of *empty regions* in multivariate space ("white spots"), that is, permissible value combinations that for some reason do not occur. These white spots can be important to study both in a descriptive and a theory driven way.

In chapter 4, the issue of cross-sectional classification is treated and a number of cluster analysis-based procedures for cross-sectional analysis are presented. The presentation also includes a basic discussion of classification and the measurement of dissimilarity/similarity between objects. The importance of considering possible outliers, which for both theoretical and technical reasons should not be classified with the others, is highlighted, and a procedure, RESIDAN, is presented for undertaking an analysis of outliers.

The classification methods presented in chapter 4 are based on the assumption that the variables involved are reasonably continuous and can be assumed to be on an approximate interval scale. Quite another starting point is obtained if the variables are discrete, with each variable just taking one of a few values. Then it becomes possible to list and study all possible value patterns. For this purpose, configural frequency analysis (CFA) was developed. In CFA, the observed and expected frequencies of all possible value patterns are studied and a body of different methods were devised for different purposes. This versatile methodology, which is not so well-known outside Germany, is introduced in chapter 5 and discussed in relation to model-based methods like log-linear modeling (LOGLIN) and latent structure analysis (LSA).

In chapter 6, we present a few selected methods for carrying out person-oriented longitudinal statistical analyses. Longitudinal cluster analysis is presented as are CFA-based methods and latent transition analysis (LTA), which is a model-based method for the longitudinal analysis of categorical data, related to LSA. A more process-oriented method is also introduced, namely i-states as objects analysis (ISOA). This method can be especially useful for small samples and for studying short-term development. The main procedure presented in chapter 6 is LICUR. It is based on descriptive classification analysis undertaken within each time point/domain separately, which are then linked in a cross-tabulation and analyzed by exact cell-wise tests. LICUR is robust and can be used in both cross-sectional and longitudinal settings.

In chapter 7, issues of validity and reliability are discussed. Such issues are, of course, always important but even more so when classification analysis is undertaken on multivariate data. Within such a methodological approach it tends to be extremely hard to formulate "solvable" mathematical–statistical models that incorporate errors of measurement and sampling errors. Some different ways of handling these difficult issues are discussed in the chapter, including the use of "brute force" computer technology based on simulation studies (e.g., verifying that the obtained results are not only a product of the capacity of a classification method to find structure even in random data). Chapter 7 is short, and it is given the status of a chapter to emphasize the importance of taking seriously issues of validity, replicability, and reliability.

Together, the methods presented in chapters 4 through 7 make possible the application of person-oriented analyses in a variety of research settings and for variables with different scaling properties.

The SLEIPNER statistical package for carrying out person-oriented analyses is introduced in chapter 8. It is written in Fortran77 and runs on a PC. The package can be downloaded from the Net.

In chapter 9, results from empirical research are reported in which the person-oriented methods presented in this volume have been applied. It deals with children=s adjustment to school seen from the perspective of patterns of bad and good adjustment in a number of important areas, as judged by the teachers. The children are studied at age 10 and again at age 13 regarding stability and change.

Finally, in chapter 10, conclusions and guidelines for future developments are given. Hopefully, by then the ambitious reader is ready to go on to analyzing her or his own data. We firmly believe that the methods presented provide a solid basis for this if they are applied with good judgment. However, it must be recognized that person-oriented methodology is only in its first or second generation of methods and that more sophisticated procedures are likely to evolve during the next 10 years.

We warn the reader who is not already familiar with the person-oriented approach against skipping chapter 2 and chapter 3 and getting directly "down to business" by quickly learning how to carry out person-oriented analyses. It is, for instance, useful to more fully understand the argument we make that systems found in nature frequently are characterized by a few typical attractor states or optimal/critical configurations of values in the variables studied, and that these can be searched for by modern typological methods. In chapter 3, a necessary background is given with regard to the principles of the methods and essential measurement characteristics. In our experience, problems tend to arise when a researcher starting from an essentially variable-oriented, theoretical perspective tries to carry out person-oriented statistical analyses; this is discussed at some length in chapter 10.

We look forward to taking you, the reader, on this journey through the person-oriented landscape and hope that you find it as exciting as we do. We hope you will come to share our conviction that we must bring back "the person" into quantitative research and that the approach presented in this book will be helpful to achieve this purpose.

Chapter 2
THEORETICAL FRAMEWORK

1. INTRODUCTION

The focus of this volume is methodological issues in research on individual developmental processes. A necessary prerequisite for the choice of appropriate methods for treatment of data in empirical research on individual development is a strong link between the methodology applied for elucidation of the problem focused on, on one hand, and the character of the structures and processes being investigated, on the other hand. The appropriate link between phenomena under investigation and the methods applied for treatment of data implies that the statistical model must match the psychological model for the phenomena under consideration. The appropriateness and effectiveness of the statistical model applied for the study of a specific problem depends on how well the properties of the psychological model are reflected in the statistical model.

An example that illustrates the issue can be drawn from models in traditional variable oriented research for the analysis of the relation between latent aggressive dispositions in individuals, on one hand, and manifest aggressive behavior, on the other hand (Magnusson, 1976). The most frequently used statistical methods for analyses of the relations between variables in personality and developmental research would assume, in this specific case, a linear relationship between latent aggressiveness and aggressive behavior as illustrated in Fig. 2.1a. Such statistical models match and are appropriate for the study of the problem with reference to a psychological model, which assumes that the stronger the latent disposition, the stronger the manifestation in actual aggressive behavior, along the whole range of the latent disposition. The linear statistical model does not, however, match a psychodynamic model for the relation between latent aggressiveness and manifest aggressive behavior. A psychodynamic model makes the following assumption:

THEORETICAL FRAMEWORK

For low to medium aggressiveness, there is a monotonic positive relation, implying that the stronger the individual's latent disposition, the stronger his or her aggressive behavior will be. When latent aggressiveness becomes very strong, the aggressive impulses are repressed and the aggressive behavior becomes inhibited. The stronger the aggressive impulses, the stronger the defense mechanisms, and the psychological model for the relation will take the form shown in Fig. 2.1b. The conclusion, essential for our reasoning here, is that the statistical linear model is effective for elucidation of the relation between latent aggressive dispositions and manifest aggressive behavior only if the psychological model shown in Fig. 2.1a is valid, but not for the empirical analysis of data with reference to the psychological model shown in Fig. 2.1b.

Thus, in order to reach the scientific goal of empirical research, the choice of the appropriate and effective methodology in each specific case must (a) be based on careful analysis of the phenomena under investigation, and (b) made with reference to an appropriate theoretical psychological frame of reference for the phenomena.

In a recent article, Harré (2000) summarized his evaluation of the present state of the art in psychology in the following formulation that has a bearing on the discussion here:

> It has been about 30 years since the first rumblings of discontent with the state of academic psychology began to be heard. Then, as now, dissident voices were more audible in Europe than in the United States. It is a remarkable feature of mainstream academic psychology that, alone among the sciences, it should be almost wholly immune to critical appraisal as an enterprise. Methods that have long shown to be ineffective or worse are still used on a routine basis by hundreds, perhaps thousands of people. Conceptual muddles long exposed to view are evident in almost every issue of standard psychological journals. This is a curious state of affairs. New pathways and more realistic paradigms of research have been proposed, demonstrated, and ignored ...

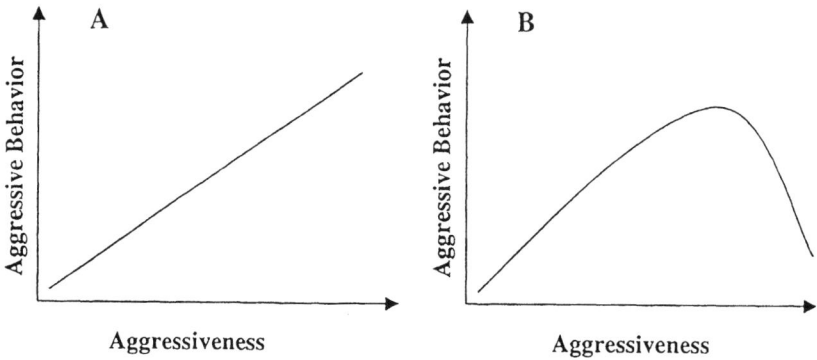

FIG. 2.1. The assumed function of actual aggressive behavior on latent aggressiveness for (a) the trait measurement model, and (b) the psychodynamic measurement model (From Magnusson, 1976).

The natural sciences have achieved their enormous success by the adoption of schemata through which the indeterminate world around us can be made to disclose some of its features. (p. 1303)

The extent to which the critical evaluation by Harré (2000) is relevant varies across psychological subdisciplines. Regardless, for us as developmentalists, there are reasons to take this critical evaluation seriously; it hits a critical point also for research in that field. Too often, developmental research is caught in the prison of piecemeal theories and/or sophisticated statistical models and methods, without the necessary reference to proper analysis of the phenomena at the appropriate level (see Cairns, 1986; Cairns & Rodkin, 1998; Magnusson, 1992, 2001; Sörensen, 1998).

The remedy of this situation is the acceptance and application of research strategies in which empirical studies on specific developmental issues are planned, implemented, and interpreted with explicit reference to an overriding, common theoretical framework. Only in this way can results from studies on specific issues contribute to the synthesis of knowledge that is necessary for real understanding of developmental processes. With reference to these propositions, the aim of this chapter is to present the main characteristics of the holistic–interactionistic perspective on individual developmental processes.

The holistic–interactionistic perspective has formed and forms the theoretical framework of the planning and implementation of studies on specific issues in the longitudinal research program, Individual Development and Adaptation (IDA), at the Stockholm Laboratory for Developmental Science. The program was initiated in 1964 by the second author of this volume, David Magnusson, and is led by the first author, Lars Bergman, since 1996. Overviews and discussions of the theoretical perspective and its research strategy implications for the program have been presented elsewhere (see, e.g., Bergman & Magnusson, 1997; Magnusson, 1985, 1988, 1995, 1998b, 1999a, 1999b, 2000; Magnusson & Allen, 1983b, Magnusson & Stattin, 1998; Stattin & Magnusson, 1996). These articles also serve as sources of relevant references on each specific issue dealt with in this chapter. (On some issues, references to these sources are given in the text.) The theoretical framework briefly summarized here has also guided the development and application of appropriate methodological tools. The methodological implications of the holistic–interactionistic perspective have been discussed at length in other connections (see Bergman, 1988a, 1988b; 1993, 1995, 1998, in press; Bergman & Magnusson, 1983, 1987, 1990; Bergman, Eklund, & Magnusson, 1991; Magnusson, 1988, 1993, 1998a; Magnusson & Allen, 1983a; Magnusson & Bergman, 1988, 1990). Chapters 3 through 10 of this volume are devoted to more detailed presentations and discussions of this issue.

2. A HOLISTIC–INTERACTIONISTIC PERSPECTIVE

The main goal of the longitudinal IDA research program is to contribute to understanding and explaining the processes underlying individual development. Two basic propositions of the theoretical approach to that goal have guided the planning and implementation of the IDA program: (1) An individual functions and develops as a total integrated organism, and (2) the individual develops as an active participant in an integrated person-environment system of higher order.

These propositions form together the main basis for the holistic view on individual functioning and development, in which the individual is the organizing principle for psychological inquiry.

The historical roots of the modern view of the individual as an integrated, undivided organism was discussed by Magnusson (1999a). In research, it is most strongly reflected in the struggle between an idiographic and a nomothetic approach and in the dispute over a clinical versus a statistical model in the study of individual differences. The holistic view reflected in typological approaches to individual differences has been and still is influential in clinical practice and psychiatric diagnoses. (The typological view is discussed in chapter 3.)

For a long time, the holistic view was considered too vague and lacking in specific content to serve as the basis for strong theories for understanding and explaining individual functioning and development. During the last 30 years, however, the holistic model has been enriched and now forms a solid scientific basis for planning, implementation, and interpretation of empirical studies on specific aspects of individual functioning and development. This situation is the result of development with respect to both content, theory, and methodology. (For an overview, see Magnusson, 1999a).

The substantive contributions come from psychological research on cognitive and noncognitive mental factors and behavior, and from biological and medical research on the functioning of the brain and the role of physiological aspects of the total functioning of individuals. A central feature of a holistic model is the integration of mental, behavioral, and biological aspects for understanding the functioning and development of the individual. The application in empirical research on individual development of an integrated, coherent, theoretical framework contributes to bridging the gap between mental, behavioral, and biological models, which has been and still is to some extent an obstacle for real scientific progress.

Important contributions to the effectiveness of a holistic model as a theoretical framework for empirical research on specific phenomena derives from the presentation of modern models for dynamic, complex processes, particularly the general systems theory (see, e.g., Thelen & Smith, 1998; Urban, 1979). In natural science disciplines, which are concerned with multidetermined stochastic processes, such as meteorology, biology, chemistry, ecology, and others, such models have had an almost revolutionary impact on both theory building and empirical research during recent decades.

Also, individual development can be described in terms of dynamic, complex processes. This makes the modern models for such processes to some extent applicable also in theory building and empirical research in psychology. Before such application is considered, it is, however, essential to have in mind that individual developmental processes are not only dynamic and complex, they are also *adaptive* (see, e.g., Lerner, 1984). The central role of potentialities and limits with respect to adaptive ability was discussed for early socialization processes by Cairns (1979), for aging processes by Baltes, Lindenberger, and Staudinger (1998), and for positive development by Magnusson and Mahoney (2002). In contrast to traditional models, often identified under the umbrella heading of contextual models, the modern holistic–interactionistic view is not restricted to the individual's adaptation to changing physical and social environmental conditions. According to the modern view, the internal, person-bound mental, behavioral, and biological factors are also involved in the ongoing individual adaptation process.

The strong role played by adaptive ability in combination with intentionality in the individual's interaction with his or her environment restricts the applicability in psychological research of the mathematical models that have been developed and applied in natural sciences. However, the general models have helped to draw attention to the following important characteristic features of a multidetermined, stochastic process that are also important for understanding the complex, dynamic, and adaptive processes of individual development.

- A basic element of the modern models is their emphasis on *processes*. Psychological research in general is mostly concerned with the relation between causal factors and outcomes. This characteristic is reflected in the most frequent designs, with the focus on the relation between predictor and criteria, and between independent and dependent variables. High prediction is regarded as an important goal of empirical research and the criterion for scientific success. The new models draw attention to the process character of the life course rather than to the outcomes of developmental processes.
- Applied in psychological research, the models also emphasize the holistic–interactionistic, integrated nature of developmental processes. The holistic principle holds for all systems of interest in research on human ontogeny, regardless of the level at which the system is operating. It holds for the mental, behavioral, and biological processes of individuals as well as for the individual as an active partner in his or her integrated person-environment system. It also holds for the environment and its subsystems, such as the peer system among youngsters or the family system. For example, the holistic perspective formed the fruitful framework for analysis and discussion of social development by Cairns (1979). Central aspects of a holistic view were discussed by Kitchener (1982) with reference to an organismic model.
- The models emphasize the holistic and interactive, often nonlinear nature of dynamic, complex processes. A central principle in the functioning and development of all living organisms is the principle of dynamic interac-

tion as emphasized by the biologist Mayr (1997). It is also a basic principle of a holistic view on individual development (Thomae, 1979). Dynamic interaction among factors involved in dynamic, complex processes is something different from and should be distinguished from statistical interaction in data within an experimental design. The models for dynamic, complex processes provide a theoretical framework for investigating and understanding the dynamic processes of interaction of operating factors within the individual, and the continuous reciprocal interaction between the individual and his or her environment in the person–environment system, within a single integrated perspective.
- Traditional developmental research is overwhelmingly focused on the study of variables and their interrelations. Emphasizing the holistic, interactive character of the processes, the modern models confirm and provide a theoretical basis for the old proposition that a particular variable's psychological significance for the functioning of an individual cannot be understood by studying it in isolation, out of its context with other, simultaneously operating variables in the individual. This proposition forms the basis for conclusions that are fundamental for planning, implementing, and interpreting of studies on specific developmental issues.

In natural sciences, the formulation of the new models has initiated a strong methodological development. For further real progress to be achieved in psychological research, it is important that, without slavishly copying these methods, we recognize this development and create methodological tools that are appropriate to the nature of the psychological phenomena that are our main concern. This implies, among other things, consideration to the important facts: (a) that developmental processes are not only dynamic and complex but also adaptive, and (b) that the individual in interaction with the environment is an intentional, active agent.

3. A MODERN HOLISTIC–INTERACTIONISTIC VIEW

From the perspective just presented, a modern holistic view emphasizes an approach to the individual as an organized whole, functioning in a dynamic adaptation process as an active element of an integrated person–environment system. At each level, the totality

> … gets its characteristic features and properties from the interaction among the elements involved, not from the effect of each isolated part on the totality.… Each aspect of the structures and processes that are operating (perceptions, plans, values, goals, motives, biological factors, conduct, etc.) takes on meaning from the role it plays in the total functioning of the individual. The whole picture has an information value beyond what is contained in the separate parts. This implies that the individual as a whole must be considered as the framework for planning, implementing and interpreting empirical research on specific aspects of individual functioning in both a current perspective and a developmental perspective. (Magnusson, 1990, p. 197)

From a developmental perspective, the functioning of an individual in a certain type of situation changes across time as a result of developmental processes in the individual and of changes in the person–environment system. Within the framework set by constitutional factors (inherited or not), mental, behavioral, and biological aspects of an individual's way of functioning change over time, as a result of biological maturation, and of learning and experience, in a broad sense. The person–environment system, of which the individual is an active element, changes also across time, partly as a result of factors in the individual's own proximal and distal environment, and partly as a result of the individual's own actions, for example, by choice of new jobs, a new partner, or moving to another place. This means that over time, the individual developmental process is driven by a nested system of mental, biological, and behavioral factors in the individual and social, cultural, and physical factors in the environment (see, e.g., Lerner, 1991; Magnusson & Stattin, 1998).

3.1. THE ROLE OF THE HOLISTIC PERSPECTIVE IN DEVELOPMENTAL RESEARCH

At first sight, the claim for a holistic perspective in psychological research may seem obvious, even trivial. Researchers have argued, even quite recently, that it is too general to serve meaningful purposes in scientific analyses of psychological phenomena. This argument demands a clarification of what a holistic model for the study of developmental processes is, and what it is not.

A holistic theoretical framework for research on individuals serves two overriding and interrelated purposes: first, it provides a common conceptual space for communication between researchers working in different subfields; second, it means that the principles and mechanisms underlying the processes that are the main target of our empirical analyses can be investigated in detail within a common theoretical framework. In natural sciences, the acceptance and application of a general model of nature has served these two purposes and have been one of the basic conditions for success in these fields.

By offering a common theoretical framework for the planning, implementation, and interpretation of empirical studies on specific aspects of individual development, a holistic model makes it possible to amalgamate results from different subfields. A *synthesis* of knowledge about different aspects of developmental processes is needed in order to overcome the fragmentation of research into subfields without integration that has hampered, and still hampers to some extent, real scientific progress (Kagan, 2000; Magnusson, 1999b).

In order to avoid misinterpretation of what we have just said, a few comments may be pertinent.

As was said earlier, the holistic view serves as the theoretical framework for planning, implementation, and interpretation of studies on specific problems. The role and functioning of a holistic model is not to offer a specific hypothesis or an explanation for all problems. In natural sciences, the Newtonian general model of nature did not answer all questions about the structure and functioning of the physical world. Furthermore, the holistic, integrated model for individual functioning and individual development does not imply that the entire system of an individual must be studied in every research endeavor. The application of a common model of nature for research in natural sciences never implied that the whole universe should be investigated in every study (Magnusson, 1998a).

3.1.1. Conclusion. Thus, in order to understand and explain the specific aspects of the processes underlying individual development, we need a general model that incorporates mental, behavioral, and biological factors in the individual, as well as social, cultural, and physical factors in the environment into one integrated, theoretical framework; that is, we need to apply a holistic model. In order to function effectively as a theoretical framework for planning, implementation, and interpretation of studies on specific developmental issues, a holistic model has to go beyond the content area of traditional, developmental psychology. An effective holistic model must build on and incorporate knowledge, not only from different subareas of developmental psychology, but also from all those disciplines that are concerned with different aspects of individual developmental processes: developmental biology, neuroscience, pharmacology, sociology, anthropology, and other related disciplines.

This conclusion has led to the establishment of a new scientific discipline, *Developmental Science*. This science is built on the basic proposition that the different elements of the integrated developmental processes form their own specific domain of content in the interface of behavioral, biological, medical, and social sciences (Cairns, 2000; Cairns, Elder, & Costello, 1996; Magnusson, 1996, 2000; Magnusson & Cairns, 1996). Effective research on issues within this domain requires its own theoretical framework, measurement models, models and methods for data treatment, and research strategies. They follow as a consequence of a holistic perspective on developmental phenomena. If taken seriously, acceptance and application of this new discipline will contribute both to more insightful formulation of problems to be empirically investigated, as well as to the application of methodological tools and research strategies that are appropriate with reference to the character of the phenomena, that is, to more solid empirical research on developmental phenomena. An obstacle to such a positive consequence of the concept of developmental science is the misunderstanding of it as a synonym for developmental psychology. As already emphasized, developmental science goes beyond traditional boundaries of psychological subdisciplines.

3.2. INTERINDIVIDUAL DIFFERENCES FROM A HOLISTIC PERSPECTIVE

A fundamental condition to be recognized in our search for generalizations about individuals is the fact that all individuals do not function and develop in the same way. This raises basic questions for developmental research: In what respects and how are individuals similar, and in what respects and how are they different? An adequate answer to these questions is a necessary condition for correct generalizations about principles and mechanisms underlying and guiding developmental processes in individuals. Two aspects of individual differences are of special interest for the choice of an appropriate research strategy and for the application of effective methodological tools in developmental research: (1) Individual differences in the organization of operating factors in a current and in a developmental perspective, respectively, and (2) individual differences in biological and psychological timing of these processes.

3.2.1. Individual Differences in the Organization of Operating Factors. In an earlier section, we claimed that the holistic view now offers a theoretical basis for planning, implementation, and interpretation of empirical studies on specific developmental issues. Within this framework, developmental processes are accessible to systematic, scientific inquiry. The basis for this proposition is that these processes are not random; they occur in a specific way within organized structures and are guided by specific psychological and biological principles (Magnusson, 1999a).

Organization is a characteristic feature of individual structures and processes at all levels; it is a characteristic of mental structures and processes, of behavior, of biological structures and processes, and of the functioning and development of the integrated individual. The circumstance that structures and processes are organized into an integrated hierarchical system is a prerequisite for the functioning of the organism as an adaptive system, currently and over time. Individual development implies continuous transformation and change in the organization of mental, behavioral, and biological structures and processes.

The process of developmental organization that takes its start at conception is guided by the principle of self-organization (see, e.g., Thelen, 1989). Self-organizing ability is a characteristic of open systems and refers to a process by which new structures emerge from existing ones. Within subsystems, the operating components organize themselves to maximize the functioning of that subsystem with respect to its purpose in the total system. At a higher level, subsystems organize themselves in order to fulfill their role in the functioning of the totality.

Within a specific system, say the cardiovascular system, each of the operating factors (e.g., systolic blood pressure, diastolic blood pressure, and heart rate) do not function and develop independently of each other. The specific role of each operating factor is determined by the role it plays in the system. The operating factors are organized and function in terms of functional configurations, in what will be referred to in the following text as *patterns*. This implies, among other things, that the important individual differences are to be found in differences in the patterning of operating factors in the system under investigation. Organization in terms of patterns is not restricted to the functioning and development of each subsystem. Also, subsystems are organized in systems of higher order, that is, subsystems function and develop interdependently. Not in a mechanistic way, but rather, as emphasized in a holistic–interactionistic perspective, in terms of processes that are effective for the functioning of the individual as an integrated organism.

Thus, the important information about an individual is in the special organization in terms of patterns of operating mental, biological, and behavioral factors at all levels of individual functioning. Within subsystems, individuals may differ in the way in which operational factors are organized and function. Individuals may also differ in the ways subsystems are organized and function. These organizations can be described in terms of patterns of operating factors within subsystems and in terms of patterns of functioning interrelated subsystems within the individual. As a consequence, for empirical developmental research, the study of developmental change in terms of person-bound patterns of relevant factors becomes a central task.

A fundamental feature of the organization of operating factors in the processes is that the number of ways in which operating factors in a certain subsystem can be organized in patterns is restricted in order to allow the subsystem to play its functional role in the totality; and the number of ways in which subsystems can be organized to form the overriding pattern for the integrated organism is also restricted (cf. Gangestad & Snyder, 1985, who argued for the existence of distinct personality types, with reference to shared sources of influence). Only a limited number of states are functional for each subsystem and for the totality.

This view implies, among other things, that complex, dynamic systems, which characterize individuals, have inherent restrictions, which implies that certain states cannot occur, so-called "white spots" (Bergman & Magnusson, 1997). Valsiner (1984) drew attention to the fact that the range of an individual's actual behavior constitutes only a fraction of what is theoretically possible. The recognition and identification of patterns occurring very seldom, or not at all, is important for understanding functional systems, sometimes even more important than finding typical, developmental sequences. What cannot occur demarcates what can occur and both aspects have to be accounted for in sound theoretical explanation of some phenomena. This in particular may be the case in research on deviant behaviors, because it is at the boundaries of what can occur that "normal" development leaves the track. Individuals may have such special configurations of values that they do not belong to any of the categories obtained in the pattern analysis. Individuals with such profiles may be of special interest in some connections (Bergman, 1988b). Cicchetti (1996) also argued that incorporating knowledge about atypical ontogenesis would enhance developmental theories, and Kagan, Snidman, & Arcus (1998) drew attention to the importance of studying individuals with extreme values. This issue will be further elaborated in chapter 3 with respect to its methodological implications.

In conclusion, the discussion in this section implies that developmental processes take place in an organized way in individuals, who function and develop as integrated organisms. In the earlier section, it was claimed that across time these processes are driven by a nested system of mental, biological, and behavioral factors in the individual and factors in the environment. These characteristics put strong challenges on empirical analyses of developmental processes.

3.2.2. Individual Differences in Biological Timing. An essential aspect of individual differences, with far-reaching implications for planning, implementation, and interpretation of empirical studies is differences in biological timing of developmental processes throughout the whole life span. Individual differences occur in this timing, within the context of the functioning of the integrated individual, with respect to somatic and morphological characteristics, to cognitive and noncognitive mental factors, to physical and mental capacity, and to general competence in handling the demands of the environment, and so forth. Some of these features are apparent and important in very early infancy; other features emerge and become essential for individual functioning later in life, in adolescence, maturity, and old age.

Differences in the rate of biological maturation among individuals of the same chronological age may have profound consequences, not only for individual differences in various aspects of functioning, but also with respect to the way the environment reacts to the individual. Such differences in developmental timing thereby influence individuals' social relationships, as well as their capacity to meet and adapt to environmental demands and to use environmental opportunities effectively. These differences become particularly striking during puberty and adolescence.

An illustration of individual differences and their consequences for the individuals and of the holistic way in which individuals function and develop is the effect of individual differences occurring among girls related to the chronological age at menarche. In the IDA program, a strong correlation was found between the age of menarche and different aspects of norm-breaking behavior among girls at the age of 14 to 15 years (Magnusson, Stattin, & Allen, 1986; Stattin & Magnusson, 1990). For example, girls maturing very early reported much stronger alcohol use than later maturing girls. Interpreted in a cross-sectional perspective, this result indicated that a group of girls at risk for antisocial development had been identified. However, at the age of 26 to 27, no systematic relation between the age of menarche and drinking at adult age was observed. But very early biological maturation had far-reaching consequences for education, family, own children, job status, and so forth. The effect could not be attributed to early maturation per se; it could be identified as the result of a net of interrelated factors, particularly the social characteristics of close friends, but also other factors linked to biological maturation, such as self-perception and self-evaluation.

Interindividual differences in growth rate have consequences for the choice of appropriate methodologies and research strategies in developmental research (see Bateson, 1978). An illustration can be drawn from the developmental curve for weight of the thymus (Magnusson, 1985). The typical growth curve is shown in Fig. 2.2 for four hypothetical individuals, A through D, who differ with respect to the

THEORETICAL FRAMEWORK 15

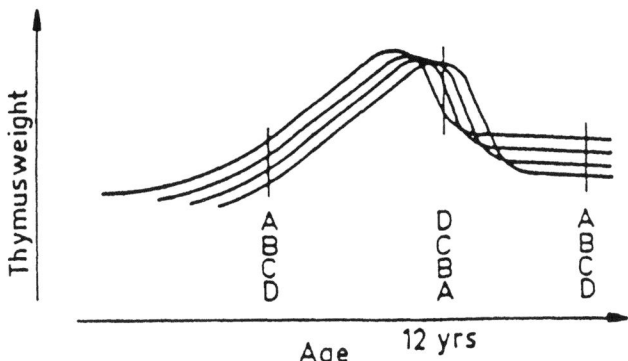

FIG. 2.2. Fictitious growth curves for four individuals, A–D, with respect to thymus weight (From Magnusson, 1988).

rate of biological maturation, as indicated by the chronological age at which the growth curve reaches its peak. (The weight of the thymus reaches its peak round 12 years of age and then declines rather rapidly to about half that weight at about 20 years of age.) For various chronological ages, Fig. 2.2 shows the rank orders of the individuals with respect to the weight of the thymus.

Thus, although the rank order of individuals with respect to thymus weight varies across ages, there is regularity and consistency in the process of growth and decline of the gland, once biological age instead of chronological age is taken as the reference variable. One implication of this fact is that any cross-sectional matrix of data for variables that reflect or are related to individual differences in biological maturation will contain a certain variance, most of the time of unknown size, which is due to such differences. The magnitude of that variance introduced in the matrix depends on the kind of variables studied and where in the developmental process the study is performed. The effect occurs, of course, independent of whether individual differences in growth rate are measured or not (Magnusson, 1993).

Thus, the existence of individual differences in growth rate for operating factors in developmental processes limits the applicability of a cross-sectional design in which chronological age is the marker of maturation. These differences may affect results to an extent that has not always been recognized and considered in research. To control for biological age instead of for chronological age is a remedy only under certain specified conditions. Biological and chronological factors are nested factors, because the expression of individual differences in growth rate is sometimes counteracted by societal rules, roles, and expectations that are bound to chronological age, such as the age for beginning and ending of compulsory school education, the age for compulsory military service in some countries, and the compulsory age for retirement.

The methodological consequences of the existence of individual differences in biological maturation are essential for dealing with developmental issues, such as the following: (a) In studies of the stability of single variables in terms of rank order stability; (b) in cross-sectional studies of the interrelations among operating person and environmental factors in a current perspective; (c) in the application of factor analysis in order to identify basic factors operating in individual development; (d) in studies of early antecedents of later stages of development, for example, in the study of the developmental background of various aspects of adult functioning. Recognizing this, researchers have asked for alternatives to the use of chronological age for the study of individual differences (cf. Baltes, 1979; Rutter, 1989; Wohlwill, 1970).

3.3. Research Strategy Implications of a Holistic View

The aforementioned reasoning leads to the conclusion that we need to formulate each specific problem in developmental processes within the framework of the integrated organism, changing over time, in order to understand and explain the processes underlying individual development. This conclusion has important consequences for research strategy in empirical developmental research.

- Individual development refers to progressive or regressive changes in the structures and/or the functioning of systems at different levels across the entire life span—from conception to death. As a consequence, a necessary research strategy implication of the process character of individual development is that individuals are observed across time, that is, the application of a longitudinal design.

  There are a number of reasons why a longitudinal design is necessary for understanding developmental processes. One is that operating factors necessarily shift over time, both with respect to which factors operate, their distinct character per se, and their significance and role in the individual's integrated interactive processes. It is only the organism that remains distinct and identifiable. Another reason is that such central issues as stability and change and causal mechanisms in individual development processes cannot be effectively investigated without observing the individual over time.

  In the definition of development just presented, two concepts are essential; *change* and *time*. Time is not the same as development but development always has a temporal dimension. Consequently, processes going on in an unchanged manner, within existing structures, do not constitute development. The implication of this reasoning is that the length of a longitudinal study and the frequency with which observations are needed cannot be decided once and for all, independent of the character of the system(s) under investigation. The frequency with which observations must be made and the length of observation period vary with the type of processes under study. For instance, understanding fetal development requires very frequent observations during a rather short period of time, whereas studying aging processes can limit the number of observations and spread them over a longer period of time.

As stressed earlier, the application of a longitudinal design, that is, following the same individual over time, is a necessity and follows logically from the view of individual development as a process. Longitudinal design is full of possible traps as demonstrated in critical analyses (see, e.g., Nesselroade & Baltes, 1984; Schaie, 1965). This implies that the proper use of a longitudinal research strategy presupposes planning and implementation with reference to careful analysis of the phenomena under study.

- A holistic model for individual development implies that mental, behavioral, and biological aspects of individual functioning, as well as social, cultural, and physical factors of the environment are incorporated into one integrated theoretical framework as formulated. It was also claimed earlier that the role of a single variable and its significance for the functioning and development of the individual is dependent on its context of other simultaneously operating factors; that is, its contribution to the understanding of the developmental processes of individuals cannot be finally investigated and understood in isolation from its context.
- Planning of empirical research on a specific issue has to cover the relevant operating factors of the system, at the appropriate level, may it be the cognitive system, the cardiovascular system, the behavioral system, the system of family relations, the integrated individual, or the person–environment system.
- As already emphasized, a developmental science approach implies that we have to go beyond what is traditionally considered developmental psychology. Important knowledge of developmental phenomena, essential for understanding the functioning and development of certain subsystems as well as of the integrated organism must also be drawn from other, neighboring disciplines in social, medical, biological, and natural sciences. The implication of this proposition is that we have to become involved in real cross-disciplinary and cross-cultural work.

3.4. Methodological Implications of a Holistic Perspective

The scientific goal of empirical developmental research is to contribute solid knowledge to understanding development processes, the psychological, biological, behavioral, and environmental factors that are involved and which principles guide the processes. What is advocated here is that research, aiming at this goal, in order to be effective has to be designed, implemented, and interpreted with reference to a common theoretical framework. The holistic–interactionistic perspective serves the purpose of such a framework.

We noted earlier that a common reaction to the claim for a holistic perspective is that it is too general to be helpful in empirical research. However, the holistic–interactionistic model does in fact place specific and important demands on the measurement models, and the methods and models for treatment of data in developmental research. These requirements have far-reaching implications for the planning, implementation, and interpretation of studies on specific issues.

A holistic theoretical framework implies that subsystems operate interdependently but often on different spatial and temporal scales and at different levels in complex, interactive, and adaptive processes; this makes the identification of operating mechanisms and underlying principles difficult. These conditions emphasize the need for careful choice and application of appropriate methodological tools in empirical research on developmental processes. However, the difficulties must not deter empirical studies on specific aspects of the processes, applying the general rules for scientific inquiry. As emphasized earlier, the processes of individual development are not random; they occur in a specific way within organized structures and are guided by specific psychological and biological principles. These circumstances make developmental processes a natural target for scientific analysis.

An analysis of the fundamental characteristics of individual development in a holistic theoretical framework leads to the conclusion that we need to apply measurement models, and models and methods for data treatment, that are more appropriate for the specific character of developmental phenomena. What further progress in empirical developmental research particularly needs is models and methods for the study of processes. In the IDA program, we have devoted much time and effort to this task. This issue will be dealt with in the following chapters.

Block (1971), as a theoretical basis for his application of the Q-sort methodology to the study of developmental issues, made a distinction between two different methodological approaches in developmental research, namely what he referred to as the *variable* and the *person approach*, respectively. As proposed by Magnusson (1999a), the basic difference between the two approaches lies in the view of a specific datum for a certain characteristic of a certain individual at the level of the *measurement model* of each of the two approaches. According to the measurement model of the variable approach, a single datum for individual A on a latent dimension k derives its psychological significance from its position on that dimension in relation to positions for other individuals, B, C, D, and so forth. According to the measurement model of the person approach, the same datum derives its psychological significance from its position on the latent dimensions k, l, m, n, and so on. These latent dimensions are assumed to represent simultaneously working factors in the system under investigation.

The difference in basic measurement models has implications for the kind of *generalizations* that can be made from results of empirical studies. Generalizations of results obtained from studies applying a variable approach refer to relations among variables, synchronically or diachronically. Using a person approach, generalizations of results from empirical studies refer to individuals in terms of characteristic patterns of operating factors at the system level under investigation. Developmentally, this type of generalization is empirically based on data reflecting stability and change in individual patterns of data from different points in time.

In this connection, we emphasize from the beginning that the variable approach and the person approach are complementary, not contradictory, in research on developmental phenomena. Both approaches are legitimate as long as they are applied with strict reference to the specific assumptions made in each of them. It is important to keep in mind that the two approaches contribute different answers to the same question. This is due to the fact that empirical research applying each of the approaches refers to basically different measurement models. The two approaches are methodologically orthogonal, not endpoints on the same methodological dimension.

The methodological implications of the variables and person approaches, respectively, have been discussed elsewhere (see, e.g., Bergman, 1988a, 1993, 1998; Bergman & Magnusson, 1991; Magnusson, 1988, 1998a). Because the rest of the volume is devoted to the implications of the person approach, this section focuses on the implications and consequences of the variable approach.

4. THE VARIABLE APPROACH

Developmental research is dominated by a variable approach. The approach is evident in many contexts, in (a) correlational studies of relations between variables in cross-sectional designs, (b) in studies of the stability of single variables over time, (c) in studies of the links between environmental factors and various aspects of individual development, and (d) in studies of the developmental background to adult functioning. Commonly used statistical models include comparisons between means, correlation, and regression analysis, and factor analysis modeling. The dominance of a variable approach is manifested in the widespread application of structural equation modeling in the search for causal relations.

4.1. Data Treatment

In a variable approach, the lawfulness of processes in individual development is studied in terms of statistical relations between variables across individuals at group level. The basis for this treatment of empirical data is a statistical model with certain specifications. A number of statistical models have been developed for different cases. The most common is the linear model, which serves as a starting point for the application of a number of statistical methods, such as Pearson correlations, multiple correlations, analysis of variance (ANOVA), and structural equation modeling. Perhaps mainly due to technical complications, nonlinear models and methods are applied much less frequently than linear models and methods.

Generally, the demand for a match between the statistical model applied in the study of a specific problem, on one hand, and the characteristics of the phenomena under study, on the other hand, is violated in developmental research using a variable approach in two interrelated ways.

1. Problems are being formulated and discussed in terms of statistical relations among variables with reference to a statistical model, but with little or no reference to an explicitly formulated view regarding the nature of the phenomena to which the data refer. Such is often the case, for example, in discussions and applications of causal models and causal relations (see, e.g., Hellvik, 1988; von Eye & Clogg, 1994).
2. The statistical models are tested with reference to data sets, the relevance of which is taken for granted without reference to the character of the real phenomena. Examples can be found in the literature on structural equation modeling (see, e.g., Bergman, 1988a, for a discussion).

4.2. Assumptions

As emphasized earlier, a necessary condition for empirical research to yield solid knowledge is that the statistical model meets the requirements of the psychological model. This proposition motivates a closer look at the assumptions that must be met for the proper use of linear regression models, which are the most frequently applied models for data in developmental research (Magnusson, 1998a):

1. Individuals can be compared on a nomothetic, continuous latent dimension in a meaningful way.
2. Individuals differ only quantitatively, not qualitatively, along the latent dimension for a certain factor.
3. Relationships among factors and their role in the totality of an individual is the same for all individuals. For example, in a multiple regression equation, each variable has the same weight for all individuals and reflects what is characteristic of the average person.
4. The interrelations among factors studied at the group level in nomothetic analyses can be used to make inferences about how the variables function within individuals.
5. The psychological significance and meaning of a certain position on the nomothetic scale should be the same, quantitatively and qualitatively, across individuals and ages.

Now the relevant question is: How compatible are these assumptions with the holistic–interactionistic model for individual development in terms of dynamic, complex, and adaptive processes? The characteristic features of developmental processes, discussed earlier in this chapter, demonstrate that the assumptions of the linear regression models are met only under very specific conditions. The goal of developmental research is to understand and explain how and why individuals develop. From this perspective, the assumption under 4 is of central importance: the assumption that the statistical linear relationship between two variables at group level can be used as a basis for conclusions about the functional relation between the same two variables within each of the individuals.

Obviously, the number and range of cases in which the linear statistical model is applicable in a relevant way is far more limited than its frequency in empirical psychological research would indicate.

4.3. An Empirical Illustration

An empirical example of a common approach to the study of a developmental problem using a linear model for analysis of data may serve as a basis for some observations. The example is drawn from a study in the IDA program of the role of early problematic behaviors among boys in the developmental processes underlying adult alcohol problems. The group being studied consisted of all boys who attended grade 6 in the school system in one community in Sweden ($N = 540$). The average age of the boys was about 12 years and 10 months. (A more comprehensive presentation of the study was given by Magnusson, Andersson, & Törestad, 1993).

With reference to a review of the relevant literature, the following possible early antecedents of later alcohol problems were chosen for analysis: *aggressiveness, motor restlessness, concentration difficulties, lack of school motivation, disharmony, peer rejections*, and *school achievement*. Each of these variables had been reported to be early indicators of later antisocial problems. Data for the first five variables were obtained by teachers' ratings, data for peer rejection were obtained by sociometric ratings, and data for *school achievement* were obtained by summing the grades in Swedish and mathematics.

Data for alcohol problems in adulthood were obtained from official records, collected from the police, the social authorities, and open and closed psychiatric care (Andersson, 1988). These data are complete for all subjects and represent the age period of 18 through 24 years of age. The information refers to arrests for public drunkenness, convictions for drunken driving, measures taken in accordance with the temperance law, and the DSMIII-R diagnosis of *alcohol abuse* and *alcohol dependence* (American Psychological Association, 1983). In total, 80 of the subjects were registered for alcohol abuse during this period.

The statistical criterion on adult alcohol problems was dichotomized, yielding two groups of males: those with and those without alcohol records.

In Table 2.1, the first column shows the coefficients of correlation for the relationship between each of the independent variables, on one hand, and the dependent variable, on the other hand, obtained as pointbiserial coefficients. Within parenthesis, the semipartial correlations are presented. Each semipartial coefficient reflects the linear relation between the variable under consideration and the criterion, when the role of the other independent variables has been partialed out from the independent variable.

TABLE 2.1

Point-Biserial Correlations and Semipartial Correlations Between the Independent Variables and the Dependent Variables (Registered Alcohol Abuse, Ages 18 to 24)

Independent Variable	Correlation	
	Point-Biserial	Semipartial
Aggressive behavior	.221	.025
Motor restlessness	.236	.036
Concentration difficulties	.262	.048
Lack of school motivation	.259	.030
Disharmony	.248	.079
School achievement	−.180	.018
Peer rejection	.055	−.049

From Magnusson, Andersson, & Törestad (1993).

As can be seen, each of the independent variables has a significant, linear relationship with the dependent variable, except one, *poor peer relations*. So far, the significant coefficients for the correlation between single, early indicators of problem behaviors and adult alcohol problems are, on the whole, in line with results from a large number of earlier studies using the same methodology.

The interesting situation appears, however, when we look at the semipartial correlations, none of them exceeds .10. This implies that data for each of the independent variables explain less than 1% of the total variance for registered alcohol abuse at adult age, when the variance common with all the other variables has been controlled for. Thus, the specific contribution of each single variable to prediction of alcohol problems at adulthood is of little, if any, use for understanding the developmental processes underlying alcohol problems at adulthood.

This empirical study is an example from a domain of developmental research in which a variable approach dominates, namely studies on early antecedents of later outcome(s). The results demonstrate some problems in application of the linear statistical model for empirical research in this and similar domains.

Statistically, the low, semipartial coefficients are only a necessary consequence of the colinearity, reflected in sometimes high intercorrelations among the variables involved in the process under investigation. Substantively, the size of the semipartial coefficients are understandable in the light of a holistic–interactionistic view. At the individual level, the variables in the analyses only reflect different aspects of the dynamic functioning of one and the same organism, functioning as a totality. This implies that many specific elements are operating jointly and simultaneously in forming individuals' functioning and malfunctioning. Thus, it is not surprising that data pertaining to one variable will also contain information about other, simultaneously operating variables, in the process. As a consequence, measures of single variables will, sometimes greatly, overestimate the unique contribution of each of them in the process of developmental change. The same conclusion holds in research on the unique role of specific aspects of the environment in developmental processes, when the independent variables in the statistical design are environmental factors. In empirical research, the risk for overestimation of "effects" is common, as a consequence of the fact that rarely more than one or a few of the variables, which together form the operating constellation of factors, are studied simultaneously.

The example also illustrates the problems connected with the fact that many, if not most, of the variables studied in empirical analyses of developmental phenomena are hypothetical constructs. This implies that each of the labels represents a fuzzy concept without clear boundaries and reflects a limited aspect of what is an integrated, complex, dynamic, and adaptive process. Hypothetical constructs of this kind, in which developmental psychology abounds, run the risk of reification, that is, being regarded as tangible, concrete and causal entities. This risk is augmented using sophisticated statistical models containing latent variables, such as structural equation modeling (see Bergman & Magnusson, 1990, for a discussion).

4.4. Inferences to Individuals in a Variable Approach

The overriding goal of empirical developmental research is to contribute knowledge about the developmental processes of individuals. Thus, the important criterion on real success is in the effectiveness with which the methodology helps us to draw inferences to individuals in the final analysis. This fundamental proposition makes it important to examine one of the basic assumptions underlying the frequent use and application of linear models in developmental research already summarized in this chapter: The interrelations among variables studied at the group level in nomothetic analyses can be used to make inferences about how the variables function within individuals. Two comments are pertinent:

1. At the level of the individual, nonlinearity, more often than linearity, is a characteristic of the relation between operating factors. For example, the effect of hormone A on the dependent hormone B is not necessarily linear. The nonlinearity in individuals' reactions across time to medical treatment, and individual differences in this respect, is another example (see, Magnusson, 1993, for a concrete illustration). The same holds true for the interaction of a single individual with his or her environment. Individuals' psychological and physiological stress reactions to increasing stimulation from the environment are often nonlinear. The inverted U-relation found between performance as well as psychological and physiological stress reactions for individuals, on one hand, and the strength of the demand

from the environment, on the other hand, is one example. The nonlinear relation in processes over situations or time between operating person-bound factors or the relation between the individual and his or her environment may also differ among individuals.
2. The results for the correlation between single problem behaviors at an early age and later alcohol problems, presented in Table 2.1, can be used as a starting point to illustrate another aspect of inferences from variable oriented studies applying a linear model to the development of individuals.

The results presented in Table 2.1 give a picture that is commonly presented in scientific journals. A large number of variable-oriented studies have reported sometimes strong relationships between single problem behaviors at an early age, assumed to be early risk factors, and adult maladjustment in terms of criminal activity and/or alcohol problems. Most of the time, these studies are concerned with one or a few of these early behaviors at a time. This circumstance formed the conditions for asking the following question: To what extent does the whole picture of pairwise correlations between conduct variables at an early age and maladjustment factors at adulthood depend on a rather limited number of persons characterized by broad syndromes of adjustment problems? The answer to this question is crucial for the correct understanding of results on single variables and of the possibility to make inferences from such studies to individual processes.

The question about the role of single variables was studied, using data for aggressiveness among boys at the age of 13 as a precursor of later criminal activity and alcohol problems (Magnusson & Bergman, 1988). The results are presented in Table 2.2. In the first step of the analysis, the relationship between ratings of aggressiveness at the age of 13 and data from official records for criminality and alcohol abuse at age 18 through 23 was studied for the whole sample by computing chi-squares for the corresponding 2 × 2 tables. The results are presented in Table 2.2a. Thus, calculated for the whole sample, there is a relatively strong significant relation in statistical terms between aggressiveness at age 13 and later criminality and alcohol abuse.

In the second step of the analyses, those boys who were rated not only as aggressive but also as characterized by at least three other of the problem behaviors, were removed from the analysis of the relation between early problem behaviors and later maladjustment. The results are presented in Table 2.2b. As can be seen from the table, the relation is insignificant for those who were aggressive but did not demonstrate severe problem behaviors in other respects. The extent to which the results presented for aggressiveness in Table 2.1 holds for other variables has to be established in further analyses.

The question being raised can now be answered: The results indicate that observed statistical relationships in a set of adjustment variables may only be an expression of the fact that a small group of individuals are characterized by a general syndrome of problems; this conclusion is valid in both a cross-sectional and in a developmental perspective.

TABLE 2.2
Longitudinal Relationship Between Aggression at Age 13 and Criminality Or Alcohol Abuse at Ages 18 to 23

			Age 18-23			
			Criminality		Alcohol Abuse	
			No	Yes	No	Yes
Age 13			$p < .001$		$p < .001$	
(a)	Aggression ® (N = 538)	Yes	383 (84.7)	69 (15.3)	405 (89.6)	47 (10.4)
		No	50 (58.1)	36 (41.9)	62 (72.1)	24 (27.9)
			n.s.		n.s.	
(b)	Aggression ® (N = 467)	Yes	373 (84.8)	67 (15.2)	395 89.8	45 10.2
		No	22 (81.5)	5 (18.5)	24 (88.9)	3 (11.1)

Note. (a)—all men (N = 538); (b)—men after removal of those belonging to severe multiproblem clusters at age 13 (N = 467). Frequencies (row-wise percentages within parenthesis). The significance of a relationship was tested using a chi-square with one df, corrected for continuity. From Magnusson & Bergman (1988).

This result has two implications. Substantively, it indicates that aggressiveness in itself, when not combined with other adjustment problems, is not a risk factor for later adjustment problems. Methodologically, it invalidates the basic assumption for the application of a linear model that results obtained at the group level are generally valid for all individuals in their developmental processes.

4.4.1. Conclusion. As emphasized earlier in this chapter in the presentation of the holistic integrated model, a basic principle in the functioning of complex, dynamic, and adaptive developmental processes is the principle of interaction among operating factors. A limiting implication of the application of linear regression models and in interpretation of results from such studies, such as the coefficients in Table 2.1, is the fact that they do not consider the existence of interactions. To a certain extent interactions can be handled within for example, structural modeling, but these possibilities are limited.

There is nothing wrong with any statistical model. The specific properties and assumptions of a statistical model are clear and cannot be disputed. The problem arises when it is applied for the study of phenomena that do not meet the basic assumptions of the psychological model. This discussion shows that the match between the linear statistical model and the psychological model is weak in many cases where the statistical model is frequently applied. Thus, effective developmental research needs complementary ways for treatment of data.

5. THE PERSON APPROACH

The person approach is a theoretical concept at the level of phenomena, at the system level. It forms the theoretical basis for an approach to methodological issues, which is complementary to the variable approach in developmental research.

The basic motive for the application of a person approach for the study of developmental issues is the holistic–interactionistic theoretical framework has been presented earlier in this chapter: It is individuals, not variables, that develop. Referring to the holistic, interactionistic framework, Magnusson and Allen (1983a) summarized the essence of the person approach in the following formulation: "The person oriented approach to research (in contrast to the variable centered approach) takes a holistic and dynamic view; the person is conceptualized as an integrated totality rather than as a summation of variables" (p. 372). In planning, implementing, and interpreting empirical studies in IDA, the person approach has played a central role as the theoretical background for discussions of research strategies and models and methods for treatment of data that are compatible with the nature of the phenomena being studied.

The distinction between the variable approach and the person approach concerns both concepts, methodological implications, and research strategy. Neither need be nor can be proved by statistical tests. Even if a variable oriented approach would provide a stronger prediction in statistical terms of adult behavior from certain measures of childhood behavior than that provided by a person-oriented approach, the latter might still contribute to a better understanding of the processes of individual development, as emphasized by Magnusson & Bergman (1990). The appropriate criterion for the choice of approach in a specific case is the extent to which each of the two approaches contribute to useful answers to meaningful questions about developmental processes.

5.1. Pattern Analysis

As already emphasized, the person approach is a theoretical perspective. It reflects a holistic-interactionistic view on individual development. In operationalization, it forms the theoretical basis for the application of empirical analysis of patterns of data for operating factors as a methodological tool for the study of individual developmental processes and of interindividual differences in these respects, as discussed. The theoretical analyses presented earlier in this chapter imply that individuals can be conceptualized, for each studied system, as belonging to different categories, each with its characteristic properties. In terms of data, each category can be described by a characteristic pattern of values for the variables that are relevant for the study of the problem under consideration. Individuals can be categorized into subgroups or sub-subgroups, on the basis of pattern similarity.

That individuals can be categorized on their specific patterns of values for relevant variables and followed over time in this respect was advocated by Magnusson, Dunér, and Zetterblom (1975) in connection with the presentation of the first empirical study using that approach. This study was concerned with the patterns of normbreaking behaviors among teenagers (pp. 113–118). Since then a comprehensive program has been devoted to the development and application of more modern methods for analysis of characteristic patterns of relevant variables as reflected in the following chapters of this volume.

5.1.1. Conclusion. From the perspective discussed in this section, the task for empirical research on individual functioning and development in terms of patterns is, in each specific case, fourfold: (1) to decide the level of the system under consideration, (2) to identify possible operating factors in the system under consideration, that is, the variables that have to be considered in the particular pattern, (3) to identify the ways in which these factors are organized, that is, the actual working patterns, and (4) to identify the operating mechanisms and the psychological and biological principles underlying developmental processes. So far the overwhelming number of studies on developmental issues has been devoted to the second task, the search for possible operating variables. A challenge for the future is to apply a research strategy that satisfies all four needs with reference to the holistic–interactionistic perspective.

Within the IDA-program, much effort has been devoted to develop and apply a coherent system of (a) a general integrated holistic model for understanding and explaining individual development; (b) a person approach as the theoretical basis for the application of pattern analysis; (c) appropriate methodological tools for the study of individuals, with an emphasis on methods for pattern analysis; and (d) data collected with reference to the overriding theoretical model for individual development. The general theoretical perspective and its application for the study of developmental issues have been presented in the first three volumes of this series. The following chapters of this volume are devoted to the presentation of recent developments of methodological tools for the study of developmental issues with reference to the perspective of a person approach.

Chapter 3
GENERAL METHODOLOGICAL CONSIDERATIONS

In this chapter, a general methodological overview and discussion is given as background to the more technical chapters to follow. In reading this chapter, the knowledgeable reader will discover that certain important methods are omitted or just mentioned briefly while other methods, especially those that are oriented toward presenting classifications, are treated at greater length. This, of course, reflects our own agenda and the demand to keep this introductory book short. It should not be regarded as passing judgment on these omitted methods; a number of which can also be quite useful within our person-oriented framework.

1. SOME METHODOLOGICAL ISSUES RAISED BY THE HOLISTIC–INTERACTIONAL RESEARCH PARADIGM

We learned about the holistic–interactionistic paradigm and the theoretical foundation of a person-oriented approach in chapter 2. We also learned that one way of viewing development is through the framework provided by the study of complex dynamic models. It was emphasized that, from this perspective, the usefulness of a standard, variable-oriented approach, based on a linear model can be more limited than is usually believed. Such an approach can be difficult to reconcile with an acceptance of the following assumptions that we believe hold in a number of research contexts:

1. The model for the relationships between different factors need not apply to every studied individual.
2. Linear relations are frequently not very useful approximations of relations that hold in reality; nonlinear relationships and interactions, even higher order interactions, often exist.

3. The variable values characterizing an individual can have their most salient meaning as parts of configurations and patterns, rather than by themselves.

These assumptions have been taken in a modified form from Bergman and Magnusson (1991, 1997) and have also been discussed in chapter 2. If propositions 1 through 3 are accepted, the implications are there for the choice of research strategy and method. For instance, theoretical formulations in terms of theoretical constructs as separate units influencing each other (often symbolized by a diagram with boxes and arrows) can be misleading. It can imply a denial of the three assumptions just presented, at least in common methodological translations.

Take the case of an application of structural equation modeling (SEM) in which the variance–covariance matrix provides the input data for the modeling. In this way, all interactions and nonlinear relationships not captured by this input matrix are disregarded, which can lead to serious errors. A major problem is then that the procedure is not self-correcting because the fit of the model is normally tested against the correlation matrix. Hence, a perfect fit of the model can be obtained but the model may still not represent the essential features of the "real" data as represented by the persons in a variables data matrix (see, Bergman, 1988a, for a demonstration of this). In addition, in many applications of SEM the same linear model is assumed to hold for everyone, which violates assumptions 1 and 2 just mentioned. In fairness, it should be said that certain newer formulations within the SEM tradition are better aligned to the three mentioned assumptions; for instance, handling certain types of interactions and nonlinearity and allowing for individual parameters in growth curves and dynamic relationships. For an overview, see Cudeck, Du Troit, and Sörbom (2001).

From the perspective presented, one would like to see increased research efforts that use methodological approaches other than the application of standard variable oriented methods. Here, different avenues are open, such as the five approaches presented now:

1. *The study of single individuals, using statistical methods and based on intensive longitudinal data.* A forceful advocate of this approach is Nesselroade (Nesselroade & Ford, 1985). For this purpose, for instance, *p*-technique and multiple time-series analysis (Schmitz, 1987) could be used. This approach offers a way of understanding the developmental process of a single individual without contaminating intra- and interindividual variation (Nesselroade & Ghisletta, 2000). This contamination largely goes unnoticed when applying ordinary methods for interindividual analysis on a sample of persons. In fact, what is there seen as interindividual variation can in part be "caused by" intraindividual variation. To give an extreme example: In a study of intelligence and personality, IQ and depression are measured on the same day. One person is temporarily in a very depressed mode due to a tragic loss just incurred and for this reason also performs very badly

on the intelligence test. This person will tend to increase the standard deviations of the intelligence and depression variables and also to increase the correlation between intelligence and depression due to his or her intraindividual variation. Of course, when using a *p*-technique and focusing on intraindividual variation, generalizing the results over individuals is not unproblematic; a problem that in certain situations can be handled by approach 2 described now.

2. *The study of latent growth curve models, allowing for individual differences in the parameters of the model.* In this way, development in the form of individual trajectories in different variables can be modeled in a way that offers a rapprochement of results pertaining to the intra- and interindividual domains. A number of new methods is now emerging within this area emanating from the SEM tradition (see, e.g., McArdle & Epstein, 1987; B. Muthén & L. Muthén, 2000). Curran and Bollen (2001) combined the latent growth curve modeling approach with the autoregressive model to achieve a more flexible modeling. Another approach is taken within the HLM tradition as discussed by Raudenbush (2001).

3. *The use of mathematical models taken from the study of nonlinear dynamic systems (NOLIDS).* Such models open up the possibility of getting closer to the *motor of change* than one usually does with ordinary statistical models. In contrast to these models, which tend to have a static focus on modeling status at different points in time, NOLIDS emphasizes the modeling of the change process using differential or difference equations. Models for complex dynamic systems within the natural sciences have resulted in the development of powerful new tools for their analysis. These tools include nonlinear mathematics, data simulation methods, the study of patterns, chaos theory, and catastrophe theory. It is important that the behavioral sciences make full use of the opportunities offered by NOLIDS because, appropriately applied, they also have implications for theory and empirical research within our domain (Barton, 1994; Vallacher & Nowak, 1994). Interest in applying NOLIDS in the study of individual development is also increasing (e.g., Smith & Thelen, 1993).

A word of caution here. As pointed out in chapter 2, the differences must be recognized between the molecular systems where NOLIDS so far have been successfully applied and the systems regulating individual development at a more molar level, which are the focus here (see Kelso, 2000, for an insightful discussion). Nevertheless, many of the ideas and concepts of NOLIDS are of key interest even if they, in many cases, will be restricted to be only conceptual tools and no actual mathematical modeling is carried out. Like with approach 1, one also has here the problem of generalizing from the single individual to a population and of how to study interindividual differences.

4. *Theoretical work on the "science of science" aspects of theory, mathematical/ statistical modeling, and estimation methods*, as exemplified by

the work of Casti (1989) and Valsiner (1984). For instance, what are the requirements for a model of a phenomenon if the model is to be compatible with certain propositions made within the holistic-interactionistic framework? This is a complex issue and it is discussed, for instance, in Bergman (2002). He outlines a number of considerations, which are relevant when choosing a method that mirrors a developmental process.

5. *Focusing on information as a Gestalt by using a person approach* as indicated in chapter 2. From this perspective, the study of typical configurations of values is relevant. The assumption of emerging types is suggested by analogies to system theoretic thinking; normally, only a small number of states are in some sense optimal and lead to a stable behavior of the system. For instance, in biological systems, often distinct types are found (e.g., of species, ecotypes; see Colinvaux, 1980). Within psychology, a similar point has been made by Block (1971) talking about "... 'system designs' with more enduring properties" (p. 110) and by Gangestad and Snyder (1985), arguing for the existence of distinct types, each sharing a common source of influence.

It is this fifth approach—the person approach—that is expounded in the present volume with the aim of explaining interindividual differences. Many of the methods presented can, of course, be used for analyzing objects other than individuals in a pattern-oriented way. For instance, the variable is regarded as the object with the different individuals' values of the variable as the profile of interest. In this way, as an alternative to conventional factor analysis, a classification of variables could be undertaken, based on the similarities between the different variables' profiles of values over individuals. In another setting, the school class could be the object of interest that is measured in a number of variables, and so on. However, in the following we only present methods in the context of a person approach with the individual as the object of interest.

To summarize the person approach in relation to a variable-oriented approach: Sometimes reality may not be continuous and rather operates to produce more or less discrete types. It may be that specific configurations of system states (i.e., value patterns that can characterize the system at a specific point in time) are in some way optimal and therefore become stable and frequently observed. Using pattern-based methods can be a more direct way of finding these important types of states than is obtained using variable-based methods.

The search for typical configurations or patterns receives some support from the study of complex systems. An important aspect of NOLIDS is the Janus-faced emphasis on typical attractor states on one hand, and the emergence of chaos on the other hand. Roughly speaking, it could be argued that if similar attractor states apply to different individuals, these might show up as frequently occurring typical value profiles, provided that the studied variables cover the essential aspects of the system under study. Or to say it differently: Certain states of the system are in some way optimal and therefore become stable attractor states, which has the effect that they are frequently observed. From this perspective, person-oriented methods like the ones presented here may be more natural than variable-oriented methods in certain settings.

In the following, an overview is given of methodological issues concerning the study of individual development from an interindividual perspective within the person approach perspective just presented. Because the concept of *type* is central, we begin with a discussion of how it is defined in the present context.

2. TYPES AND TYPOLOGY

The words *type* and *typology* have caused confusion and even resentment within psychology. In fact, Cattell (1957) discussed no less than 45 meanings of the concept *type* in psychology. The concepts are also used with varying meanings within other sciences such as sociology and biology. The reader is referred to Bailey (1994) and Blashfield (1980) for overviews. Waller and Meehl (1998) made a number of careful distinctions with regard to type and typology, preferring the use of the terms *taxon* for, roughly speaking, a "meaningful" type and *taxometrics* as a generic name for (their) procedures for finding taxa. In the following, a brief discussion is given of the typology and type concepts to clarify how these concepts are defined here and used by us.

By a typology, we mean here a set of class descriptions that is of some general or theoretical use for dividing persons into different classes for a specific purpose. In this book, we consider only mutually exclusive and nonoverlapping classes, although we recognize that in some settings, overlapping classes can be highly relevant (Wiener-Ehrlich, 1981). If an empirical classification, for instance, the clusters resulting from a cluster analysis of a sample of individuals, fulfills the mentioned condition, the clusters indicate a typology. Then it is not the clusters and their members per se that constitute the typology but rather the generic properties of these clusters. Each cluster is then a type. A type is sometimes referred to as a "natural cluster." Often, but not necessarily, the properties of a type are stated in terms of a profile of values in the studied variables. For instance, the cluster centroids (i.e., profiles of means for the variables in the clusters) for a set of natural clusters would be one way of presenting the types that constitute a typology.

To give an example, Bergman and Magnusson (1991) studied patterns of boys' extrinsic (≈ externalizing) problems at age 13 in which the scores on "problem load" in six different problems constituted an individual's profile. A cluster analysis of the boys' profiles of values in the six variables was then undertaken from which eight clusters emerged. For instance, one of the clusters was labeled *conduct problems*, and the boys belonging to this cluster were characterized by all of the following problems: *aggression, motor restlessness, lack of concentration,* and *low school motivation.*

They did not have either of the two remaining problems. (That is, the cluster centroid had high mean scores for the four first mentioned problems and low scores for the last two problems.) This cluster, and a number of others, were found at both age 10 and 13 and in two different samples of boys as well as for girls. At least partly, the eight clusters can be said to indicate a typology of extrinsic adjustment problems and the conduct problems cluster to indicate a type within this typology.

An empirical classification is characterized by two properties:

1. The general characteristics of the classes or clusters emerging in terms of their typical characteristics. Usually one looks at the cluster centroids but sometimes differences between the clusters/classes in external variables may be highly informative. For instance, in the aforementioned example of establishing a typology of extrinsic adjustment problems, differences between clusters with regard to later outcomes is an important aspect of the validation process.
2. The allocation of individual members to the different classes or clusters. This is usually achieved directly as a product of the quantitative analysis. For instance, in a cluster analysis, the main result is a classification of the individuals. Another way of assigning class membership is to have a defined procedure for assigning persons to classes (often constructed from analyzing an initial sample) and then apply this procedure to another sample of persons. For instance, the cluster centroids resulting from a cluster analysis of a large initial "reference" sample are used in the following way: For each person in a new sample, measured by the same variables, the similarity of his or her value profile to each cluster centroid is measured and the person is assigned membership in the cluster to which he or she is most similar.

It is the first property that most directly relates to the issue of typology and type. Allocating the sample members to the "right" cluster in the presence of sampling error and errors of measurement tends to be a more difficult task than identifying "true" centroids, which is what is needed to establish a typology. Hence, it may be easier to demonstrate the existence of a typology than, for instance, to pursue research linking individual types, based on the typology, to other external variables. In the first case only number 1 needs to be involved (albeit for more than one sample) but in the second case, it may be necessary to also properly assign individuals to types (both number 1 and number 2) in order to carry out the study.

A typology can either be hierarchical or nonhierarchical. The usefulness of a hierarchical typology should be noted. It permits an overview, because the researcher can move down the classification tree to a more global level, and it permits looking at a more detailed picture by moving up the classification tree. A class at a lower level usually includes several classes at a higher level. This means that the interpretation of the classes at a specific level can be extended by comparing the results to those obtained at a more detailed level and to those obtained at a less detailed level. This flexibility is an advantage when compared to many other methods. For instance, in standard factor analysis, no comparable property holds for comparing factor solutions with different numbers of factors. A thorough analysis of the meaning of a hierarchic classification and how it is to be secured and validated deserves more attention from researchers within developmental science than they so far have received. Here we can learn much from biology, where this issue has been extensively studied.

It is important to realize that many different types of approaches are possible for generating a typology besides cluster analysis of dimensional data (i.e., cluster analysis of profiles of values in the variables of interest). Other important approaches are:

1. Classification analyses based on (dis)similarities between persons obtained by other methods than comparison of two individuals' values in a variable profile. For instance, raters evaluate the similarity between each pair of persons in the relevant aspects, and the average of their ratings is used in a matrix of similarity between all pairs of persons. This matrix is then used as the input data in a cluster analysis.
2. Raters sort people directly into classes based on subjective information available for each subject.
3. By making all variables discrete so that each takes just a few different values, all possible pattern combinations can be studied and (unexpectedly) frequently occurring value combinations will then give information about types. This is done in, for instance, configural frequency analysis (CFA), which is presented in chapter 5. From a CFA perspective, Krauth (1985) emphasized the importance of identifying combinations of variable values that emerge above chance level. His line of reasoning started from the CFA framework in which each observed frequency was compared to the expected frequency computed from the marginal frequencies of the variable values that made up the pattern. He pointed out that this is an objective method for identifying types when analyzing value patterns for discrete variables. Without denying the usefulness of this approach to type identification, it has limitations as a general procedure for identifying types. From Krauth's (1985) perspective, the interpretation of a frequently observed value pattern which is not a type in the sense of a significantly overfrequented cell in a CFA analysis is that it is not a "real type," because the observed frequency could be predicted by the marginal frequencies. From his position, you say that the marginal frequencies are *given* entities not to be explained or accounted for. But one could argue that the process under study both produces the marginal frequencies and the cell frequencies and that, from this perspective, any replicable, very frequent value combination deserves to be called a type.

4. The typology is theoretically derived. (To be considered as saying something about reality and not just as a conceptual tool, the typology, or at least aspects of it, then needs to be followed by empirical verification.) For instance, based on Weber's (1947) thinking about the type concept of bureaucracy, Udy (1959) constructed a 16-cell typology based on the absence/presence of each of four key characteristics (see Bailey, 1994). Bailey also pointed to the importance of considering the ideal type, which normally is nonexistent in the empirical world but is useful in that it shows a theoretically derived type in its purest form, like one might choose a perfect coin in mint condition as a reference exemplar, although in the empirical world, all coins of that type in circulation are less than perfect.

Regardless of approach, it is, of course, important to carry out a study of the validity and generalizability of a proposed typology, whether it is based on theoretical considerations, empirical classification, or on both. These issues are discussed in chapter 7.

We now discuss two frequent lines of criticism against a typological approach:

1. The first line of criticism is the argument that a typological representation of k-dimensional data for n individuals is an oversimplification of the available information as compared to the representation given by a dimensional system of reference, treating the k variables as separate pieces and instead analyzing the $k \times n$ data matrix (e.g., Anastasi, 1968; Ekman, 1951, 1952). This criticism can be relevant in a case where the typological information is created directly, for instance, by ratings by a clinical observer as in the old typologies. Then no dimensional data ever exist and the purported loss or distortion created by the typological approach is difficult to evaluate. However, in modern typological analyses based on dimensional data, the truthfulness of a representation of the multivariate data by a classification can be measured and other methods applied for comparative purposes. Besides, the demand for a faithful representation of the essential features of the basic data should also be directed against results from using common variable-oriented methods, as discussed before in relation to the overreliance one sometimes has on the correlation matrix as containing all necessary information.

2. The second line of criticism says that a typology claims to represent individuals as being fixed or unchangeable, which goes against well-established knowledge about the plasticity of human development. This is to put up a "straw man." By typology, we mean the following: Although a certain degree of stability and generality is implied, the primary interest is in the changing typologies during development and the changing type membership of the individual during his/her development. We are interested in both stability and change and there is nothing fixed or innate in a typology.

What has just been said in number 2 brings the issue of a longitudinal typology into focus. Based on the preceding discussion, it is seen that a longitudinal typology could be one or several of the following:

1. Developmental types arrived at theoretically.
2. A set of empirically derived cross-sectional typologies, covering different ages.
3. A typology, empirically based on a genuinely longitudinal analysis. The quantitative analysis could then be carried out either by directly studying and classifying the complete multivariate trajectories of the individuals or by first undertaking cross-sectional classifications, which then are linked longitudinally for the individuals.

We mainly discuss the third kind in later sections of this volume. For further perspectives and empirical examples concerning typologies, see Asendorpf (2000), Bergman (2000), Block (1971), Eysenck (1953), Gustafson & Ritzer (1995), Krauth (1985), Misiak and Sexton (1966), Pulkkinen, Männikö and Nurmi (2000). See also Robins, John, and Caspi's (1998) discussion of basic personality types.

3. THE MEASUREMENT OF PATTERNS

An *individual value pattern* consists of the values in the variables constituting the pattern. This pattern is the basic unit of analysis and interpretation in many types of person-oriented analyses. For instance, it is used for calculating the degree of dissimilarity between all pairs of individuals that form the basic information in many types of cluster analysis used for grouping people. A number of aspects of measurement are discussed from this pattern-oriented perspective.

3.1. Measurement in Standard, Variable-Oriented, Multivariate Studies in Relation to the Person Approach

It is very common in the behavioral sciences to undertake studies involving many variables measured for a sample of persons. Very frequently, different variables are measured in different ways and considerable efforts are made to secure that valid and reliable measurements are obtained. It is often seen as desirable to have all variables on approximate interval scales so that powerful statistical methods can be used that demand variables of this type. Often the scales for the different variables are dissimilar and not really comparable (for instance, intellectual performance, as measured by the total score on the DBA test and socioeconomic status [SES] for a child as measured by the father's level of education and status of vocation, represented by one of seven ordinal SES groups). These differences in scaling are usually not seen as a major problem because the main function of each scale/variable is (a) to indicate the relative standing of the individuals in the sample, and (b) to indicate approximately the size of the differences between the different individuals' values in the variable. Stevens' (1946) classification system of measurements into four levels (nominal, ordinal, interval, and ratio) with their respective admissible quantitative operations usually provides the theoretical measurement framework but often a fairly relaxed attitude is held with regard to the necessity of assumption (b) to be valid. However, Stevens' system has been subjected to discussion and criticism, both with regard to the implications for the choice of statistical method (Townsend & Ashby, 1984) and with regard to the usefulness of Stevens's four categories of measurement (Velleman & Wilkinson, 1993).

This brief sketch of how some aspects of measurement frequently are regarded in a variable-oriented context was given to provide some background to the following conclusion: In a variable-oriented context when a multivariate study is carried out, frequently the variables are scaled one by one and made comparable to each other, either by means of linear transformations to a common scale (e.g., z scores are constructed) or by using a statistical method whose results are invariant to linear transformations of the involved variables (e.g., computing correlation coefficients). This is the measurement heritage we tend to bring along when studying patterns but it can be a treacherous heritage. In a person-oriented perspective, it is the pattern as a whole that carries the information, not the parts regarded separately. This means that the different parts of the profile must be comparable. Two ways of accomplishing this are (a) bringing all variables to the same scale by linear transformations, or (b) constructing the measurements of all the variables in a coherent multivariate measurement procedure, which ensures that they are comparable. If possible, this is the preferred approach. Both (a) and (b) are discussed now.

3.2. Patterns and Linear Transformations

It was pointed out that for many standard variable-based methods, the results do not depend on whether one or another type of scaling of an involved variable is used, as long as the scales are linearly related. In other words, the results are invariant under linear transformations of the involved variables. However, when undertaking a pattern analysis, the situation is usually less favorable. For instance, in a cluster analysis, a similarity or dissimilarity matrix is analyzed. Measures of (dis)similarity are normally not invariant under linear transformations. If the standard deviation of one or more of the variables constituting the individual value pattern is changed, normally the measure of (dis)similarity changes. This holds for the most frequently used measure, namely the averaged squared Euclidean distance (see chapter 4 for a presentation of different coefficients of (dis)similarity).

Perhaps surprisingly, this lack of invariance also holds when the correlation coefficient is the measure of similarity. It is even sensitive to changes in the means of the involved variables. On the surface, this may seem wrong because it is well known that the correlation coefficient is invariant under linear transformations of the involved variables. However, if such transformations are done in the present context, it would mean separate linear transformations of the values in different variables for a person who is treated as a variable in this case. In other words, the correlation coefficient as a measure of similarity is calculated for each pair of persons by considering them as the two variables and the variables as the cases. Hence, if an "original" variable is linearly transformed, this means in terms of the similarity coefficient that for one case (i.e., one original variable, now regarded as an object in the calculation of the person correlations), the values are linearly transformed. To this the correlation coefficient is not invariant.

So a decision to standardize or not standardize the variables can considerably change the results that will be obtained. Normally, when variables are used that have different types of "natural" scales and ranges of variation, standardization should be undertaken. If that is not done, what typically happens is that the variable with the largest standard deviation will tend to "dominate" the profile and, for instance, decide the resulting classification from a cluster analysis based on the profiles to a larger extent than the other variables.

However, in some cases, an essential function of the patterns may be to capture differences in scatter and level for the different variables at a given point in time and for the same variable measured at different points in time (Bergman & Magnusson, 1997). In such situations, a standardization should not be undertaken. Instead some procedure for multivariate scaling should be used, which is discussed in the next section.

3.3. Multivariate Scaling for Pattern Analysis

3.3.1. On the Limitations of Relative Scoring. From a person-oriented perspective, issues of multivariate measurement have been given insufficient attention when studying individual development in a multivariate sense. The sensitivity of the results of a pattern analysis to the scaling of the variables was also pointed out. As already indicated, variable-based methods are often applied, the results from which do not depend on whether one or another type of scaling is used—as long as the scales are linearly related. Examples are the frequent use of correlation techniques and many applications of structural equation modeling. Sometimes this invariance to linear transformations is desirable but the limitations on the generalizability of the results should be spelled out. To give an example: If adjustment problems are studied using such an "invariance approach," one has to assume that it is unimportant for the study that different adjustment problems are differently common in the sample and/or that the same adjustment problem measured at different ages may have a different frequency. To make this point more concrete, consider the following example:

As parts of a study of typical patterns of intrinsic (i.e., internalizing) adjustment problems, Bergman and Magnusson (1984a, 1984b) studied five different adjustment problems characterizing each of 466 girls, studied at the age of 10: *feelings of low peer status, low self-esteem, doesn't like schoolwork, doesn't like school generally,* and *psychosomatic reactions.* For the sake of brevity, the scaling is discussed for only the last two variables. *Doesn't like school generally* was composed of six items from a pupils' questionnaire and was identified by factor analysis. Each item had three or four scale steps with 1 indicating the positive extreme for that item and the highest score indicating the negative extreme. For example, the first item was "Do you think school is fun?" with the response alternative, *always,* coded 1, *often,* coded 2, *occasionally,* coded 3, and *never,* coded 4. First, an index, *doesn't like school generally* was formed by summing the scores on the six items. The theoretically possible minimum and maximum values are 6 and 20, respectively. The frequency distribution of this index is indicated in Table 3.1 together with the corresponding quasiabsolute scores (explained below).

All psychosomatic items were scored 1–4, with 1 indicating an absence of psychosomatic reactions of the type asked for in the item. For instance, the first item was, "Do you have a headache in the morning before you go to school?," with the same response alternatives as given in the example above. Also for Psychosomatic Reactions, an index was formed by summation of scores (three items were included). The theoretically possible minimum and maximum values were 3 and 12, respectively. The frequency distribution of this index is indicated in Table 3.2 together with the corresponding z scores and quasiabsolute scores (explained below).

TABLE 3.1
Frequency Distribution of Raw Scores and Quasiabsolute Scores for the Index, *Doesn't Like School Generally**

Raw score	Corresponding z score	Corresponding quasiabsolute score	Relative frequency in percent
6-7	−1.78 − −1.27	0	15.7
8-9	−.76 − −.25	0	37.0
10-11	.26 − .77	0	34.7
12-13	1.29 − 1.80	1	9.7
14-15	2.31 − 2.82	2	2.6
16-17	3.32 − 3.84	3	.2
18-19	4.35 − 4.85	3	.2
20	5.36	3	.0
Total			100.0

*$n = 466$, $M = 9.49$, $sd = 1.96$.

Note. The analyses made in Table 3.1 and Table 3.2 are complementary to those made by Bergman and Magnusson (1984a, 1984b) and are based on a slightly different sample (complete data demanded and no imputation performed).

For the moment ignoring the quasiabsolute scores, a number of conclusions relevant to the issue of multivariate measurement can be drawn from looking at Table 3.1 and Table 3.2. First it can be seen in Table 3.1 that the vast majority of girls really endorse statements indicating that they are positive or at least neutral in their attitudes about school. Only the 3% with a score of 14 or higher can be said to be clearly negative because 13 is the score obtained if answering on the average, neutral. However, 12.7% of the girls obtain a z score larger than one standard deviation above the mean, which would be regarded by many as indicating a negative view of school in that respect. Among these 12.7%, the majority were girls who did not express a negative attitude to school. Small interindividual differences that probably have no psychological significance and could easily have been created by response sets or errors of measurement are here "blown up" by the z transformation. We also see, due to the non-normality of the distribution (it is positively skewed), that unusual but not extremely rare raw scores are given very high z values.

Now, looking at Table 3.2, it is seen that a depressingly high percentage of the girls (48.6%) have a score of five or higher in the index, with 5 indicating that they either experience one symptom frequently or two symptoms more occasionally, and a higher score indicating more severe psychosomatic symptoms. However, the z score corresponding to five is only .27, which by many would not be seen as indicative of a problem. A comparison between the z scores for the two indices also shows that the same z score only means the same for the two variables in a very narrow sense and, if the "real" meaning of the variable scores are considered, the z scores cannot be used for comparing values between variables. Please note that the principal conclusion about the inability of a standardized scale to offer a panacea

TABLE 3.2
Frequency Distribution of Raw Scores and Quasiabsolute Scores for the Index, Psychosomatic Reactions*

Raw score	Corresponding z Score	Corresponding Quasiabsolute Score	Relative Frequency
3	−1.11	0	29.4
4	−.42	0	21.9
5	.27	1	18.9
6	.96	2	23.4
7	1.65	3	3.0
8	2.33	3	2.1
9	3.02	3	.4
10	3.71	3	.6
11-12	4.40 – 5.09	3	.2
Total			100.00

*$n = 466$, $M = 4.61$, $sd = 1.45$

for making scores for different variables comparable applies even if the two indices were normally distributed, which they are not here. To ensure comparability, often some other type of scaling is needed that enables one to make meaningful comparisons where some kind of absolute meaning of the raw scores is taken into account. One such approach is discussed now under the heading of Quasiabsolute Scaling.

3.3.2. Quasiabsolute Scaling. To recapitulate: In certain situations, one may not want to assume linear invariance of the involved variables and prefer a multivariate scaling of all the involved variables so that the values compared between variables and times of measurement retain a more absolute meaning than is accomplished by standardized scores computed separately for each variable and measurement occasion. When one wants to take this extra meaning into account, many standard statistical methods cannot be used because they make no use of this extra meaning. For instance, the results of a standard correlation analysis are the same whether z scores or raw scores are the input to the analysis.

The issue of multivariate measurement was discussed by Bergman and Magnusson (1987, 1991) in relation to the measurement and classification of profiles of adjustment problems studied longitudinally. For their purpose they constructed a *quasiabsolute scaling procedure* applied to all variables at all measurement occasions. They did not claim that the scaling provided absolute prevalences of the involved adjustment problems (hence "quasi"). They intended, within the constraints of their study, to obtain profiles of adjustment problems that contained relevant information about the prevalence of different problems between variables and measurement occasions, using a comparable tally for all variables.

Raw information about each adjustment problem (sometimes from more than one data source) was used in the quasi-absolute scaling and transformed into a four-step scale with the following scale values:

0 = no problem
1 = tendency to problem
2 = presence of problem
3 = pronounced problem

The aim of the study was only to discriminate in the negative end of the adjustment spectrum for reasons explained by Bergman and Magnusson (1991). The procedure by which the quasiabsolute scaling was done involves both a subjective component, using independent raters, to give each datum of raw information its appropriate weight and a mechanical, objective set of rules based on these weights for computing the quasiabsolute scores based on the raw data. The outcome of such a procedure is illustrated in Table 3.1 and Table 3.2 and for details the reader is referred to Bergman and Magnusson (1984a, 1984b). For instance, one conclusion based on the results of Table 3.1 and Table 3.2 is that, within the framework provided by their scaling procedure, psychosomatic problems were much more frequent for the 10-year-old girls than were problems with not liking school. In the pattern analyses that were carried out, the quasiabsolute scaling procedure was applied to all variables to provide a ground for comparing values in the different variables by presenting them in the profile in a common metric derived from the theoretical perspective we had. This perspective included the view that different problems could be differently frequent at a given age and the same problem could be differently frequent at different ages and that this must be reflected in the scaling of the variables. This state of affairs is reflected by a quasiabsolute scaling procedure but not by an ordinary standardization procedure.

3.4. Measuring Change

Consider first the case of a single variable. It is well known that the measurement of change can lead to problems, both with regard to reliability and validity (Bergman, 1972; Harris, 1963; Werts & Linn, 1970). Within the framework of classical test theory, a change score can be written as follows:

Change score = true change score + error change score

Assume that the observed scores are standardized to z scores separately at each of the two time points. We then have further:

The variance of the true change score = the sum of the variances of the true scores at the two time points minus two times the covariance of the two true scores.

We then have each true variance equal to the reliability (because the reliability can be expressed as the ratio between the true variance and the total variance, and the total variance is 1.0 due to the standardization).

Because usually the same variable measured at two occasions is highly correlated with itself, the variance of the true change score will tend to be quite small. Because the error scores at the two time points are assumed to be independent, the variance of the error change score will be twice the variance of the error score at one time point. Hence, for a change score, more of the total variance is usually error variance than for a score referring to a specific time point. The reliability of a change score tends therefore to be considerably lower (see Lord, 1963). In order to have a high reliability of the change score, it is necessary that the correlation between the two time points is low. But if this is the case, one might start to wonder whether really the same thing is measured at the two points in time. This creates what Bereiter (1963) called the "unreliability-invalidity dilemma" (p. 4).

Here we have presented an outline of a complex problem, which also includes the interpretation of regression effects and implications for relating change to other variables. It is beyond the scope of this chapter to dwell more on this point and the interested reader is referred to the previously mentioned sources and to Rogosa and Willett (1985). For the purposes of this book, we only want to draw the following conclusion: If the variables under study contain measurement errors (which usually is the case), the formulation of a pattern of change scores in the variables of interest is a questionable strategy. The strong influence of errors of measurement on this profile combined with the sensitivity of most types of pattern analyses to errors in the variables constituting the pattern is almost a recipe for "cooking" misleading results.

The following two strategies for avoiding the problems just mentioned should be pointed out:

1. Avoid computing change scores and use instead scores pertaining to the different time points in the analyses. This is the main strategy followed in this book.
2. Consider the unreliability–invalidity dilemma in conjunction with the fact that most variables used in developmental studies have really been conceived in a cross-sectional perspective. An alternative approach might then be to construct variables designed to directly measure the process under study as a complement to the usual variables that are designed to give a snapshot of the situation at a specific time. For instance, in some situations, it can be meaningful also to ask the subjects about their estimate of the change they have experienced or even about the rate of change they have experienced. In fact, there are examples of situations when such information obtained at a single point in time is more valid than conventional change information obtained by comparing means from two points in time (see Wikman's, 1991, demonstration of this with regard to the change in working environment in Sweden during the 1970s). Of course, this should not be seen as a general plea for using retrospective data instead of longitudinal data. Only in special situations are such change estimations useful and then normally as complementary information to the longitudinal data.

3.5. Missing Data

In a person-oriented analysis, all variables in the pattern are simultaneously analyzed. Frequently, a substantial proportion of the subjects in the sample have missing data in one or several variables included in the profile. This can create problems because the analysis usually demands complete data in all variables, and subjects with missing data will have to be deleted from the analysis. Complete data are then bought at the cost of losing many subjects, perhaps with almost complete data, and possibly creating a drop-out bias.

The seriousness of missing data depends on the structure and size of the partial and total dropout, the character of the involved variables, and the aim of the study (see, for instance, Bergman & Magnusson, 1990; Cox, Rutter, Yule, & Quinton,

1977; Groves, 1989). Sometimes the most reasonable solution is to "guess" missing values for subjects having almost complete data, a procedure called *imputation*. For this purpose, an array of methods are available, usually based on linear models (for an overview, see Pierzchala, 1990). However, in a pattern-oriented setting, it seems natural to use a twin approach. A missing value is then replaced by the value in that variable for a twin subject that has complete data (El-Khouri & Bergman, 1992). A procedure for imputation has been implemented in the SLEIPNER statistical package, which is presented in chapter 8.

It should be emphasized that what is created using imputation is, of course, a *temporary file* for a specific analysis. The data should not be changed by this procedure.

4. AN OVERVIEW OF PERSON-ORIENTED METHODS FOR STUDYING INDIVIDUAL DEVELOPMENT

In this section, a brief overview is given of a number of different person-oriented methods and possible approaches within this paradigm. The overview partly builds on a presentation given by Bergman and Magnusson (1997). Some of the presented methods are presented in later chapters and others are just briefly indicated here as a guide or menu for the reader and to provide a framework. Our perspective in this presentation is restricted to the study of interindividual differences. Methods for the study of nonlinear dynamic systems, which we believe will become important in the future for carrying out a person-oriented approach, are left out. For a more extensive overview, the reader is referred to Bergman (1998).

In Fig. 3.1, a pictorial overview is given of common, pattern-based methods for studying individual development from an interindividual perspective. The classification tree of methods is incomplete and only methods of special interest in the present context are classified at a more detailed level. The two classes of methods focused on are in capital letters.

4.1. Model-Based Methods

In Fig. 3.1, a distinction is made between model-based and descriptive methods, although the borderline is not always clear. Here, *model-based* means that there is a model according to which the observed data are assumed to be generated. An example of a model-based method with latent variables is latent transition analysis (LTA), which was developed within the framework of latent class analysis for analysis of categorical data (Collins & Wugalter, 1992). Parameters are estimated, describing latent statuses and their evolution over time, and the model's fit to data can be tested (see chapter 4 and chapter 6.) An example of a model-based method without latent variables is loglinear modeling (Bishop, Feinberg, & Holland, 1975), where the logarithms of the cell frequencies are modeled according to the "effects" of belonging to specific categories in the different variables. Also here the model's fit to data can be tested (see chap. 5). Examples of tailoring this method to the study of change are given by, for instance, Clogg, Eliason, and Grego (1990).

GENERAL METHODOLOGICAL CONSIDERATIONS   45

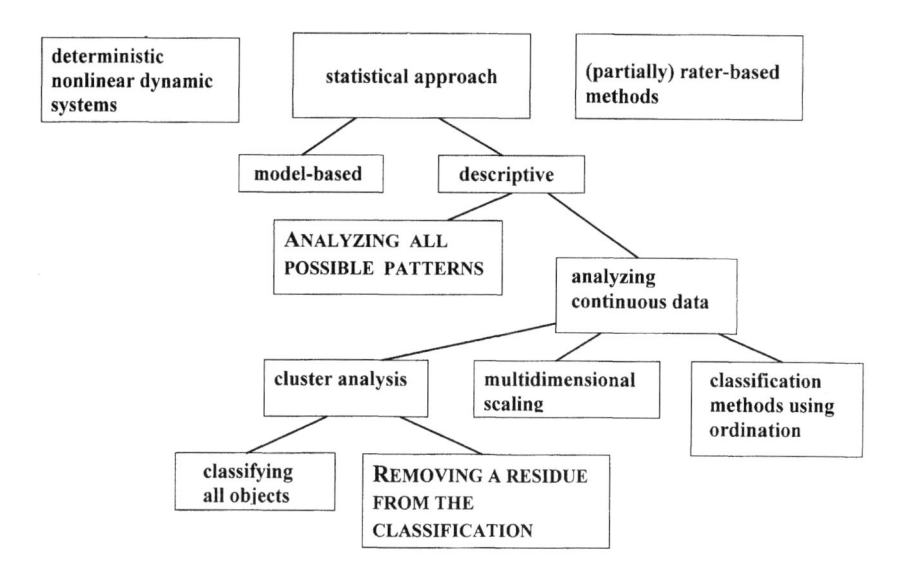

FIG. 3.1. Overview of common methods for analyzing individual pattern development.

Although model-based methods are highly useful in certain situations, they are secondary in the methodological arsenal presented in this book. The main reason for this is that we want here to present a basic set of robust methods for person-oriented analysis without introducing the complications of complex methods; they entail strong assumptions for which the tenability tends to be nontransparent.

4.2. Descriptive Methods

It should be emphasized that "descriptive" here simply means "not model-based" in the sense the term was introduced. Also within a descriptive framework, like the one we focus on, hypothesis testing can and will be carried out, not for a whole model of the data but rather of important aspects of the expected structure in the data.

A graphical presentation of similarities between profiles can sometimes be useful in developmental research, for instance, based on multidimensional scaling (Wood, 1990). However, the application of such illustrative methods is not discussed because they normally are best suited for describing a fairly small number of subjects. The interest here is mainly on interindividual differences studied for fairly large samples. Only in one way we introduce MDS here, namely for the purpose of giving a graphical representation of the similarities between different clustering solutions (see chap. 9).

4.2.1. The Cross-Sectional Perspective. Although our main interest is developmental, it is a useful base to first consider the cross-sectional analysis of patterns. Classification in a cross-sectional perspective is treated rather extensively in chapter 4. There the focus is on the cluster analysis family of methods for classifying objects on the basis of their (dis)similarities. A number of different major types of cluster analysis are presented, mainly agglomerative hierarchical methods. Which method of cluster analysis is best, of course, also depends on the data set at hand and the specific problem under study. Methods allowing overlap between clusters are potentially attractive but may lead to various interpretational problems and are not further pursued here (Wiener-Ehrlich, 1981).

Methods other than cluster analysis can be used for achieving a classification. For instance, it was briefly mentioned that model-based classification using latent class methods could be useful in certain situations. They are briefly discussed in chapter 4. Although our bias here is descriptive, it should be pointed out in defense of a model-based approach that, for instance, Meehl (1992) was critical of cluster analysis, which he claims only sort subjects into clusters usually to obtain homogenous groups, possible without necessarily identifying "natural" clusters that he calls "taxa." Latent class procedures could be used that take into account properties of taxa and try to identify them. He also indicated procedures based on what he calls a system of coherent cut kinetics (Meehl & Yonce, 1992).

Instead of aiming at a classification by grouping individuals on the basis of their patterns of values in continuous variables, one could follow Gustav Lienert's configural frequency analysis (CFA) approach (see Krauth & Lienert, 1973). It is a set of methods for studying all possible value patterns. The involved variables have to be discrete, often dichotomized or trichotomized, to make manageable the number of value patterns to be examined. Lienert and his co-workers developed CFA in a number of ways; for a basic introduction, the reader is referred to Krauth and Lienert (1982). A more recent overview is given by von Eye (1990a). CFA has a resemblance to some other techniques for analyzing higher order contingency tables like, for instance, log-linear modeling (LOGLIN). Compared to LOGLIN, CFA is a simpler and more explorative method and it can be used also in situations with cells containing zeros. Ignoring the special features of CFA with regard to design of configurations and measurement, it can be viewed as a special type of analysis of cell residuals; CFA is presented in chapter 5.

4.2.2. The Longitudinal Perspective. Consider first the classification issue from a longitudinal perspective. The developmental process can then be studied in the following two ways:

1. For each individual, a longitudinal pattern is formed that includes his or her pattern of scores in the variables at all measurement occasions and longitudinal types are classified directly based on this information. Ideally, this means that full account is taken of each individual's developmental trajectory in the

studied variables. This could be done by longitudinal cluster analysis, as discussed in chapter 6. It could also be done by applying i-state sequence analysis (ISSA), in which an a priori taxonomy of theoretically expected common types of individuals' developmental multivariate trajectories is used to structure the data set and then, within each set, looking for typical developmental sequences (Bergman, 1995). It could also be done by applying i-states as objects analysis (ISOA). In this approach, the information from a given age is considered as a "subindividual" and first a common classification system is created for profiles pertaining to any given age. Based on this classification, stability and change in class membership is then studied (Bergman & El-Khouri, 1999). Under certain assumptions, the ISSA and ISOA methods can be more powerful and extract more information than conventional methods, especially when small samples and many measurement occasions are involved. However, ISSA and ISOA are mainly suited for studying short-term development. ISOA is introduced in chapter 6. That chapter also discusses the potential problems of a direct longitudinal classification and emphasizes the frequent usefulness of the linking procedure now presented.

2. At each age, a classification is made and the results of the different classifications are linked, usually by forming cross-tabulations of classifications at two adjoining ages. Development can then be studied with regard to (a) The flow over time of individual class membership (individual stability and change), and (b) The evolvement of the classification structure (structural stability and change).

   This general procedure can be specified in different ways; in chapter 6, the Linking of Clusters after removal of a Residue (LICUR) procedure is presented. It is, as we see it, fairly robust and generally applicable and can also be used for comparing the results between different domains of data pertaining to one measurement occasion.

Leaving classification methods aside and following the CFA rationale of studying patterns of value combinations for discrete variables, methods have been developed within the CFA paradigm for handling a large variety of developmental situations, some of which are discussed in chapter 6. This includes the study of repeated measurements designs (von Eye, 1990b).

4.2.3. Some Methods for Analysis of Special Aspects of Patterns. Instead of considering the complete value patterns in a pattern analysis, as has been discussed, various specific properties of the patterns can be studied. Two such types of analyses are the following:

1. Sometimes the key features are the maximum and minimum scores of the value profile. The variable taking the maximum value and the variable taking the minimum value in an individual's profile may be considered the

cardinal features of the profile with the other scores providing the background. Of course, this implies that the scales of the different variables must be commensurable. The categorization of the profiles of scores into the different possible maximum–minimum combinations and the frequency of the different combinations give information about the individuals' profile status. Stability and change in individuals' maximum–minimum variable combinations may also tell us about the most characteristic features of how patterns evolve (see Bergman, 1998).

2. An individual's profile of scores may be even or uneven—it may have a large or small profile scatter. This can be studied in different ways, for instance, by measuring the variance around the mean of the scores in all variables constituting the profile. Again, the scaling of the involved variables must be commensurable to allow for meaningful interindividual comparisons. Profile scatter can in one measure summarize an important property of the individual pattern (see Bergman, 1998).

In the following, MAximum–MINimum (MAMIN), a method related to number 1, is indicated. Because this method, which is used in chapter 9, does not fit into the other methodological chapters, it is described here in more technical detail than the other methods in this chapter.

Sometimes a special interest might be ascribed to the two variables showing the maximum and minimum values of an individual's profile. This information might summarize an important property of the system under study. Here the MAMIN method is presented to carry out such an analysis. It must then be assumed that the variables are approximately continuous and on an interval scale, and they must all be comparably scaled (most commonly based on standardized scores). In the following, MAMIN is introduced for the case with three variables in the profile. The reader can easily generalize the method to a situation with a larger number of variables in the profile.

With three variables there are six possible maximum–minimum combinations (the variables are denoted in Table 3.3 with X, Y, and Z).

Here the total number of observations is n and the observed frequency of each value combination is f. Under an independence model the frequencies of all the expected frequencies are the same ($= (1/6)n$). Deviances from the null hypothesis could be approximately tested based on a chi-square with 5 degrees of freedom. Specific cells could be approximately tested based on standardized residuals (Haberman, 1973) or using the binomial distribution. Following the CFA paradigm, it could, for instance, be tested if a specific maximum–minimum combination is a significant type. This can be done by finding in the binomial distribution the probability of observing the maximum–minimum combination at least as many times as it has been observed with the total number of observations being equal to n and the probability of observing the event equal to 1/6. Using the same rationale, antitypes can be searched for by finding the

TABLE 3.3
Possible Maximum–Minimum Combinations for the Three Variables Case

Maximum–Minimum Combination	Observed Frequency	Expected Frequency
X max Y min	fxy	(1/6)n
X max Z min	fxz	(1/6)n
X min Y max	fyx	(1/6)n
X min Z max	fzx	(1/6)n
Y max Z min	fyz	(1/6)n
Z max Y min	fzy	(1/6)n

probability of observing a maximum–minimum combination at most as many times as it has been observed.

A complementary analysis can be made of the two variables with the *most* similar values (Table 3.4). There are three such combinations.

Types and antitypes of similar variable combinations can be tested using the same rationale that was just outlined for the maximum–minimum combinations.

At a first glance, the analyses suggested here might appear as only more crude variants of the correlation coefficient. This is not true. MAMIN is based on the whole profile of values and the results complement those found by, for instance, cluster analysis and an ordinary correlation analysis. The fundamental difference from ordinary correlations is seen in that all the results produced by MAMIN normally change when a variable is added to or deleted from the value profile in difference to the correlations that remain the same except that some correlations are deleted or added.

In many practical applications, variables are not completely continuous, leading to the possibility that, within a subject, more than one maximum–minimum combination can be found (or that more than one pair of variables are "most similar"). There is no obvious solution to this problem. One approach is to delete subjects with ties of this type. Another one is to count more than one maximum–minimum instances. Then the number of observations will, of course, exceed the number of subjects.

TABLE 3.4
Possible Most Similar Variable Pairs in the Three Variables Case

Variable Combination	Observed Frequency*	Expected Frequency
X and Y	fxy	(1/3)n
X and Z	fxz	(1/3)n
Y and Z	fyz	(1/3)n

4.3. The Study of "Anticlasses"

The search for typical patterns can be complemented with a search for what Bergman and Magnusson (1997) called "white spots," the patterns that occur seldom or not at all. Within the confinement of phase space (i.e., what theoretically can be observed), it can be of great interest to locate not only the "dense" regions, where there are many observations, but also to locate the empty or almost empty regions, although there are no "technical" reasons for why they should be empty. Why are these classes of patterns/developmental trajectories not characteristic of anyone? Unfortunately, a mapping of the boundaries of areas containing nonoccurring developmental trajectories is seldom made, despite the obvious relevancy for theory testing. Research along these lines has been discussed, for instance by Lewin (1933), who analyzed boundary conditions in terms of "region of freedom of movement" (p. 598). Cairns and Rodkin (1998) presented a "prodigal analysis" for highlighting pathways for persons who do not follow the normative developmental pathways of the configural subgroup to which they belong. To conclude: The concept of white spots offers additional ways of testing theories in terms of predictions of what should *not* happen in development according to one's theory. This could be done cross-sectionally or developmentally, for instance by looking for pathways of pattern development that for some reason have not been trodden. What has just been said also underlines the importance of studying extreme cases, as discussed by Kagan et al. (1998).

A number of approaches are possible for analyzing white spots, like searching for antitypes within CFA and the identification of a *residue* ($\approx$ unclassifiable subjects) within a cluster analytic framework. The residue concept has the following background: It has long been recognized that multivariate outliers can disturb the results of cluster analysis and it has been suggested that in some situations, it might be useful not to classify everybody (Edelbrock, 1979) but to leave a (small) residue of unclassified subjects. In addition to technical reasons for this, theoretical reasons have been suggested by Bergman (1988b), who pointed out that there often exists a small number of "unique" individuals due to extreme environmental conditions and particular genotypes, and that they should not be forced into a cluster. A procedure, RESIDue ANalysis (RESIDAN), for the formation and analysis of a residue is presented in chapter 4 and it can also be used for the purpose of analyzing white spots.

4.4. Variable-Oriented and Person-Oriented Methods as Complementary Approaches

To reiterate: When studying individual development, do not confuse a person-oriented *theoretical* approach with a person-oriented *methodological* approach using pattern analysis. Of course, it is in most cases natural to use pattern-based methods when person-oriented research is carried out but the method is not equal to the person approach, which is a more encompassing concept including theory, method, empirical analysis, and the interpretation of the results. It is probably safe to state that there has also been an overemphasis on using standard variable-based methods also to try to account for interactions and this research has sometimes been called person-oriented. Normally, it is more straightforward to take care of complex interactions by concentrating on profiles of values rather than by introducing interaction terms within a variable-oriented framework. Such an approach, if carried out ambitiously, tends to become extremely complex. Cronbach (1975) compared it metaphorically to entering a hall of mirrors.

Pattern-oriented and variable-oriented methods are both competitive and complementary. We argue that the complementary aspects should be emphasized. For example, in a new area of research, variable-oriented methods are used to help in delineating systems to study and to find operating factors, and so forth. Then typical configurations of values in these factors are looked for using person-oriented methods. This might lead to new theories, which sometimes can be tested by variable-oriented methods, in which specific hypothesized interactions can be incorporated as new variables, and so on. Additionally, the simultaneous application of pattern-oriented and variable-oriented analyses can be useful and thought provoking, not least because the pictures provided by these two approaches can be hard to reconcile or even to align for comparison. It is a little like the difficulty of combining reports of an event by a deaf person and a blind person. But just like in this simile, the combined information from the two types of analyses may tell you things you cannot understand by just having one type of information. It may also reveal method-bound constraints in the generalizability of the results you would not be aware of if you had just made one type of analysis.

4.5. Some Computer Programs for Carrying Out Pattern Analyses

Many of the analyses presented in this book can be accomplished within the major statistical packages with some juggling around. Most person-oriented analyses presented, including imputation, can be conveniently accomplished by the SLEIPNER statistical package that will be available on the Net. In later chapters, when describing methods that cannot be implemented by the use of the standard packages or by SLEIPNER, we try to indicate where a computer program can be found for carrying out the analysis.

Chapter 4
CLASSIFICATION IN A PERSON-ORIENTED CONTEXT

1. INTRODUCTION AND OVERVIEW OF THE CHAPTER

Classification of individuals into distinct groups is one of the focal subjects implied by the person approach. Generically, classification has a broad domain of reference that stretches across many disciplines, including psychology. The relevance of classification to the person approach has been presented elsewhere (chap. 3), and it was also concluded that other strategies implementing that approach are possible. However, the longitudinal multivariate strategy of investigation on which we rely in this book, with its focus on types, states, individual stability, structural stability, and so on, seems to us to be naturally realized in connection with classificatory concepts and methods. Of course, within a classificatory paradigm, several methodologies are also possible; the central issues and concepts usually remain isomorphic across these methodologies. For our purpose, we focus on cluster analysis and on methods derived from a cluster analytical view. In this chapter, we restrict our attention to cross-sectional classification, which in later chapters is used as a building block for longitudinal analyses.

We choose cluster analysis because it offers a framework where conceptual entities belonging to the method proper find correspondence in those belonging to the domain of investigation. At the risk of oversimplifying, clusters in the language of the method would correspond to classes or types in the domain of investigation, proximities to similarity in a psychological sense, and so forth.

We start this presentation by delimiting the concept of *(dis)similarity*, which is at the heart of the type of classification with which we are concerned. This is followed by a brief introduction to some ways of measuring dis(similarity), which are applicable in cluster analytical contexts. We then describe the RESIDAN approach (Bergman, 1998) for removing certain cases called outliers from the set of cases we want to classify. Theoretical reasons for removing outliers are discussed by, for example, Edelbrock (1979) and Bergman (1988b). This is followed by a description, in general terms, of cluster analysis in terms of major subsets of methods with common properties. For reasons of brevity, very short summaries are given of these techniques but a larger section is devoted to a technical description of the hierarchical agglomerative methods, which are more commonly used than others and that are at focus in the person-oriented approach presented in this volume. We also illustrate somewhat semiformally the mechanics of one possible algorithm that implements these methods. Next, some key issues in classification in general and of cluster analysis in particular are brought up, which contribute to the quality of a resulting classification. We believe that viewing the classificatory endeavor as a black box accepting data at one end and producing classes at the other, without proper evaluation of the input, the process, the output, and their correspondence to the psychological reality one is trying to capture, is detrimental for the whole approach and indeed for any classification.

Latent class analysis is also briefly introduced as one alternative to cluster analysis for conducting a classification analysis. This class of methods despite its importance is not further pursued in this book beyond this brief presentation, which is aimed at orienting some readers into alternative avenues other than the ones offered by cluster analysis.

The conceptual, reciprocal translation between the language of the method and that of the domains of the theory and the empirical world is, of course, not straightforward (it very rarely is!). A typology (and its classes) is itself a model for describing what we perceive psychologically and with our instruments. Consider for instance, the reciprocal translation between a hierarchy of cluster solutions to a typology of states or syndromes. This reciprocal translation demands that the correspondence between the entities described in the statistical domain and the ones inherent in the psychological model has been established. Any conclusions derived from a clustering solution should be made without losing sight of the assumptions governing that correspondence. These issues are discussed and we conclude the chapter with some reflections on man as a classifier.

There are two major ways in which classification problems present themselves. In the first, the task is to recover (or construct) some classification scheme based on a set of data. In the second way, classification denotes the "identification" processes through which one would identify (assign or allocate) an object as belonging to one of a number of classes in an already existing classification scheme.

Classification approaches of the first kind partition input data, presented as cases, into constituent groups of cases that are coherent and separated; a major direction in this sense constitutes cluster analysis. Other and similar approaches have been referred to in different fields as techniques of Q-factor analysis, typology, grouping, clumping, classification, numerical taxonomy, unsupervised pattern recognition, and conceptual clustering.

Classificatory endeavors of the second sort are sometimes referred to as assignment or identification diagnosis and include techniques for discriminant analysis and techniques for the formation of regression trees. The objective of these approaches is to derive classification rules from samples of classified cases and to apply these rules for assignment purposes for other samples.

In this volume, the concern is with the first type of classification, where data are used to find a classification structure for the studied sample of individuals. In the following, a brief summary is presented of selected methods of cluster analysis. For more complete, technical, and substantive overviews, see Anderberg (1973), Everitt (1974), Hartigan (1975), Gordon (1981), Shepard (1988), Miller (1987) and Blashfield and Aldenderfer (1988). A recent and thorough review is given by Arabie and Hubert (1996).

2. SIMILARITY AND DISSIMILARITY

Similarity in classification is fundamental and functionally many faceted. At one level, it is readily and intuitively understood by everyone, given the important role it plays in human categorization, recognition, concept formation, judgment, and other cognitive processes. On another level, a load of work has been put in to bring clarity into the nature of the similarity concept that is assumed, analyzed, and discussed in a variety of domains such as philosophy, logic, mathematics, and psychology, to name a few.

Similarity may be captured formally in a mathematical or statistical sense. It can be illustrated on a pair or pairs of objects, or it can be observed as a rule, used with some frequency, by an agent, in certain situations, in judging precepts of a pair of objects. For most classificatory purposes, the power of generalizing from instances is a function of how strong the observed similarities are.

The case for identical cases having perfect similarity with regard to cue attributes is simple from a classificatory point of view; they are trivially grouped together. The same applies for groups of cases that are identical. The kind of situations where identity is sufficient for a total classification of all cases is, however, not frequently encountered and one often has to adopt a more relaxed notion of similarity. Once identity is abandoned, similarity changes its nature from being a binary-valued characteristic to a multivalued one, and in some sense continuous. Thus, the following becomes a necessary prerequisite for most classificatory endeavors: the ability to perceive, conceive, or measure *multivalued* similarity between two cases or two groups of cases, that is, some level of disparity is allowed to exist between two cases that for all other purposes are considered similar. One consequence thereof is that one is able to characterize a given group by a similarity level that is "typical" of all pairs of cases in that group. Thus, three different situations may be encountered:

1. Classification is based on identity; cases belonging to the same group are all in some sense identical and the similarity level is absolute or total.
2. A predefined notion of similarity is used to constrain the formation of the groups. No pair in the group may differ more than what is a priori "acceptable." The similarity level is thus set to reflect a prior belief in what constitutes a homogenous group.
3. There is no a priori defined tolerance for disparities between pairs of cases belonging to the same group, i.e., no typical level for similarities between pairs of cases in a group is set. The similarity level is allowed to freely vary for different groups.

One consequence of number 2 is that some of the cases may not be classified at all, and depending on the chosen level of tolerance, some groups may not be formed or discovered altogether. These are groups who may well be separated from other groups but within which pairs are less similar than is a priori considered appropriate. But groups that are formed under these conditions conform necessarily and in chorus to one notion of homogeneity equally imposed on all of the groups. In number 3, however, all the cases are grouped but the resulting groups may differ with regard to the degree of homogeneity characterizing each group. In both 2 and 3, the resulting classifications goes beyond that of number 1, which is obviously no more than a simple frequency count of an ideal exemplar.

2.1. Measuring Proximity

Measuring the degree of proximity (similarity or dissimilarity) between all pairs of cases or groups of cases is fundamental to the types of cluster analysis we are discussing. A proximity matrix is essential in most classification endeavors. Thus, a matrix of dissimilarities (or similarities) is often employed and summarizes all the relevant relationships within the set of cases to be classified, such that each pair of cases will have an associated numerical dissimilarity value $d(x_i, x_j)$, or similarity value, $s(x_i, x_j)$, which depicts the extent to which the ith and jth cases resemble one another.

To measure proximity a set of relevant features is implied. A class has its members sharing "criterial" features that distinguish them from nonmembers of that class. Of course, it is often the case that there is no single criterial feature involved but a collection of features that are more or less criterial. This raises the important question of how to decide what that collection is and what it means for a collection to be criterial. In "statistical" (probabilistic) classifications, clear-cut definitions of a category are lacking. Instead, statistical relations between features and categories imply a probabilistic membership function for the incorporated cases, such that cases having some features or some combination of features are more likely to belong to a certain category rather than another. For an extensive analysis and a formal model of proximity, in general, and psychological similarity, in particular, see Gregson (1975).

A wide range of different measures of proximity has been proposed in the classification literature. Similarity measures between patterns of variables exist with varying characteristics for a wide range of variable types. Some of these are of limited usefulness, and others are closely related to one another. For reviews or lists of proximity measures, see Cormack (1971), Anderberg (1973), and Diday and Simon (1976). Here, we chose to explicate the mechanics of measuring the Euclidean distance by reference to two more general metric distances, namely the Minkowski and the Mahalanobis (1936) metrics. The Euclidean distance is focused on here because of its metric properties and because it takes into account both the profile level and the profile form when comparing patterns. If the interest is only in profile form, the correlation coefficient can be used instead. Then, the correlation is computed between the two patterns[1] and represents a measure of similarity.

The terminology in this section concentrates on describing proximity measures for a pair of cases described by a set of variables, but much of the description is also relevant for constructing proximity measures for pairs of variables (see also Anderberg, 1973). For measures relevant for comparing cases in terms of mixed types of variables, see, for example, Lerman and Peter (1985).

Measures of dissimilarity are often called dissimilarity coefficients and are often defined without any loss of generality to lie in the range $[0, \infty]$. Measures of dissimilarity and similarity are closely related in an inverse way. Dissimilarity measures can readily be transformed into similarity measures by means of various transformations, for example, $s(x_i, x_j) = \dfrac{1}{1 + d(x_i, x_j)}$ or $s(x_i, x_j) = c - d(x_i, x_j)$ for some constant c. However, the reverse is not always true, because dissimilarity measures may or may not be viewed as "distances" satisfying the triangle inequality (Everitt, 1974). Formally, the function d (as is the function s) is a mapping from the set of all pairs into one-dimensional Euclidean space (i.e., from $X \times X$ to the real numbers). Furthermore, it is required that the function d satisfies the following conditions:

1. $d(x_i, x_j) \geq 0$ **for all** $x_i, x_j \in X$
2. $d(x_i, x_i) = 0$ **for all** $x_i \in X$
3. $d(x_i, x_j) = d(x_j, x_i)$ **for all** $x_i, x_j \in X$

If the function d also satisfies (4) $d(x_i, x_j) + d(x_j, x_l) \geq d(x_i, x_l)$ then it is called metric or distance.

---

[1]Normally, the correlation coefficient is computed between variables. Here, cases and variables exchange roles.

One widely used metric function d is the Euclidean distance defined as:

$$d^{(2)}(x_i, x_j) = \left[\sum_{k=1}^{p}(x_{ik} - x_{jk})^2\right]^{1/2}$$

where x_{ik} denotes the value taken by the kth numeric variable on the ith case and p denotes the number of variables. The Euclidean distance is in fact a special case of the more general Minkowski metric given as:

$$d^{(r)}(x_i, x_j) = \left[\sum_{k=1}^{p}|x_{ik} - x_{jk}|^r\right]^{1/r}, \quad r > 0$$

which when reduces $r = 1$ reduces to the well-known city block metric:

$$d^{(1)}(x_i, x_j) = \sum_{k=1}^{p}|x_{ik} - x_{jk}|$$

The Euclidean distance is often criticized for being unsuitable particularly for variables that are measured in different units and that have different variances, and also if the variables are extremely correlated. However, Euclidean distance can be rendered scale invariant simply by standardizing the data before computing the distance. Another approach might be to scale down the variables that have greater range by using some weighting function that could be incorporated in the measure of dissimilarity itself (e.g., see Lance & Williams, 1966; or Cronbach & Gleser, 1953). To explicitly account for any correlations that might exist between variables, another generalization of the Euclidean distance, the Mahalanobis distance $d^{(M)}$, can be used. $d^{(M)}$ can be expressed as

$$d^{(M)}(x_i, x_j) = \left[\sum_{k,l}^{p}(x_{ik} - x_{jk})c_{kl}(x_{il} - x_{jl})\right]^{1/2}$$

where c_{kl} is the component that is found in row k and in column l of the inverse of the $p \times p$ variance–covariance matrix C of the variables involved. If the matrix is diagonal, that is, $c_{kl} = 0$ when $k \neq l$, then the use of $d^{(M)}$ corresponds to the use of the Euclidean distance on rescaled axes. If the matrix is the identity matrix, that is, $c_{kl} = 1$ when $k = l$ and $c_{kl} = 0$ otherwise, then $d^{(M)}$ reduces to the Euclidean distance used on standardized data.

The city block metric is useful for combining variables with varying scale levels. This is manifested, for instance, in that two cases, say x_i and x_j, which are three units apart on one variable and one unit apart on another have the same distance between them as two other cases, say x_l and x_k, which are two units apart on each variable. This is to be contrasted with the use of Euclidean distance which would render x_l and x_k less dissimilar than x_i and x_j, would be. In fact, for the analysis to be undertaken, a relevant consideration for deciding on an appropriate value of r in the Minkowski metrics is the emphasis that one would wish to give to large differences on a single variable; higher values of r give relatively more emphasis to the larger differences.

3. HANDLING OUTLIERS IN CLUSTER ANALYSIS

Prior to cluster analysis, there is a preliminary phase where the variables are chosen, data collected, coded, registered, and checked for errors. When the data are coded, care is usually taken in choosing the input medium, in deciding on suitable scales, in choosing appropriate missing values, in deciding an appropriate format, and sometimes in choosing the order of the variables when the order is deemed necessary for, for example, interpretation purposes.

An important decision concerns whether all studied subjects should be classified. From both a theoretical and technical standpoint, Bergman (1988b) argued that, often, it is not reasonable to expect all subjects to fit into one of a small number of homogeneous groups and that in many situations, not every one should be classified. In the clustering literature, this issue has been discussed using the term *coverage* to indicate the proportion of the sample classified (Edelbrock, 1979). Thus, in many situations, the outlying subjects should be identified and placed in a residue group to be analyzed separately, and the classification be carried out for the remaining subjects in the sample.

There may also exist enough knowledge about a domain of study to predict the existence of outliers of a certain type. Detecting these can be seen as confirmatory of the theory that has led to that prediction. But if no prediction can a priori be made with regard to the existence of outliers in the data set, genuine outliers that are detected may then complement our understanding of the studied domain. The relation of the concept of *outliers* to that of white spots, which was introduced in chapter 3, should here be noted. An outlier can be regarded as being in the borderland between what is observed and a true white spot, which is not observed at all. However, the situation is different when outliers are artificially introduced in a data set (see section 3.1). The success or failure of an outlier detection test hinges then directly on the appropriateness of the assumed white spots declared by these outliers, that is, whether the theory is correctly specified.

The RESIDAN methodology is used here for detecting and removing multivariate outliers prior to clustering (Bergman, 1988b). It has been implemented in SLEIPNER, our statistical package for person-oriented analysis, which is presented in chapter 8.

There are also technical justifications for removing outliers from data prior to cluster analysis. Many clustering techniques are sensitive to the presence of outliers

(Milligan, 1980). Hierarchical agglomerative clustering algorithms of the linkage type are especially vulnerable because outliers can bias the hierarchical structure at any merging level during the clustering process. This kind of vulnerability is evident because of the focus of most clustering algorithms, on maximizing internal cohesion and/or external isolation. These two objectives do not always play in concert and the problem is aggravated in the presence of an outlying case.

3.1. The RESIDAN Method

Early methods for identifying residue cases incorporated the identification process in the classification phase. For example, the nonhierarchical clustering method introduced by Lorr and Radhakrishnan (1967) produced a group of residue cases that were not classified. Wishart's RELOCATE procedure (Wishart, 1987), which starts with a given classification and relocates each case to the best fitting cluster could be asked to create a residue group of unclassified cases. But the RESIDAN method proposed by Bergman (1988b) removes outlying cases *before* cluster analysis.

In practice, four phases constitutes the proposed method: the choice of parameters, the identification phase, the classification phase, and the evaluation phase. In the first phase, the result is a function of the decisions that have to be made as to

a. whether or not to standardize the variables (the same choice should normally be made when the cluster analysis proper is performed);
b. the type of dissimilarity measure used;
c. the threshold value, T, supplied by the researcher and at which two cases are considered similar. This value is usually subjective but could be related to the data set so that it reflects an "average" value of similarity between two cases belonging to the same cluster;
d. the number of cases K required to be similar to a specific case, in order to keep it in the data set (and not to consider it as a residue case). For $K = 1$, a case is considered a residue if it is not similar to any other case. For $K = 2$, a case is considered a residue if it is similar to at most one other case, and so on; and
e. the weights to be assigned to the variables.

The *identification phase* starts by

a. computing the dissimilarity matrix for the whole data set (i.e., dissimilarity values are computed between every possible pair of cases); and then
b. identifying those cases for which there are at most $K - 1$ similar cases; and then
c. removing the identified cases from the original data set and placing them in a residue.

Subsequently, in the *classification phase,* a cluster analysis is performed on the reduced data set, preferably with the same choices made earlier with regard to scaling variables and type of dissimilarity measure.

In the *evaluation phase,* the outliers are scrutinized for errors of measurement; those that are found with errors are totally removed. The remaining outliers can then be analyzed separately and in light of the results from the classification phase. For example, by noting for each residue case the cluster to which it is most similar, next most similar, and so on, and/or studying each pattern in light of one's theoretical expectations, atypical patterns can be looked for in the residue or tentatively explained in light of the classification results.

A more direct and confirmatory way for testing a theoretically expected atypical pattern is by including it as an "artificial case" in a cleansed data set (a data set with all the residue cases removed). If a residue analysis is performed with the result that the artificial case is being identified as a residue case, then one's hypothesis is confirmed, otherwise the residue set would have been empty.

Normally, one should not expect a residue set that is more than, say, 3% the sample size. Small *Ts* yield larger residue sets and so do large *Ks*. Also, because this procedure contributes to reducing the chaining problem in cluster analysis by removing intermediate cases, large *Ks*, especially in combination with small *Ts*, may result in the elimination of small elongated clusters. Generally, $K = 1$ or $K = 2$ is recommended. The reader is referred to Bergman (1988b) for a detailed presentation of the RESIDAN method.

4. SELECTED METHODS FOR CLUSTER ANALYSIS: AN OVERVIEW

One fundamental doctrine that guides classification poses certain demands on the separation property and coherence of the outcome classes. Classes are required to be as much separated from each other as possible and, at the same time, it is wished that they are as coherent as they can be. Governed by this doctrine, cluster analysis denotes grouping techniques aimed at establishing these goals. The aim is to allocate a set of objects to a set of mutually exclusive and exhaustive groups (partition) such that cases within a group are similar to one another whereas cases in different groups are dissimilar. Input to a cluster analysis is usually a set of measurement vectors, each being an instantiation of a variable vector representing a case. Output from a cluster analysis can be a hierarchy of partitions or one single partition, depending on the method used. When a hierarchy of partitions is obtained, one is usually chosen according to some criteria but for certain purposes, other more or less fine-grained partitions may be chosen from that hierarchy.

Classification methods, in general, and cluster analysis, in particular, should not be made into black boxes that transform input data of any kind into classificatory schemes. We want to join others in advocating caution and careful considerations of the purpose of the intended classification and of the assumptions one is making about the entities involved. See section 6. for an overview of considerations for achieving a useful classification.

Cluster analysis can be undertaken for various reasons, depending on the special field of application and the specific goal set by the researcher. These includes finding a true typology, model fitting, prediction based on groups, hypothesis testing, data exploration, hypothesis generation and data reduction. The literature abounds with clustering techniques, sharing to a varying degree common views and/or answering to specific requirements and adopting special criteria. Some of the divisions of these techniques (not necessarily mutually exclusive) frequently listed in the literature are given in this chapter.

There has been considerable work done on introducing statistical theory in cluster analysis and on exploring the statistical properties of traditional techniques. For instance, the concept of *ultrametricity*, a cornerstone in hierarchical cluster analysis, first introduced in the mid-1960s, has been a focus of a variety of analyses, helping to shed light on the interrelations between various hierarchical techniques. Advances have also been made in validating hierarchies, partitions, and individual clusters, as well as for the absence of structure in a data set (see Gordon, 1996). The comparison of classification trees is another area where considerable work has been done to seek consensus trees and to assess agreement and differences between trees. Other approaches relate cluster analysis to elements of graph theory (e.g., Frank & Harary, 1982) thus providing new means of evaluating the results from cluster analysis and providing guidelines on how to increase the efficiency and tractability of clustering algorithms. Also, efforts have been made to incorporate elements of statistical theory into clustering with advances made in the area of mixture models and in classification methods based on the latent class model of Lazarsfeld and Henry (1968), for example, De Soete and DeSarbo (1991) and De Soete (1993).

4.1. Hierarchical Methods

The utility of cluster analysis in general and of the hierarchical methods in particular derives from its power to discover embedded structures in the data and its ability to describe in a meaningful way the classes thus formed. The goals of cluster analysis are met if the provided solution is as optimal as possible when measured with respect to the isolation between classes and the compactness of each class. The objective of hierarchical techniques is to investigate the structure of the data at several different levels by successively fusing sibling groups or alternatively splitting parent groups. Two main subcategories of these techniques include the agglomerative methods and the divisive methods.

4.1.1. Agglomerative Methods. Hierarchical agglomerative methods are generally more favored than their divisive counterparts. They are unidirectional, bottom-up, merging at each step the two structural units (i.e., clusters) in the data set that satisfy some criterial function. Agglomerative methods start by assuming each individual case to be a cluster and at each step, those two clusters that are most similar in some defined sense are fused. The process continues until there is only one cluster left containing all cases. The question then is to decide at which level the partitioning is optimal or makes sense.

The different agglomerative clustering methods differ mainly in the way similarities between entities in the analysis are handled and computed and some methods are only defined for measures satisfying certain metric properties. Common methods include the nearest neighbor or single link method (Johnson, 1967), the furthest neighbor or complete linkage method, the centroid method (Sokal & Michener, 1958), median method, group-average method (Sokal & Michener, 1958; Lance & Williams, 1966), McQuitty's methods (McQuitty, 1956, 1964, 1966), Lance and Williams beta-flexible method (Lance & Williams, 1966) and Ward's method (Ward, 1963). Agglomerative methods are by far more studied than their divisive counterparts, partly because of the computational complexities involved in the latter methods. In section 5., some technical aspects of such methods are described.

4.1.2. Divisive Methods. Divisive methods split clusters with the process starting at the other end where the data set then defines one cluster and the objective is to optimally split that cluster into two separated and internally homogenous clusters. The process continues by splitting each cluster in a similar fashion until all clusters are singletons. The techniques that are used for deciding which cluster to split are either monothetic (based on variables considered one at a time, an instance of which is association analysis; e.g., Lambert & Williams, 1966), or polythetic (based on all variables considered simultaneously; Macnaughton-Smith et al., 1964).

4.2. Partitioning Methods

Optimization-partitioning techniques involve starting with some partition of the data and then, unlike the hierarchical techniques, cases are shuffled back and forth between the different clusters until some clustering criterion is optimized. Here, the clusters obtained after relocation form a partition of the set of cases with no information resulting on the hierarchical structure of the data. One inherent property of all methods falling under this category is that even for small data sets, there are far too many possible partitions to consider all possible partitions. The steps commonly found in most of these techniques reflect the execution of some method for initiating clusters, methods for allocating entities to initiated clusters, and of reallocating cases to clusters by shuffling them back and forth until a criterion is optimized.

The main difference between the methods in this group is in the way clusters are initiated and the way reallocations are performed. Examples include the k means method (MacQueen, 1967), random search (Fortier & Solomon, 1966) and steepest descent (Gordon & Hendersson, 1977).

4.3. Density Search Methods

Density or mode seeking techniques search for regions of high densities in the p-dimensional hyperspace defined by p variables. Here the focus is on finding regions of the space where the points are very dense. Most of those methods adopt an initial strategy similar to the single linkage method but try to circumvent the problem of chaining frequently encountered in single linkage by capitalizing on the idea of continuity and discontinuity of closeness of a prospective point or cluster in the space. Examples of such techniques are the taxmap method (Carmichael & Sneath, 1969), the cartet count method (Cattell & Coulter, 1966), and mode analysis (Wishart, 1969).

4.4. Some Other Methods

A variety of methods do not naturally fall in any of the already mentioned categories. Some have the distinctive feature of allowing for overlapping clusters as in Jardine and Sibson's (1968a, 1968b) and Shepard and Arabie's (1979) methods. Other methods, such as, for instance, Q-factor analysis, which is frequently used in psychology, use factor analysis techniques to find clusters with the role of variable and cases interchanged. Instances of other techniques are given by Rohlf (1970), Ling (1973), Ross (1969) and Andrews (1972).

5. HIERARCHICAL AGGLOMERATIVE METHODS: TECHNIQUE

In most hierarchical agglomerative methods, the following apply: At the onset, each case, denoted x_i, where $1 \leq i \leq n$ and n is the total number of cases in the data set, is considered as a cluster, denoted $\{x_i\}$. The starting partition, denoted Π_1, is then a set of n clusters each comprising one element. Thus, $\Pi_1 = \{\{x_1\}, \{x_2\}, ..., \{x_n\}\}$. Next, a coarser partition Π_2 is obtained by merging two clusters from Π_1. Again, a coarser partition Π_3 is obtained by merging two clusters from Π_2 and so on until all the elements belong to only one cluster, that is $\Pi_n = \{\{x_1, x_2, ..., x_n\}\}$ is obtained. Thus, the result from an agglomerative clustering algorithm is a sequence of partitions $\Pi_1 \to \Pi_2 \to ... \to \Pi_n$ such that if $\Pi_i = \{C_1^i, ..., C_{N_i}^i\}$ and $\Pi_{i+1} = \{C_1^{i+1}, ..., C_{N_{i+1}}^{i+1}\}$ are some partitions in that sequence then $N_{i+1} = N_i - 1$ and $N_i = n - i + 1$, $i = 1, ..., n$.

Usually, dissimilarity (or similarity) between clusters governs the selection of a pair of clusters in Π_i that are to be merged. Thus, dissimilarity between two clusters $d(C_k, C_l)$, $C_k, C_l \in \Pi_i$ is defined and computed for all pairs of clusters in Π_i. A pair (C_t, C_u) is selected for the next merge whose dissimilarity value is least among all the computed dissimilarities. Thus, for a given partition $\Pi = \{C_1, ... C_N\}$ the pair (C_t, C_u) is selected which satisfies the following relation $d(C_t, C_u) = \min d(C_k, C_l)$, $1 \le k, l \le N$, $k \ne l$.

Next an algorithm is presented. In this description, a dissimilarity measure is assumed but the reasoning is largely analogous for a similarity measure.

5.1. Algorithm

Input: A set of n cases $\{x_1, x_2, ..., x_n\}$ and a measure of dissimilarity $d(x_i, x_j)$, $1 \le i, j \le n$.

Output: the series of partitions $\Pi_1 \to \Pi_2 \to ... \to \Pi_n$.

1. $N = n$ *Initialize the number of clusters to be equal to the number of cases present.*

2. **For** $i = 1, ..., N$ **do**   *Create N clusters where each cluster contains one distinct case.*
   $C_i = \{x_i\}$

3. $\Pi_1 = \{C_1, ..., C_N\}$ *Define the first partition in the hierarchy as the collection of all the N(=n) newly created clusters.*

4. **For** $1 \le i, j \le n, i \ne j$, **do**   *Define the distance between all distinct pairs of clusters as the distance between the corresponding singleton cases contained in them, that is, compute a dissimilarity matrix between all pairs of cases.*
   $d(C_i, C_j) = d(x_i, x_j)$

5. Current = 2   *Initialize a counter to reference the current merging level and the resulting partition.*

6. **If** $(N > 1)$ **do**

   a. Find (C_t, C_u), $C_t, C_u \in \Pi_{current}$ such that
   $d(C_t, C_u) = \min d(C_k, C_l)$, $1 \le k, l \le N$, $k \ne l$
        Find in the current partition the least dissimilar clusters.

   b. $C_p = C_t \cup C_u$ *Merge the last found two least dissimilar clusters.*

   c. $\Pi_{current} = \Pi_{current} - \{C_t, C_u\} + \{C_p\}$
        Update the current partition by removing C_t and C_u and adding C_p.

d. For all $C_i \in \Pi_{current}, C_i \neq C_p$ **do**
   Compute $d(C_p, C_i)$

   Update the dissimilarity matrix by removing the t and u columns and rows from the dissimilarity matrix and replacing them with the updated dissimilarities between the newly formed group and all other groups. This type of updating is described in the next section.

   e. $N = N - 1$

   f. *Current* = *Current* + 1
   g. Repeat 6

7. **Stop**

5.2. Updating Dissimilarities

The different methods of agglomerative clustering that were just mentioned differ mainly in their ways of computing and updating distances between clusters; namely in their way of accomplishing *compute* $d(C_p, C_i)$ in Step 6. Here we illustrate this for five common methods.

1. The single linkage defines the distance between clusters as the distance between their nearest neighbors. Thus,

$$d(C_p, C_i) = \min d(x, y) \text{ such that } x \in C_p \text{ and } y \in C_i$$

2. The complete linkage defines the distance between clusters as the distance between the most distant pairs of points, each belonging to one of the clusters, that is, their furthest neighbor. Thus,

$$d(C_p, C_i) = \max d(x, y) \text{ such that } x \in C_p \text{ and } y \in C_i$$

3. The average linkage defines the distance between two clusters as the average distance between all pairs of points, one taken from each of the two clusters. Thus, if the number of elements in a cluster C is denoted by $|C|$ then

$$d(C_p, C_i) = \frac{1}{|C_p| \cdot |C_i|} \cdot \sum d(x, y) \text{ such that } x \in C_p \text{ and } y \in C_i$$

4. The centroid method defines the distance between two clusters as the distance between the centroids of the clusters (the cluster centroid is defined as the set of means for the cluster in all variables and is here denoted with M). Thus,

$$d(C_p, C_i) = d\big(M(C_p), M(C_i)\big) \text{ such that}$$

$$M(C) = (M_1(C), M_2(C), \ldots, M_v(C)) \qquad (1)$$

and

$$M_j(C) = \frac{\sum_{x_r \in C} x_{rj}}{|C|}, \; j = 1, \ldots, v \text{ where } v \text{ is the number of variables.} \quad (2)$$

5. The Ward method fuses clusters which when combined result in a minimum increase in the error sum of squares, i.e., in the total within-group sum of squares (ESS). ESS is defined then as the sum for all groups of the sum of the squared Euclidean distances between the elements of each group and the group's centroid (see formulas 1 and 2 in the previous section). At a certain fusion level, ESS is computed and its value is then compared to the ESS resulting from fusing together two clusters. If there are g clusters then there are $\binom{g}{2}$ possible fusions that can take place and for each possible new partition a new ESS can be computed. The pair of clusters, which fusion results in the least increase in ESS, is then chosen for fusion and so on. It turns out that instead of directly computing all possible increases, this state of affairs can be translated in terms of dissimilarity comparisons between clusters. The dissimilarity matrix is then updated only for those entries relevant to the last formed cluster, that is, between the newly formed cluster and each of the remaining clusters. This updating of dissimilarity can be accomplished in the following way:

$$\text{if } C_p = C_t \cup C_u \text{ then}$$

$$d(C_p, C_i) = \frac{|C_t| + |C_i|}{|C_t| + |C_u| + |C_i|} d(C_t, C_i) + \frac{|C_u| + |C_i|}{|C_t| + |C_u| + |C_i|} d(C_u, C_i) - \frac{|C_i|}{|C_t| + |C_u| + |C_i|} d(C_t, C_u)$$

and the dissimilarity between two clusters each containing one element is usually taken as the squared Euclidean distance (or the average squared Euclidean distance).

In real implementations, a recurrence relation between distances can be used to compute the distance between a cluster C_i and a new cluster C_p formed by the fusion of clusters C_t and C_u. Thus, in the course of forming the clusters, the dissimilarity matrix is used to choose the next amalgamation and also provide values that are input into the recurrence formula, which then updates the matrix with regard to the newly formed cluster. This recurrence relation has the following form:

$$d(C_p, C_i) = \alpha_t d(C_i, C_t) + \alpha_u d(C_i, C_u) + \beta d(C_t, C_u) + \gamma |d(C_i, C_t) - d(C_i, C_u)|.$$

The parameters $\alpha_t, \alpha_u, \beta$ and γ are given for some hierarchical methods in Table 4.1. The β-flexible method can also be noted in Table 4.1 (Lance & Williams, 1966). It produces solutions that depend on the value of β supplied by the researcher and appears to be a well functioning method with the value of β set to between $-.15$ and $-.25$. For a more formal and complete presentation of the techniques discussed in this section, see, for example, Miyamoto (1990).

6. SOME PRACTICAL CONSIDERATIONS FOR ACHIEVING A WELL-FUNCTIONING CLASSIFICATION USING CLUSTER ANALYSIS

A number of technical issues are important to consider in order to obtain useful results from a cluster analysis (see also Bergman, 1998):

1. The issue of scaling and standardization of the variables must be resolved in a satisfactory way.
2. The choice of a sound clustering algorithm is of obvious importance, preferably trying two different ones (e.g., Ward's [1963] method and average Linkage). Sometimes cluster analysis is criticized on the ground that dif-

TABLE 4.1
Different Clustering Methods With Their Corresponding Values for α_t, α_u, β and γ to be Instantiated in the Recurrence Relation for Updating Group Dissimilarities.*

	α_t	α_u	β	γ
Nearest neighbor:	$1/2$	$1/2$	0	$-1/2$
Furthest neighbor	$1/2$	$1/2$	0	$1/2$
Centroid	$\dfrac{n_t}{(n_t + n_u)}$	$\dfrac{n_u}{(n_t + n_u)}$	$-\alpha_t \alpha_u$	0
Group average	$\dfrac{n_t}{(n_t + n_u)}$	$\dfrac{n_u}{(n_t + n_u)}$	0	0
Ward	$\dfrac{n_t + n_i}{(n_t + n_u + n_i)}$	$\dfrac{n_u + n_i}{(n_t + n_u + n_i)}$	$\dfrac{-n_i}{(n_t + n_u + n_i)}$	0
β-flexible	$\dfrac{1}{2}(1-\beta)$	$\dfrac{1}{2}(1-\beta)$	β	

*n_t, n_u, and n_i denotes the number of elements in C_t, C_u, and C_i respectively, i.e. $|C_t|$, $|C_u|$, and $|C_i|$

ferent algorithms produce partly different classifications of the same data. This criticism appears to be largely misplaced for two reasons: (a) if a high quality analysis is carried out and the specific aspects of the classification that is at focus are properly considered, large method differences in results are not common (cf. Morey, Blashfield, & Skinner, 1983); and (b) different clustering algorithms focus on somewhat different aspects of classification, and a moderate difference in the resulting classification is no more surprising and alarming than is the observation of a moderate difference between the arithmetic mean and the median computed for the same data. Maybe even less so, considering the complex multivariate reality that is described by the resulting clustering solution.
3. Only variables with a reasonably high reliability should be included.
4. Only a limited number of variables in the profile should be included if the analysis aims at finding homogenous clusters (say, no more than eight variables).
5. One should be ready to retreat from the demand of classifying everybody.
6. The difference between a primary goal of assigning cases to clusters and a primary goal of identifying natural clusters should be noted. Homogenous clusters tend to be related to "natural" clusters but they are not equivalent. A researcher may have a definition of what is meant by natural cluster that puts less emphasis on homogenous clusters than we have done in this volume. In this case, Ward's (1963) method, for example, may not be a good method. Also the use of the explained error sum of squares to aid in deciding the number of clusters might be suboptimal in some situations. It often decreases with the number of variables in the profile. However, cluster recovery in relation to an external criterion classification of natural clusters tends to increase when more dimensions are added to the description of each case (Milligan & Cooper, 1985). This is only to be expected because a larger number of dimensions often contain more information about the clustering structure. One might then erroneously judge a classification based on many dimensions as inferior when compared to one based on fewer dimensions. Please note that the other LICUR stopping rules might be useful in such situations (the LICUR method is described in chap. 6).
7. Another problem that may arise when the hierarchical agglomerative methods are used has to do with ties. These occur when there exist several pairs of cases equally similar to each other and that are all equally eligible for fusion. In this situation, the cluster solution may vary (usually only slightly) depending on which pair is selected (in some implementations, this may depend on the order in which the cases are presented). This problem is most likely to arise if the variables are discrete and one way of resolving it is by some form of variable standardization (see also, Gordon, 1996).

It should be obvious from the aforementioned that, as always, issues of reliability and validity are important. The reliability and internal validity issues are perhaps even more important than in many other situations, considering the absence in cluster analysis of a tenable, mathematical–statistical framework in which errors are modeled. Reliability and validity issues are treated in chapter 7.

The validity of a classification outcome is more or less a function of the choice of the variable vector, the scaling of the variables, the choice of method, the choice of proximity measure, the sample of cases under investigation, and, when relevant, the choice of the solution. Superfluous or irrelevant variables distort the domain in which classification takes place and will also likely render the results useless. Not attending to scaling problems will unduly inflate the importance of some variables when measuring proximities between cases or clusters. Different methods are biased toward recovering clusters of certain forms and thus may impose a structure on the solution different from the "real" one. The proximity measure may not be optimal for the method used and the sample of cases may not be representative and/or may include outlying cases (so called outliers). In short, there is a good ground in classification for saying that one reaps what one sows.

7. LATENT CLASS ANALYSIS

Another important family of methods in classification goes under the name of latent structure analysis, where a latent variable is inferred from manifest (observed) variables. In this family, methods for latent class analysis, latent trait analysis, and latent profile analysis are incorporated. The rationale is the same for all these models but they differ with regard to the type of variables they handle and the nature of the latent variable to be characterized. For instance, when the observed variables are continuous, the type of analysis involved is either factor analysis or latent profile analysis, depending on whether the latent variable is continuous (factor analysis) or discrete (latent profile analysis). But if the observed variables are discrete, the analysis is a latent trait analysis if the latent variable is continuous, and a latent class analysis if the latent variable is discrete. Latent class analysis is briefly described here. This approach is basic to latent transition analysis described in chapter 6.

In latent class analysis, the cases are described by a vector of categorical variables and one starts by examining the covariations among these variables. It is then believed that one is able to explain these covariations by reference to a nonobserved, latent categorical variable. If such a variable can be determined, its discrete values will decompose the original data set into classes in which whatever remains of the relationships between the observed variables could be attributed to chance (the assumption of local independence).

Two important types of probabilities lie at the heart of the analysis: The *latent class probabilities* and the *conditional probabilities*:

The latent class probabilities are reflected by the relative sizes and the number of classes assumed in the model. Initial guesses of those are input to the analysis and the number of classes is selected for which a model of best fit is found. The latent class probabilities are then updated accordingly at the end of the analysis.

The classes are not uniquely characterized in latent class analysis in the same general sense that clusters are described in cluster analysis. Instead a case belonging to a class is characterized on each variable in a probabilistic fashion. That is, for each class there is an associated set of conditional probabilities, which states for each member of that class its probabilities of having a certain value on a certain variable. Nevertheless, these probabilities are often sufficient to differentiate between the classes in an intelligible manner, as they tend to contrast in the different classes.

When a successful exploratory latent class analysis has been conducted, the end result is a characterization of the latent variable where each class is characterized by relative size and conditional probabilities in the sense described in the foregoing section. These probabilities are also used to assign cases to the resulting classes for further analysis. Thus, for a certain case (or usually a configuration of variable values corresponding to more than one case), the probability of that case being in each of the latent classes is computed, and the class associated with the highest probability is then chosen as a host for that case. Thus, in the assignment process, an explicit and probabilistic element is involved, which is usually not encountered in other classification methods, for example, cluster analysis. Because misclassifications may result as a consequence, it is customary to estimate the error rate associated with these assignments (see Clogg, 1979, 1981a, 1981b).

8. CLUSTERS, TYPES, AND CLASSES

The question of whether structure and classes are "natural" or whether they are purposely formed or accidentally imposed on the domain of study is not an easy one to answer. This issue was discussed in chapter 3. The success or failure in recovering a natural class is a function of the domain in which classification is applied and is highly dependent on the preciseness with which the attributes or variables are chosen and measured. The latter is a difficult task and one that is only perfected upon careful theoretical considerations, iterations, and refinement, thus adding and removing variables until the set is considered suitable enough for the intended classification.

With regard to the domain proper, Meehl (1992), in an effort to explicate what he called taxonicity, distinguished between natural and "arbitrary" classes in the sense that the former is a manifestation of the domain of study, being taxonic and in it "nature is carved at its joints," whereas the latter is one that may be specified for a particular purpose by some rational conjunction of properties that need not correspond to a class that is "really out there." In the words of Meehl (1992): "All taxa are classes, but not all classes are taxa" (p. 123).

In particular, Meehl is concerned with detecting taxonicity. For this purpose, he advocates a system of "coherent cut kinetics" (Meehl & Yonce, 1992), a specially tailored taxometric approach, where numerical consequences of making a taxonicity assumption, together with other auxiliary statistical conjunctures, are tested. The reasoning is that if the test fails, then something is wrong with the model, but if the test succeeds, then the assumed model is corroborated. The idea is that by subjecting a model of assumed latent taxonicity to a variety of tests, the model is either refuted by any one single test or the convergence of evidence from different tests is taken as strong evidence in favor of taxonicity (see also Waller & Meehl, 1998).

Whether the classes are natural or arbitrary, it is implied by the classification paradigm that the classes that are formed must have some perceived properties that may qualify them for later usage. One such property relates to the "utility" of a classification as perceived by the producer of the classification and by his or her peers. Because it is a perceived and not necessarily an inherent property it originates as a consequence of the producer's ability to employ a relevant procedure to discriminate between a useful (sensible) classification and nonuseful classifications.

It is probably not surprising that much of the attention paid to issues such as class validity is found in biology, given the methodological traditions set by Linneaus as early as in the 18th century. But even when the question of validity is undecided, the structure can still be useful for a variety of reasons, for example, for data simplification, hypothesis generation, and or prediction. In the behavioral sciences, one approaches this question dogmatically by accepting a given classification if it makes sense, and one is often content with the result as long as it helps in simplifying/summarizing the data, in generating hypotheses, prediction, explanation, and or generalization; in short if it is useful. It is not infrequent that these usages are not explicitly stated at the onset of classification and that they become interwoven in the analysis and interpretation of the results.

Besides the characterization of a class as natural, the following considerations may be helpful:

(a) Classes can be a priori. Theoretical classes can be expected to exist because some underlying theory or expert consensus or plain intuition predicts it. The manifestation of "strong" prototype cases in the sample is one instance where such intuitional considerations are warranted.

(b) Classes can be illusory. For instance, the human classifier may be led to erroneously believe that a structure exists in the sample and or the population when that structure is really superimposed by the classification tool or an artifact of an erroneous choice of attributes.

If classes with regard to some doctrine are believed to exist in a population, then the natural starting point would be some kind of an intentional definition that would list those attributes we intuitively believe the class to have. This list would then form the starting point for an enumeration of the variables that are believed crucial for the classes to manifest themselves in the population. Obviously, in many situations, a complete enumeration is not feasible, and even if it were, the cost of measuring all the cases in the sample on all the variables may be prohibitive. So one has to be content with a subset of relevant attributes.

9. MAN AS A CLASSIFIER

The intuitive appeal of classification is probably due to its being a basic cognitive faculty important for survival. How can then the psychological reality of man's classificatory ability shed light on classification as a tool of research? There is no straight answer to this question. All these many facets of human classificatory ability are intriguing. This is exhibited by past and ongoing research, at least with respect to modeling that ability in relation to recognition tasks, recall, and classification of new cases when a classification scheme already exists.

After the pioneering work of early psychologists in establishing cluster analysis as an important method for classification, important feedback has found its way back to psychology from cognitive scientists with pure interest in artificial intelligence (AI) and who were inspired by the cluster analytic research paradigm (e.g., Ahn & Medin, 1992). Despite the enormous increase in computing power offered by modern technology, computers are still insufficient in face of the demands imposed by many classification problems. The modifications of the classical clustering methods and the use of ad hoc and sometimes semiformal heuristics for simplifying a classification are some of the de facto approaches that have been used by methodologists and computer scientists to alleviate the problem. How convenient it would be if research in psychology about man as a classifier were to furnish the answers to how to obtain optimal classifications! After all, there may be no better source than man himself.

A simple and basic use of man as a classifier that often has been used in psychophysics is to use raters to rate the degree of similarity between cases. The use of human raters in conjoint with an automated classifier has also been suggested (Bergman & El-Khouri, in prep.). The interaction of human goals and conceptual capabilities with the information and structure available in the environment is an important characteristic of categorization by man (Ahn & Medin, 1992). By capitalizing on the strength and sophistication of this interaction, more human-oriented classification systems may be engineered. With a working model of the human raters' classificatory potential and with the power and stability of a computerized classificatory system that supports the rater, the better of two worlds may be achieved. The supremacy of man to machine in areas where little or no computing is involved cannot be overstated, for instance as when qualitative background knowledge is crucial or when shift in context is required.

No doubt, many classification schemes are learned especially in childhood but it is not clear whether leaning is always "rote learning" with regard to the formation of object categories. A child may construct his own categories before he learns the labels that apply to those categories. The ability to produce classifications may be inherent in human nature and it is not surprising that theories of mental models have this ability as one of its focal points. The starting point is that man is a prime producer of classification schemes that he readily uses in almost all mental and other everyday activities. But he is also a consumer of myriad classification schemes he encounters and rotely learns both in childhood and in adulthood. No matter what type of mental model is preferred, the ease and flexibility with which new knowledge is patched together with existing knowledge is evident throughout most of our life. Classificatory structures lie at the heart of many models and it is probably safe to conjecture that there is a gain in presenting facts and knowledge whenever possible in a manner that is consistent with these structures. Accordingly, results from classification analyses may be preferred to those from traditional statistical methods because they are more natural to grasp, integrate (or resist), and use.

When regarding man as a classifier we discern at least three important points that extend to the general field of classification, namely:

1. We are to some extent "hard wired" to develop, elaborate, and consume classification-based results; a fact that makes a classification approach to research natural in many settings, not the least within psychology.
2. The flexibility and versatility of man as a classifier could be utilized in research to a larger degree than is the case today, for instance by using rater-based cluster analysis, in which subjective classification is combined with the support of an objective computer-based and statistical methodology.
3. The way ordinary, quantitative, statistical classification is undertaken can be inspired by research findings from the study of man as a classifier. For instance, the flexibility and power of hierarchical structures should be noted as well as the possibilities offered by a dynamic interaction between classifying cases *de novo* and adding additional cases to an already existing classification structure.

Chapter 5
ANALYZING ALL POSSIBLE PATTERNS

1. INTRODUCTION TO CONFIGURAL FREQUENCY ANALYSIS

The idea of a classification analysis based on multidimensional data is to group the individuals according to their value profiles. Usually it is then assumed that the variables are approximately continuous and can be treated as being on an approximate interval or ratio scale. We saw in the preceding chapter that cluster analysis could then be used to accomplish the classification. However, one or both of the following two conditions can apply in a specific context:

1. The scale levels of the variables do not permit the use of a standard cluster analytic approach based on interval scale data (e.g., some variables are on an ordinal scale or are pure categorical variables).
2. There are reasons to believe that the clusters resulting from a standard analysis will not give an adequate representation of the individual profiles.

If it is meaningful to make all the variables discrete, each taking just a few values, then it can be good idea to study directly all the different theoretically possible value combinations instead of giving an indirect presentation of the individual profiles in the form of class membership based on a cluster analysis. This idea was first put forth by Zubin (1937) and later taken up by Gustav Lienert in Germany and developed by him and others into a large set of procedures for analyzing data of this kind (see Krauth & Lienert, 1973, 1982). The new type of analysis was called configural frequency analysis (CFA) with a "configuration" referring to a theoretically possible value combination and "frequency" referring to how frequent a specific configuration is. CFA was originally developed in Germany and the results published in German. However, useful presentations of CFA in English are given in Krauth and Lienert (1982), in von Eye (1990a), and in von Eye, Spiel, and Wood (1996). Von Eye is also responsible for many newer developments of CFA.

To explain the basic idea: Consider three dichotomous variables, each taking the values 1 or 0. Eight different configurations then exist: 000, 001, 010, 011, 100, 101, 110, and 111. For each configuration separately, the observed frequency is compared to the expected frequency under some null hypothesis of no relationships in data. An observed frequency is significantly higher than the expected one at level α if, under the null hypothesis, the probability of observing a frequency as large as or larger than the one observed is less than or equal to α (one-tailed test). This is called a *type*. An observed frequency, which is significantly smaller than the expected one, is called an *antitype*.

The expected frequency can be computed in different ways, depending on what the specific null hypothesis is. We are mainly concerned here with the most common situation when, under H_0, it is assumed that all variables are independent. The expected frequency for a specific pattern is then obtained by multiplying the sample size by each of the marginal proportions for the specific values for each variable in the pattern. In some situations, other assumptions can be relevant under H_0.

How is the observed frequency (= obs) of a configuration compared to the expected one (= exp)? In some contexts, it is useful to compute a difference and in other contexts to compute a ratio. To give one example of the latter case: The patterning of risk factors is studied using CFA on a number of dichotomized risk variables, and an indication of a risk is rather infrequent for all risk variables. It can then be natural to compute the ratio between the observed and expected frequency of a specific risk pattern (= configuration) to locate risk configurations that stand out.

How does one decide whether an observed frequency is significantly more frequent than expected by the independence model? Different models are possible and the following basic rationale are focused on here: Under H_0, it is assumed that each observation is the result of a trial, which with probability p results in the occurrence of the specific configuration and with probability $1-p$ results in the nonoccurrence of the specific configuration; p is estimated by the ratio between the expected frequency and the sample size. Denote the sample size with n. We then have a probabilistic situation with n independent trials, each with a fixed probability of p for the event, "realization of the configuration," to occur. The probability of w occurrences of the configuration is then given by the binomial distribution:

$$\text{Probability of w occurrences} = \binom{n}{w} p^w q^{n-w}$$

$$\text{where } q = 1 - p \text{ and } \binom{n}{w} = \frac{n!}{w!\,(n-w)!} \text{ with } n! = 1 \cdot 2 \cdot 3 \cdots n \qquad (1)$$

A 5% region for rejecting the null hypothesis and accepting the alternative hypothesis of an existing type is obtained by computing the probability according to (1) for $w = n$, $w = n - 1$, and so on until the sum of these probabilities gets as close as possible to 5% without exceeding this figure, indicating that the border value for the critical region has been reached. If the observed frequency is larger than or equal to this border value, then the result is significant at the 5% level. The reversed procedure is used in testing for antitypes. The following z approximation assumed to follow the standard normal distribution could be used if the expected value is not too small:

$$z = (\text{obs} - \text{exp} - 0.5) / (npq)^{1/2} \text{ for a type} \qquad (2)$$
$$Z = (\text{exp} - \text{obs} - 0.5) / (npq)^{1/2} \text{ for an antitype}$$

If the z value according to (2) is larger than 1.65, a significant type/antitype has been found (one-tailed test). (See von Eye, 1990a, for a discussion of different significance tests and the quality of different approximations.) A crude but simple approximation is obtained by computing the chi-square component, which roughly follows the chi-square distribution with one df:

$$\text{chi-square component} = (\text{obs} - \text{exp})^2/\text{exp} \qquad (3)$$

2. AN EXAMPLE OF THE APPLICATION OF BASIC CONFIGURAL FREQUENCY ANALYSIS

In Table 5.1, fictitious data are presented referring to a study of gender, adjustment in school, and spatial ability score. Also presented are the results of some basic variable-oriented analyses. It is seen that the maladjustment score mean is higher for boys than for girls and that the spatial orientation score mean is much higher for boys. There is a moderate-low correlation between maladjustment and spatial orientation for the whole sample and also for each gender.

In order to take into consideration the whole pattern of values in the three variables, a CFA was carried out. First variable 2 was dichotomized and variable 3 was trichotomized. The results of this analysis are presented in Table 5.2.

Two types were expected a priori for theoretical reasons, namely 1 1 1 and 2 2 3. For the configuration 1 1 1 (girl, low maladjustment score, low spatial orientation), it is seen that obs = 4 and exp = 20 × 0.4 × 0.4 × 0.4 = 1.28 (see bottom of table where the marginal relative frequencies are given). The following binomial probabilities are obtained for configuration 1 1 1, which has $p = 1.28/20 = .064$:

Prob ($w = 4$) = 0.028, Prob ($w = 5$) = 0.006, Prob ($w = 6$) = .001, Prob ($w = 7$) = .000. The probability of w being equal to or larger than 4 is then, under the null hypothesis, .028 + .006 + .001 + very small probabilities that can be ignored = .035. Rejecting H_0 if obs is at least 4 then gives an approximate 5% significance test. Here

TABLE 5.1
Fictitious Data for $n = 20$ and $k = 3$*

2 52 29	
2 51 43	
1 47 37	
1 41 39	
1 59 37	**All**
2 36 27	Means: 1.6, 48.3, 50.6
2 44 59	sd:s: .5, 10.9, 15.6
2 35 62	$r_{12} = .28 \quad r_{13} = .55 \quad r_{23} = .38$
1 56 48	
2 41 67	**Boys**
1 44 56	means in v2 and v3: 50.8, 57.5
2 55 67	$r_{23} = .30$
2 61 61	
2 56 75	**Girls**
2 54 71	means in v2 and v3: 44.6, 40.3
1 35 31	$r_{23} = .25$
2 74 63	
2 50 66	
1 48 36	
1 27 38	

*(v1 = gender; 1 = girls 2 = boys, v2 = maladjustment score, v3 = spatial orientation score)

obs = 4, which is significant at the 5% level. Using the approximation given in (2) renders the following result:

$$z = (4 - 1.28 - .5) / (20 \times .064 \times .936)^{1/2} = 2.03$$

This value is larger than 1.65, which is the critical value for a result to be significant at the 5% level (one-tailed test) and, hence, the same conclusion is reached using this approximation. The crude chi-square approximation gives a chi-square of $(4 - 1.28)^2 / 1.28 = 5.78$, which is far in excess of the critical value of 3.84. The other expected type, 2 2 3, is not a significant type as seen in Table 5.2.

Frequently one also wants to explore whether any of the remaining configurations has an observed frequency that indicates a significant type or antitype. In this case, there are ten remaining configurations. However, to accomplish this, a large number of dependent significance tests have to be carried out (ten tests for types and

TABLE 5.2
Results of a Configural Frequency Analysis of the Data in Table 5.1 With Variable 2 Dichotomized (1 = 0–49 and 2 = 50–74) and Variable 3 Trichotomized (1 = 0–39, 2 = 40–60, 3 = 61–75)

Configuration	Observed	Expected	Chi-square	Binomial probabilities
111*	4	1.28	5.78	.0356
211	1	1.92	.44	.4150
121	2	1.92	.00	.5850
221	1	2.88	1.23	.1947
112	0	.64	.64	.5218
212	1	.96	.00	.6261
122	2	.96	1.13	.2491
222	1	1.44	.13	.5725
113	0	1.28	1.28	.2664
213	2	1.92	.00	.5850
123	0	1.92	1.92	.1329
223	6	2.88	3.38	.0570

Marginal relative frequencies:
Variable 1 1 . . = .40   2 . . = .60
Variable 2 . 1 . = .40.   . 2 . = .60
Variable 3 . . 1 = .40   . . 2 = .20   . . 3 = .40
*p < .05

ten tests for antitypes). Therefore, the significance levels have to be adjusted in order to achieve protection against the so-called mass significance problem (if not, pure chance could easily give spurious significances). For this purpose, a procedure devised by Holm can be used, which is an improved Bonferroni correction approach (Holm, 1979). Let us assume that k tests are to be made with a guaranteed significance level of α. First, the tests are made and the results listed from the most significant result according to the nominal significance level to the least significant result. Beginning at the top of this list, it is then seen if this result is significant at the α/k level. If this is the case, it is significant at the guaranteed α level. Then it is seen if the next result is significant at the $\alpha/k - 1$ level. If this is the case it is significant at the guaranteed α level. Then it is seen if the result after that is significant at the $\alpha/k - 2$ level. If this is not the case, the procedure is ended and no more result is significant at the guaranteed α level. Applying this procedure to the results in Table 5.2, all remaining nominal p values are first listed: .133, .195, .249, and so on. Because the smallest p value obtained is larger than .05/20, which is demanded at the guaranteed 5% level, no more significant type or antitype is obtained. The figure 20 demands an explanation: In Table 5.2, the probabilities are given for an observed frequency as large as or larger than the one obtained if obs > exp and the probability of an observed frequency as small as or smaller than the one obtained if obs < exp. For each tested configuration, we thus carry out two tests, one for types and one for antitypes. This gives 10 tested configurations × 2 = 20 tests after the two theoretically predicted types and the two theoretically "impossible" antitypes for the two predicted type patterns have been removed. In Table 5.2 (and in the SLEIPNER output on which the table is based), for each configuration, only the test with the lowest probability is given (i.e., a type test if the results point in the direction of a type and an antitype test if the results point in the direction of an antitype). The other probability is always larger than .50 and, hence, always nonsignificant.

The reader might wonder why this artificial data example was chosen and not a more interesting "real" data set with more cases and variables. The reason is that in this simple case, it is possible for the reader to hand calculate all the results produced and to completely overview all the data. We believe this is fundamental in order to develop a sound understanding of the basics of CFA. In chapter 9, we perform a CFA analysis of real data in a higher dimensional space.

3. MORE ABOUT SIGNIFICANCE TESTING IN CFA

As exemplified, often it is useful to divide the significance tests into two sets, one small *confirmatory set*, where the significances are interpreted directly, and one large *exploratory set*, consisting of all the remaining possible tests with the significance levels corrected by the Holm procedure. It is a compromise between the need for a guaranteed α level and the need to not waste power unnecessarily. It should be noted that when a very large number of significance tests is carried out for a sample size that is not large and the Holm correction is applied, the degree of precision of an approximate test becomes more than an academic question. In such cases, the approximations can give quite misleading results (Bergman & von Eye, 1987; von Eye & Bergman, 1986). As a crude rule of thumb, the z approximation given in (2) is reasonably accurate for expected frequencies above 10. For the data set presented in Table 5.2, it is not satisfactory. The chi-square approximation is very crude but it is sometimes convenient to compute it first to see if there is a necessity for applying a more accurate formula. However, most CFA computer programs can perform the binomial test and do not have to rely on approximations. This is also the case for the CFA test included in our statistical package, SLEIPNER, introduced in chapter 8. A comprehensive statistical package for CFA analysis has been developed by von Eye (1987). Another one is presented by Krauth (1993) in his book that also contains his programs (the book is in German). His package can perform a large variety of different CFA tests. Lehmacher (1981) developed a more powerful method for significance testing based on the assumption of fixed margins but this is not discussed here.

CFA has justifiably been criticized for the low information value of a significant result that is obtained when using the total independence model. It is of some value to reject the null hypothesis of total independence but the alternative accepted is really not the "validation" of a specific significant type but a more general rejection of independence. Therefore, it can be highly informative to compute the expected frequencies according to a more refined null hypothesis model; for instance, by applying a log linear model, where all main effects and all pair-wise interaction effects are incorporated but no higher-order interactions.

4. INTERACTION STRUCTURE ANALYSIS WITHIN CFA

In interaction structure analysis (ISA) within CFA (Krauth & Lienert, 1982), the variables are first divided into two sets and then the interactions between the two sets are studied. This is done by listing all the possible configurations for each of the two sets and then analyzing the two-way contingency table between the two sets, looking for significantly overfrequented cells (types) and significantly underfrequented cells (antitypes). This could be made for one or a few theoretically interesting set splits or, more exploratively, for all splits. In our simple example with three variables, there are only three possible splits: 1.23, 2.13, and 3.12. Often ISA is useful when the variables can be divided into a set of independent variables and a set of dependent variables. Then all possible such set splits are made and the resulting cross tabulations examined for types and antitypes. In cases with many variables, large sets of ISA analyses are possible, which can provide detailed information about the interaction structure.

Turning back to our data set, we might regard gender as an independent variable and maladjustment and spatial orientation as the dependent variables. Then there is only one possible ISA analysis, namely 1.23, that is, gender × maladjustment, spatial orientation. This leads to the cross tabulation presented in Table 5.3. The overall chi-square is nonsignificant and if each cell is tested using the z approximation given in (2), no significant type or antitype is obtained even before the (conservative) correction has been carried to adjust for the fact that $2 \times 12 = 24$ dependent tests have been made. For instance, the cell 1×23 has obs = 0 and exp = 2.4, which gives chi-square = $(0 - 2.4)^2 / 2.4 = 2.4$ using (3), so far from the critical 5% value (3.84, nominal level) that the less inaccurate z approximation is not necessary to compute. However, it should be pointed out that for such small expected frequen-

TABLE 5.3
ISA of the Data Presented in Table 5.2 With Gender as the Independent Variable and Maladjustment, Spatial Orientation as the Dependent Variables

	Value Pattern in Maladjustment and Spatial Orientation						
	11	12	13	21	22	23	
Gender							
1	4	0	0	2	2	0	8
2	1	1	2	1	1	6	12
	5	1	2	3	3	6	20

cies as in Table 5.3, exact tests are preferable and such tests can be carried out using the EXACON module in the SLEIPNER program to be presented in a later chapter.

5. CFA RELATED TO OTHER METHODS

Let us first say that CFA has been extended to a large variety of different settings and the reader is referred to the above-mentioned sources for further information. In chapter 6, we briefly discuss some variants of CFA useful for longitudinal analysis.

How does CFA relate to other techniques for analyzing higher order contingency tables like, for instance, log-linear modeling (LOGLIN)? In LOGLIN, the logarithms of the cell frequencies are modeled according to the "effects" of belonging to specific categories in the different variables and the model's fit to data can be tested (Bishop et al., 1975). In CFA some type of model of "no relationships" is tested, either globally for all variables or regionally for groups of variables, but there the emphasis is on the types and antitypes, that is, on the *deviances* from the null model. In practice, CFA can often be described as an analysis of residuals produced by some simple log-linear model. It then tends to be more explorative and more focused on higher order interactions than LOGLIN.

There are also model-based methods for classification of categorical data. One such family emanates from the latent structure analysis of Lazarsfeld (Lazarsfeld & Henry, 1968) based on binary items. In this methodology, briefly discussed in chapter 4, it is assumed that there exists a number of latent classes that make up the sample and that within each such class, there are no relationships between the variables (local independence). This line of thinking has been developed by Collins and Wugalter (1992) in various ways, including provisions for carrying out longitudinal analyses and is briefly introduced in chapter 6. The strength of the latent structure approach is the construction of a testable model including a model of the errors, which is not developed in CFA. The weakness of this modeling approach is a number of "stiff" assumptions that have to be made to carry out the analysis and the usually low power of detecting a misfitting model for moderate sample sizes. The strength of CFA is the closeness to the multivariate reality one wants to understand.

Finally, contrasting CFA to cluster analysis, which was discussed in the previous chapter, it is obvious that the main division point between the methods is whether one wants to regard the variables as more or less continuous (approximately interval scaled) or as essentially noninterval scaled or even categorical. In the first case, standard methods for cluster analysis based on interval scaled data can be a natural choice; in the second case, they cannot be used. Then there are alternative types of cluster analysis designed for ordinal or categorical data but CFA can be a natural choice. Also when the data are considered to be approximately interval scaled, CFA can be a useful complementary approach as long as the discretization of the variables is defensible, which would depend on the specific case.

6. A FINAL LOOK AT WHAT WE HAVE LEARNED ABOUT THE STRUCTURE IN THE DATA IN TABLE 5.1

Finally, let us return to the data given in Table 5.1, which we have analyzed, using CFA with the results presented in Table 5.2 and Table 5.3. Due to the simplicity of the data set, it can be represented in a two-dimensional plot with the maladjustment score on the x axis and the spatial orientation score on the y axis. This is done in Fig. 5.1, where girls are denoted with dots and boys are denoted with squares.

It is seen in Fig. 5.1 that there is a clear structuring of the data set with one dominant feature for the girls (low spatial orientation score, low maladjustment score) and one dominant feature for the boys (high spatial orientation score, high maladjustment score). The first one was picked up by the significant type obtained in the CFA analysis and indicated by the broken encirclement. The other dominant feature was only a tendency ($p = .057$), but is also indicated by a broken encirclement. It would also partly have been picked up if a cluster analysis had been carried out based on the two continuous variables and treating gender as a third continuous variable (a questionable procedure) as indicated by the encircled areas indicating

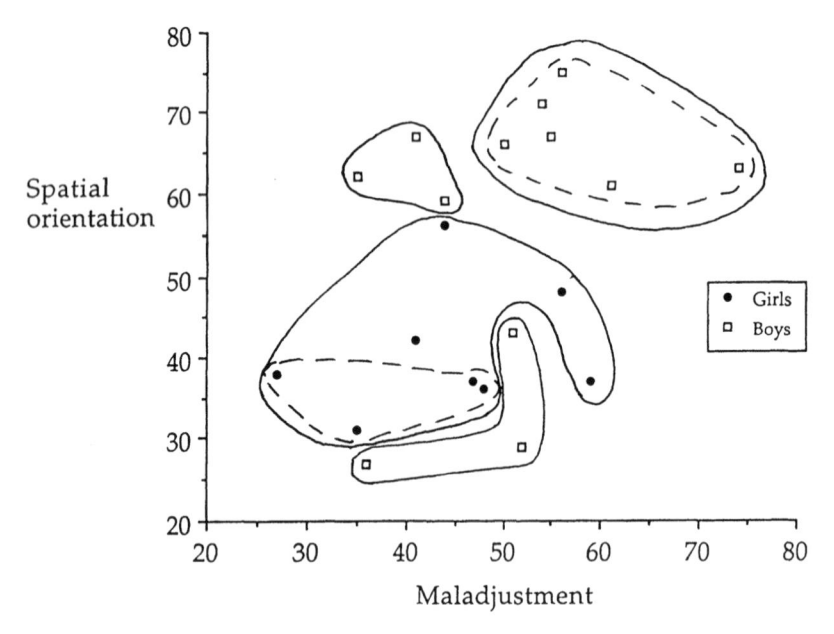

FIG. 5.1. A plot of the data presented in Table 5.1 with maladjustment score on the x axis, spatial orientation score on the y axis, boys denoted by squares, and girls denoted by dots. Encircled areas indicate the four clusters emerging in a cluster analysis of the two continuous variables and gender. Areas encircled with broken lines indicate a significant type/tendency to type in CFA.

the four clusters in a 4-cluster solution using Ward's method. All girls constituted one cluster and there were three clusters for boys, one of which corresponds exactly to the type "223."

The features of the data structure just discussed would not have been picked up by the simple variable-oriented analyses we started with in Table 5.1 but could have been picked up by more sophisticated variable oriented methods. Nevertheless, we think the simple example given illustrates the potential of CFA for finding interesting higher order interaction structures in a data set. In the case of a large sample and a large number of variables, CFA also retains much of its simplicity in description and interpretation in contrast to variable-oriented methods, which tend to have severe difficulties in handling higher order interactions.

Chapter 6
SOME METHODS FOR STUDYING PATTERN DEVELOPMENT

1. STUDYING THE DEVELOPMENT OF SINGLE INDIVIDUALS

This chapter focuses on the study of interindividual differences in pattern development. This is logical in the present context in which generalizations are to be made to populations of individuals and in which interindividual differences are thought to be profound and of prime interest in themselves. However, it should not be interpreted that we consider the study of the single individual to be unimportant; on the contrary, it can be argued that this study is at the heart of understanding individual development, both in its own right, and as a basis for careful generalization, in which studies of many such single cases are integrated. In the context of studying short-term changes in behavior, this argument was put forward by Jones and Nesselroade (1990). It is also relevant in the context of the study of long-term development (Nesselroade & Ghisletta, 2000; Valsiner, 1986). In this latter case, methodological tools such as latent growth curve analysis and time-series analysis are available for studying individual trajectories, as indicated in chapter 3.

However, in many situations one does not have the intensive longitudinal data needed for carrying out analyses of the types just mentioned. Moreover, the main goal may be to understand interindividual differences in pattern development; this goal calls for the use of a variety of analyzing strategies. We believe the arguments provided in chapter 2 and chapter 3 justify the search for homogeneous subgroups of persons with regard to pattern development. Without being the only possible approach, it is the one we focused on in this chapter. Methods with this purpose are now presented.

2. MODEL-BASED AND DESCRIPTIVE METHODS FOR STUDYING PATTERN DEVELOPMENT

A wide variety of different methodological possibilities exist for studying interindividual differences in pattern development. As indicated in chapter 3, we distinguish between model-based and descriptive methods, although the line between these two is not always clear. An example of a model-based method without latent variables is loglinear modeling (Bishop et al., 1975). Examples of tailoring this method to the study of change can be found in Clogg et al. (1990). Examples of model-based methods with latent variables are latent class analysis and Markov chain models.

Collins and Wugalter (1992) presented a method called latent transition analysis (LTA). With this method, a model can be constructed with an array of latent classes representing latent status at a given time. The latent statuses are used for constructing what they call "stage-sequential dynamic latent variables" (p. 131). Among other things, transition probabilities for the latent statuses between adjacent time points are estimated by the model. LTA has been extended in various ways, enabling the user to test a variety of models about pattern development. Errors of measurement in the indicators can also be handled by the model. However, in order to apply the model, a number of strict assumptions must be made (see Collins & Wugalter, 1992) and the power to reject a "bad" model often seems to be low for small samples. It is probably fair to say that LTA is most useful when a very "strong" model can be tested (i.e., a model with almost all parameters fixed).

Although, for obvious reasons, model-based methods are highly useful in many situations, they are not pursued further in this chapter. We concentrate instead on methods that are essentially descriptive, and that are more basic and flexible. These methods usually involve fewer assumptions about the properties of the data and can serve as basic tools. We consider this restriction to more descriptive methods as necessary to enable us to present in sufficient detail a number of useful methods within the confinements of a short book. Besides, to a certain extent, the approaches presented here can also incorporate specific hypothesis testing about development.

The interest in pattern development can take many different forms besides classifying individuals' development on the basis of their patterns of values on relevant (continuous) variables. If the variables constituting the patterns are discrete and have just a few different values, all possible value patterns could be analyzed using configural frequency analysis (CFA). Some possibilities along these lines will be presented in section 4. In some cases interest is focused on special aspects of patterns like profile scatter and profile extremes. For a further discussion of such aspects, the reader is referred to chapter 3 and to Bergman (1998). Graphical representations of similarities between profiles can sometimes be informative in developmental research, for instance using multidimensional scaling (MDS; Wood, 1990). They are normally best suited for describing a limited number of objects and will only be used here to compare cluster centroids (see chap. 9).

In section 3, we focus on methods for classification of pattern development when the patterns comprise value profiles in variables assumed to be continuous.

3. CLASSIFICATION-BASED METHODS FOR STUDYING INTERINDIVIDUAL DIFFERENCES IN INDIVIDUALS' VALUE PATTERNS ACROSS DEVELOPMENT

The main emphasis here is on classification-based methods for studying interindividual differences in the development of individuals' value patterns. We distinguish between three ways in which the developmental process is studied:

1. A longitudinal pattern is formed and longitudinal types are identified directly in the classification. Ideally, this means that full account is taken of each individual's specific pattern of change.
2. At each age, a classification is made and the results of the different classifications are linked, usually pair-wise (the time i classification is linked to the time i + 1 classification). The individuals' class membership over time is then studied.
3. First a common classification system is created that can be applied to each age separately. To accomplish this, the information from each age is considered a subwhole and all subwholes from all ages are combined to constitute a sample of objects that are classified. Then each individual is given his or her sequence of class memberships according to this classification (one class membership for each age). These sequences are then analyzed.

In the following pages, all three of these strategies are discussed. The second we believe to be the most robust and perhaps the one that is most generally applicable.

3.1. The Direct Identification of Typical Longitudinal Patterns

To focus directly on typical longitudinal patterns is attractive because, in a way, these patterns *are* what constitutes pattern development. Two analytic strategies are:

1. The direct clustering of complete longitudinal patterns representing all the information from all the time points studied.
2. The application of an ordination strategy by which the number of dimensions are reduced (principal components analysis is often used for this purpose), followed by a classification analysis of the factor scores, often using cluster analysis (e.g., Mumford & Owens, 1984).

In some respects, a longitudinal classification approach is preferable to the snapshot-and-linking approach described in the next section in that the former approach more closely represents the individuals' multivariate trajectories of change. However, in practice this genuinely longitudinal approach can be problematic. For example, in cluster analytic applications, in which data from all ages are included in the value profile, very heterogeneous clusters are often obtained that are difficult to interpret. In cases with many measurement occasions, one might, for instance, have to accept subjects' classification to the same developmental cluster due to fairly high overall similarity, despite these subjects having a different outcome or a different starting point.

Consider the results presented by Bergman and Magnusson (1986) as an empirical example of the cluster heterogeneity that can be obtained when using longitudinal cluster analysis. The authors studied the development of about 500 boys' patterns of extrinsic adjustment problems (six problems measured at two points in time). Both longitudinal cluster analysis and cross sectional cluster analysis followed by linking were applied (see Bergman, 1998, for a more detailed description). Bergman and Magnusson (1986) concluded that the longitudinal analysis resulted in interpretable results reasonably similar to those obtained using the other strategy. However, in contrast to the cross-sectional approach with linking, the longitudinal cluster solution rendered a fairly heterogeneous clustering solution with many clusters (11), a fairly large residue (5%), and a moderate explained error sum of squares (62%). The authors concluded that, in this case, the complexity of the individuals' developmental patterns was too high to be adequately summarized by a single longitudinal cluster analysis. With more than two time points, this heterogeneity problem tends to be aggravated.

In the aforementioned discussion, it was assumed that both the level and form of the profile were relevant. However, if only profile form is the focus of interest, a direct longitudinal classification might work better than otherwise, as the strain on the classification system is reduced (less information has to be summarized by the cluster membership variable). Block (1971) offered an interesting example of the potential of a longitudinal classification strategy in his longitudinal study of personality types. He used judges to perform Q-sorts of the saliency of a large number of personality characteristics for a sample of persons at different ages. Ratings on these characteristics constituted an individual's profile to be analyzed. First, the similarity between each pair of individuals was computed, using the Pearson correlation coefficient (with the two persons as variables and the rated characteristics as cases). Second, Q-factor analysis was used. Five factors (personality types) were extracted for the boys, and six factors were extracted for the girls. Block makes a number of methodological observations when discussing his results:

1. In studying "the whole personality," it was not relevant to measure similarity with regard to level, scatter, and form; only form was relevant.
2. A balance has to be struck between a fine-graded classification rendering too few cases for statistical analysis for certain types, on one hand, and a classification with just a few types leading to unwanted heterogeneity in the resulting classes on the other hand.

3. Constructing classifications separately at the different ages and then connecting them would raise interpretational problems and may miss the original goal of a longitudinal typology.
4. By including in the profile identical items (both in content and in number) from the adolescent years and from adult age, a balance is achieved and a high degree of similarity between two profiles can be interpreted as similar personality development for two individuals.
5. It is important to allow for the possibility that not everyone will fit into any of a small number of types. Hence, a residue of unclassified persons was formed.

Block's strategy for constructing a longitudinal typology appears relevant in his setting and is probably also useful in other situations in which only profile form is of interest. However, his approach means that interindividual differences are only examined with regard to *ipsative* stability and change. In this case, one must assume that level differences between individuals in the dimensions under study are unimportant and that the ranking of the saliency of characteristics contains all relevant information for the different individuals. In other words, one must disregard individual differences in the level or degree of expression of different characteristics; it must be assumed safe to ignore that persons might be more or less "even" in the level of expression of the different characteristics. In our opinion, his arguments *against* cross-sectional classification followed by linking are less convincing than his arguments *for* a direct longitudinal classification (see Block's, 1971, detailed discussion on pp. 109–120; and the discussion in Bergman, 1998).

3.2. Cross-Sectional Classification Analysis Followed by Linking Over Time Using LICUR

Here we present a method for the cross-sectional analysis of profile data followed by pairwise age linking of the results. It is our goal to provide a reasonably sufficient toolbox for basic analysis of pattern development from an interindividual perspective using this snap-shot-linking approach. We focus on the LInking of ClUsters after removal of a Residue (LICUR) rationale that was first presented in Bergman (1998). In chapter 9, empirical examples of the application are provided.

It should be pointed out that different procedures for cross-sectional classification analysis followed by linking are possible, and that the method selected should be based on the specific case. However, it is also useful to have a standard method that is applicable in a variety of situations and that can also serve as a reference procedure. Here we confine ourselves to the case in which value profiles based on interval scaled data are to be analyzed. It is further assumed that both the form and level of the profile are to be taken into account and that it is important to obtain clusters that are reasonably homogeneous. For this purpose, the LICUR method is presented. The LICUR method involves three steps. The first step is to identify a residue separately at each age (see chap. 4 for a description of the RESIDAN approach to create a residue). The second step is to cluster analyze the subjects separately at each age (see chap. 4 for a general discussion of cluster analysis). The third step is to relate the classifications at adjacent ages to one another. These three steps are now detailed.

3.2.1. The Removal of a Residue. First the RESIDAN approach is used separately at each age to remove a residue, which itself is analyzed separately. Support for this procedure was provided in chapter 4 in which it was suggested that, in many situations, there exist both technical and theoretical reasons for not classifying everybody. RESIDAN, a semiobjective procedure, was suggested for the a priori identification and analysis of a residue of unclassified individuals. This includes the study of unusual or nonexistent value patterns, possibly in the context of identifying so called "white spots" (see chap. 3). Most commonly, the residue contains 1% to 2% of the subjects.

3.2.2. Age-Specific Hierarchical Cluster Analyses. At each age, a cluster analysis is undertaken on the subjects remaining after the residue analysis. A variety of different methods for cluster analysis were discussed in chapter 4 and to a certain extent the choice of method should, of course, depend on the data set and the specific problem under study. Ward's method and k-means relocation are reported to be widely used and often well-functioning methods. The cluster analysis procedures in LICUR are based on these two specific methods. First Ward's hierarchical cluster analysis method is applied and an optimal number of clusters is chosen. Four criteria guide in this decision:

1. The solution selected has to be judged as theoretically meaningful and the last cluster fusion judged not to join two distinct and theoretically interpretable clusters.
2. The number of clusters should preferably not exceed 15 and cannot normally be expected to be fewer than five.
3. A sudden drop in the explained error sum of squares of the solution (ESS; see chap. 4) may indicate that a solution with too few clusters has been reached.
4. The explained ESS for the chosen cluster solution should preferably exceed 2/3 of the total ESS for the one-cluster solution. This criterion ensures reasonably homogeneous clusters and could be complemented by setting a ceiling for the largest acceptable standard deviation of any variable within a cluster. Admittedly, the figure of 2/3 "explained" is arbitrary but, in our experience, it is a figure that is often surpassed by "successful" classifications. However, it should be kept in mind that the more variables that make up the subjects' value profiles, the more difficult it tends to be for the clustering algorithm to find homogeneous clusters for a given num-

ber of clusters. The criterion described here can be relaxed in cases with many variables and when the focus is on the identification of "natural clusters," and not necessarily on assigning the subjects to the "correct" class.

Of course, other criteria are possible for deciding the number of clusters as well as for evaluating the quality of a clustering solution (see chap. 7; also, Milligan & Cooper, 1985).

3.2.3. Relocation Cluster Analyses. As discussed in chapter 4, the hierarchical property of a cluster solution is often very important. If this is the case, then each cross-sectional analysis stops here. However, when the emphasis is on obtaining clusters that are as homogeneous as possible, the Ward cluster solutions are used as start values in k-means relocation cluster analyses. Subjects are then relocated to minimize the ESS. The hierarchical property of the clustering solution is then lost. Our practical experience is that frequently this loss is too high a price to pay for (usually only slightly) more homogeneous clusters. That hierarchical solutions enable the researcher to move up and down the classification tree is extremely valuable. In hierarchical solutions, differently detailed classifications can be used in different analyses and the results easily compared. This, in a way, helps in solving the difficult question of deciding on the number of clusters.

3.2.4. Linking of Results Between Ages. Finally, the classifications obtained at each age are linked by cross-tabulation of age-adjoining classifications and is tested for significant types and antitypes of cluster membership combinations, preferably by using exact cellwise tests. The number of clusters at each age is usually in the range of 5 to 15, resulting in large contingency tables with several expected frequencies being very low for moderate sample sizes. Testing for significant cluster combinations (over- or under-frequented cells) is then problematic using ordinary chi-square-based statistics, as the normal approximations are not accurate. It is then advisable to use exact cellwise tests building on the Fisher fourfield hypergeometric distribution test. This can be done using the EXACON procedure in the SLEIPNER statistical package presented in chapter 8 (see also Bergman & El-Khouri, 1987). The importance of using a more exact test is underscored by the frequent need to make corrections for the mass significance problem, as a large number of cells are usually tested in this way. Exactness in the nominal significance levels becomes important and even a fairly good approximation is often not sufficiently good because the error size will increase with the number of tests made (Bergman & von Eye, 1987; von Eye & Bergman, 1986).

The correction for the mass significance problem can be made in the following way:

1. First one or maybe two cells are identified for which one has a theoretical expectation of a type or an antitype. They are tested at the nominal significance level.

2. Then for the rest of the cells, each is tested for types/antitypes using a procedure for adjusting the nominal significance levels (e.g., Holm's procedure; see chap. 5).

In order to make the results as clear as possible and to focus on the essential aspects, it can be useful to present the categories at each of the ages with arrows between the categories indicating the significant types at adjoining ages, instead of the complete cross tabulations. This form of presentation is exemplified in the analyses presented in chapter 9.

After having carried out a LICUR analysis, the ambitious researcher would like to obtain an idea of the degree to which the results obtained are dependent on the method used and on the characteristics of his or her particular sample. For this purpose, Ward's method could be replaced by the average linkage method or beta-flexible UPGMA clustering, and the LICUR analysis repeated. The results could also be repeated on another equivalent sample or, if that is not available, on a random sample of, say, 75% of the original sample. Of course, such deliberations are influenced by the specific case (for instance, subsampling applies only if the group studied is considered to be a sample from a population). If the sample is small, there can be considerable sampling variation in the results as well as an "overfit" of the results to the peculiarities of the specific sample. In this situation, a rule of thumb might be to interpret only the largest clusters; it cannot be expected that reliable results will be obtained down to the level of a fine-grained classification for small samples. Here one can make use of the facilities available in SLEIPNER for drawing random samples and for establishing the amount of structure typically found in random data. A discussion of reliability and validity issues within classification analysis is given in chapter 7.

It should be pointed out that the LICUR procedure might be useful also in a cross-sectional situation where, instead of studying a sample at, for example, two different ages, two different variable domains are studied for the same sample and each domain is classified separately.

3.3. Analyzing Sequences of Subwholes

In this section a method for analyzing sequences of subwholes is introduced. The information from each age is considered a subwhole and all subwholes from all ages are first combined to constitute a sample of objects that are then classified. Each individual is then given his or her sequence of class memberships according to this larger classification (i.e., one class membership for each age). These sequences are then analyzed. The method for accomplishing this is called i-states as objects analysis (ISOA). Because it builds partly on a theoretical/methodological conceptualization taken from the study of nonlinear dynamic systems, this background is introduced briefly first.

3.3.1. Introduction. As pointed out in chapter 2 and chapter 3, the developmental track of an individual can be viewed as being determined by a complex dynamic system with both deterministic and stochastic components; a process that is partly unique to the individual. These characteristics are reflected in strong interactions and in nonlinearity in data across individuals. Operationally, these features suggest that individuals be studied based on their patterns of individual characteristics relevant for the study of the problem under consideration.

Individual development can be conceptualized as a process characterized by *states* with change taking place in (continuous) time. A state is regarded here as a value of a variable vector characterizing the system at a given point in time and is called an *i-state* when referring to a specific individual. When discussing a person approach, Bergman and Magnusson (1997) asserted that a variety of evidence supports the notion that nature often operates in such a way that certain states are in some ways optimal or functional and therefore become attractor states, which are stable during longer time periods and therefore are observed often. Many systems studied are assumed to be *time independent*, that is, the only information of importance for predicting the future of a system is its present system state. Once that is known, time itself is no longer of any importance.

Assuming the same system is examined during the entire time period of study and that the same system characteristics are measured, led Bergman (1995) to suggest ISOA. In ISOA, it is assumed that a limited number of (true) different possible i-states exist and that, in theory if not in practice, they can all be observed at all points in time. The first task is to determine what typical states exist (they are assumed to roughly correspond to the concepts of attractor states within the study of dynamic systems). The task is then to describe how memberships to these typical states changes over time for the individuals in the sample. The method is described briefly now and more fully in Bergman and El-Khouri (1999). For a discussion of principles in studying dynamic systems, the reader is referred to Casti (1989); and for examples within developmental psychology, in particular, to Barton (1994) and Smith and Thelen (1993).

3.3.2. Outline of ISOA. In summary, the idea behind ISOA is borrowed partly from the study of dynamic systems within physics in which certain systems can be viewed as *time-independent*, that is, only the system state at the present time predicts future development, not time per se, and not previous history. This suggests that, using a classification approach, it can be meaningful to first classify states disregarding the time dimension and then use this classification to describe individual development.

In the following discussion, we assume that p continuous variables have been measured at k occasions for n subjects. We further must assume that the essential characteristics of the system under study do not change over time (i.e., only short-term development can be studied using ISOA).

A strategy for carrying out ISOA is the following:

1. Break down each subject into k subsubjects, each being characterized by its value profile in the p variables at a given occasion.
2. Compute the dissimilarities between the $n \times k$ subsubjects. So far, we have only used average squared Euclidean distance when applying ISOA but other methods for computing the dissimilarity could be used, depending on the specific problem under study and the character of the information available.
3. Remove a small number of subsubjects characterized by being (almost) unique, that is, being dissimilar to (almost) all other objects, following the RESIDAN procedure described earlier. The states they reflect are considered as either being "nonexistent" (i.e., products of errors of measurement) or rare and uninteresting from the viewpoint of describing what is typical.
4. Perform a cluster analysis on the remaining subsubjects. If homogeneous clusters appear, they provide a compact description of typical states. These become the basic units of information to be used in further analysis and description.
5. Then "complete subjects" are again formed by constructing the longitudinal cluster membership information. Each individual's longitudinal sequence of categories is studied according to the categorization of typical states. That is, each individual is described by the time-ordered sequence of cluster memberships according to number 4. In other words, the sequence of each individual's i-states is transformed into a sequence of state category values. Frequent category combinations are identified and interpreted as well as nonoccurring combinations ("white-spots").

ISOA can give the user the following three kinds of information:

1. Insight into what typical system states exist. From a dynamic systems view, this provides a map of possible system states, and from the viewpoint of a person-oriented analysis, this provides a common system for classifying profiles of values for each age.
2. Information about how the frequencies of the different typical system states change with time, that is, information about structural stability and change (albeit in a limited sense).
3. A description of individual stability and change viewed against the backdrop of the state classificatory system generated by the method. This includes the possibility of studying developmental routes not followed.

It is a strength of ISOA that in its basic analysis, a fairly large number of subsubjects can be analyzed even for small total samples of subjects when there are many measurement occasions. This situation is rather frequent and the ISOA method can be an efficient way of using all the information available. In a limited sense, the method allows for the quantitative evaluation of structural stability and change, both at a detailed level and at a more global level. At the global level, it seems natural to compare the percentages belonging to the different typical states at the different ages using, for instance, city block metric. ISOA can sometimes also be used for studying individual stability and change between as few as two measurement occasions.

Here we focused on the dissimilarity or similarity between i-states as providing the input information for the classification analysis. Please note that this approach is fairly general and does not require the kind of dimensional data used in conventional analyses of dynamic systems. This is implicit in some of the previous mentioned reasoning. There are many ways of constructing the dissimilarity matrices. For instance, raters could be used to produce dissimilarity estimates for each pair of i-states based on the available (perhaps qualitative) information. Of course, this does not mean that the problems of scaling are irrelevant. They should always be taken seriously and must be attended to carefully in each specific situation, as discussed in chapter 3 (see also Bergman & Magnusson, 1991; R. B. Cairns & B. D. Cairns, 1994).

As pointed out, the ISOA method is maximally useful in situations in which no qualitative developmental change takes place. The appropriateness of the method stands and falls with the assumption that it is permissible to compute measures of the degree of (dis)similarity between each pair of i-states both within and between individuals. For example, if pronounced changes occur in the meaning of the variables included due to fundamental developmental changes, then ISOA is less useful. However, the method can adequately reflect certain changes (e.g., the emergence of new states and frequency shifts in states). In cases with strong developmental change and changing meaning of the variables included, the LICUR procedure introduced previously, is a viable alternative.

ISOA is now incorporated in the SLEIPNER statistical package, and an example of an ISOA analysis is given in chapter 9.

4. STUDYING PATTERN DEVELOPMENT BY MAPPING ALL POSSIBLE VALUE COMBINATIONS

An obvious approach to studying pattern development is to in some way reduce the number of possible patterns and then to analyze all patterns and how individuals develop as reflected by changing value combinations in these patterns. In this way, some of the difficulties inherent in classifying patterns are "solved" because all patterns can be retained during the complete analysis. The reader has by now recognized that this is the idea behind the CFA approach presented in chapter 5. There, CFA was introduced in a cross-sectional setting as a method for analyzing all possible and observed value patterns in discrete variables.

The CFA approach has been extended in various ways to permit the analysis of developmental or repeated measurement data (see Lienert & zur Oeveste, 1985; von Eye, 1990b; and von Eye et al., 1996). In the context of direct analysis of longitudinal pattern data, we briefly mention the following two procedures:

1. The first procedure is to simply analyze all the observed value patterns at all ages simultaneously using CFA. In this case, similar problems to those

described in section 3.1 are likely to arise and there is often also a problem of extremely sparse frequencies in the cells defined by the configurations.

2. In the second category of procedures, first the change scores between each adjacent pair of ages are formed for each variable (sometimes after an ordination procedure has been applied); and second, these change scores are subjected (after dichotomization or trichotomization) to a CFA. This leads to a dramatic reduction in the number of possible and observed value patterns that, in most cases, makes this approach more practically feasible than number 1. However, it should be noted that raw score change scores are notoriously unreliable and this, to a certain extent, also carries over to dichotomized or trichotomized change scores. Large errors of measurement in the change scores can obscure existing types and antitypes. The low reliability of change scores has to do with the frequent high correlation between the time 1 and time 2 scores due to shared true variation. Therefore, the variation in the change scores tends to be error variation to a larger extent than the variation in the scores at time 1 or time 2. This was discussed in chapter 3.

A variety of different methods for describing change or development have been developed within the CFA tradition and the reader is referred to the aforementioned references and to references given in chapter 5 for a description of such methods, including more elaborated variants of number 1 and number 2 just presented. In chapter 9, we also present an empirical example in which we undertake some analyses of the types discussed here.

When applying a cross-sectional analysis with linking between ages, a CFA approach may also be useful. Many different approaches have been developed within the CFA tradition, including methods for testing for types of stability. The interaction structure analysis presented in chapter 5 can also be modified to apply to cross-tabulations across age, and so forth. Lienert and Bergman (1985) introduced a similar strategy called Longisectional Interaction Structure Analysis (LISA), which can also be used with a combination of configural frequency data and classification data.

A simple procedure that is sometimes useful is the following. Carry out a CFA at each age and then, on the basis of these analyses, reduce the number of categories at each age by merging certain unusual and "uninteresting" configurations. Then cross-tabulate the remaining categories between adjacent ages, following the rationale indicated in step 3 of the LICUR procedure presented in this chapter. In chapter 9, some analyses of this type are carried out. Hildebrand, Laing, and Rosenthal (1977) developed a method for testing (composite) hypotheses of relations between categorical variables. This method can be used for verifying if theoretical predictions of overfrequented and underfrequented cells hold up when cross-tabulation data of the type discussed here are available. This is one way of moving in the direction of theory testing, starting from the largely descriptive framework presented here.

Chapter 7
EXAMINING THE GENERALIZABILITY OF RESULTS

The need for taking issues of reliability and validity seriously exists in all scientific endeavors and, of course, here also. This can be taken as self-evident and needs no special motivation. However, in the present context, there are two additional reasons for highlighting the importance of reliability and validity:

1. The approach presented here and the methods used to carry it out are considered by many "nonstandard." The user of this approach may therefore encounter a certain skepticism that can be overcome by an especially careful analysis and presentation of aspects of reliability and validity.
2. Some of the technical methods used, foremost, cluster analysis, are not formulated in the form of a mathematical–statistical model, which incorporates errors of measurement and sampling errors. Hence, their effects are hard to evaluate. It is also documented that under certain conditions, results from cluster analysis can be distorted by such errors (see Milligan, 1980.)

Cronbach, Gleser, Nanda and Rajaratnam (1971) pointed to the importance of interpreting the reliability and validity of results in terms of their generalizability under varying conditions. This is also our view and in the present context, we highlight the following seven major facets of trustworthiness and generalizability:

1. The similarity to the results obtained if other methods were used to analyze the same data. For instance, to what degree does the obtained cluster solution differ from the classification obtained by using another clustering algorithm?

2. Quality of the representation of the inherent structure of the data at hand. For instance, the degree of correspondence is studied between the classification obtained and the basic input data as represented by the dissimilarity matrix.
3. The similarity to the results that would have been obtained if there were no errors of measurements.
4. The similarity to the results obtained for the population from which the studied subjects are considered to be a sample.
5. The similarity of the results to those obtained for other populations of subjects.
6. The similarity of the results to those obtained for different age periods than the studied one.
7. The similarity of the results or obtained for a similar set of variables.

Of course, it depends on the specific situation which of the seven facets are most relevant. With the enormous increase in computational power during the last several years, it is possible to study certain aspects of the facets using data simulation. To some extent, we can now solve by "brute force" problems of error estimation that we cannot solve using analytical methods.

In the following, several methods for studying these facets are suggested and discussed.

We concentrate on the most common situation in which we have access to information on k interval scaled variables for n subjects and the classification method used is cluster analysis. The profile of values for the subjects in these variables is assumed to contain the necessary information for deciding to which class a subject belongs. We also assume that both the level and form of a profile contain relevant information. Certain aspects of the material we now present can be generalized to other contexts but for the sake of brevity, we do not go into that in this volume.

Let us first consider facet 1. The method-generalizability of an obtained classification can be studied in a number of ways, three of which are presented below:

1. Classifications can be produced using other methods and the different classifications compared. For instance, if the original classification was the result of a cluster analysis, a number of additional cluster analyses are performed using other clustering algorithms and possibly also using other dissimilarity measures. The results using these different methods are then compared. There exist a number of methods for comparing different classifications of the same subjects (see, e.g., Dubes & Jain, 1979; and Morey et al., 1983). One set of methods is based on a four-field table formed with the total number of observations being equal to the number of pairs of subjects. In this table, the observations are classified into whether they belong to the same cluster or not in classification 1 (first dichotomous category

variable) and whether they belong to the same cluster or not in classification 2 (second dichotomous category variable). The relationship between the two dichotomous category variables is then compared. One such measure of relationship that appears to be useful is the modified Rand index (Hubert & Arabie, 1985). This index is computed by the SLEIPNER statistical package.
2. A more straightforward but also less sophisticated way of comparing two classifications is to cross-tabulate the two cluster solutions. However, as soon as the two classifications do not exhibit a reasonably good one-to-one match with regard to the centroids, the interpretation of such a table becomes difficult. The SLEIPNER statistical package can be used for analyzing this cross-tabulation after writing cluster memberships to a new results file and then using the EXACON module.
3. It should be noted that the two methods described in number 1 are focused on comparing the classifications per se, that is, how similar they are in assigning the subjects to clusters. However, in line with the reasoning presented in earlier chapters, sometimes this is not appropriate, in particular, in situations in which the classification is used primarily as a means of identifying typical cases. The purpose, in this case, is to find "natural clusters," defining types by their centroids. Here, the two classifications are compared only with regard to their centroids. This can be accomplished using the following simple matching procedure: First, the two clusters are paired (one from each classification) that have the smallest dissimilarity as measured by the average squared Euclidean distance. Then, the procedure is repeated for the remaining clusters and ends when one (or both) of the classifications does not contain any more clusters. The mean of the average squared Euclidean distances of the cluster pairs can be used as an index of the similarities between the centroids in the different classifications. This procedure is implemented in the SLEIPNER statistical package under the name of CENTROID.

Let us now consider facet 2. The quality of the representation of the dissimilarity matrix by the obtained classification can be evaluated in different ways and a variety of different indices exist (see Milligan, 1981a, for an overview). (Of course, using such methods is also one way of studying facet 1 just discussed.) We only mention the following two indices here:

1. *The point biseral correlation.* The units in this calculation are the pairs of subjects. The dissimilarity coefficient is calculated for each pair and it is noted whether the two subjects in the pair belong or do not belong to the same cluster in the classification. Then the point biseral correlation is computed between the dichotomous variable and the dissimilarity value.

2. *The percentage of the total error sum of squares "explained" by the classification (denoted with EV).* This is an index we have found useful in our applications. It should be pointed out that EV is less generally applicable than the point biseral correlation and the assumptions made in the introduction to this section must hold. The rationale behind EV is the following: Using value profiles of interval scaled variables and average squared Euclidean distance as measuring dissimilarity, a measure of class heterogeneity is given by the error sum of squares within clusters (denoted with Ec). Ec is computed as follows. First, for each subject in a cluster, the sum of all squared deviations from the centroid is divided by the number of variables. This adjusted sum is summed across subjects in the cluster and across all clusters to obtain Ec. The total error sum of squares for the whole sample is denoted as Et (= Ec if there is only one cluster). EV can now be calculated as

$$EV = 100 \times (Et - Ec) / Et$$

EV indicates the percentage of the total error sum of squares "explained" by the classification and is sometimes called the explained ESS. A figure of 100 indicates a perfect class homogeneity (all subjects in the same cluster have identical profiles) and a figure of 0 indicates the complete absence of cluster homogeneity (the variability among profiles belonging to the same cluster is the same as the total variability disregarding cluster membership). The term, *error sum of squares,* may be somewhat confusing because it is used in an unusual context. However, the name is logical because, from a classification point of view, all deviations within a cluster indicate an error in the classification from a homogeneity perspective. Computing Ec separately for each cluster and dividing by the number of subjects in the cluster results in a homogeneity coefficient for each cluster. The lower this coefficient, the more homogeneous the cluster. If z-standardized data are used, a crude rule of thumb is that the homogeneity of a cluster should be under 1.00.

What value ranges of the point biseral correlation and of EV indicate a satisfactory "fit" between the classification obtained and the structure of the data? It is, of course, impossible to give a general answer to this question. First, it depends on whether the finding of typical cases or the assignment of subjects to clusters is the primary focus. In the second case, high values on the two indices are important. Second, EV tends to increase when a larger number of classes are used in the classification and tends to decrease as the number of variables in the value profile increases. Third, EV typically vary between successful classifications in different areas. In our applications, we have formed a rule of thumb that for a profile that is well measured and does not contain very many variables (not more than seven), we consider an EV in the range of 67% as indicating a classification with reasonably homogeneous classes.

Both these indices are computed by the SLEIPNER statistical package along with others.

With regard to facet 3, many different approaches can be used to determine the degree to which errors of measurement have affected the results. Unfortunately, no approach is totally satisfactory and, as always, what can be achieved depends on the assumptions that can be made about the error generating mechanism. Methods that sometimes are useful include the following three:

1. It has sometimes been pointed out that it can be of interest to find out whether the observed cluster structure is compatible with what could be expected in similar data sets in which all relationships have been removed. If this is the case, the results can be regarded as "uninteresting" in the sense that they are only what could be expected to result from analyzing a random data set. We would at least like to establish that the "quality" of the obtained cluster solution is superior to what could be expected if random data were analyzed. The quality of a structure could be summarized by some index of what has been accomplished by the clustering solution, for instance using an internal criterion measure like EV. Two simple approaches are:
   a. Consider the observed index value for the real data set as one observation from a distribution of index values, with each one having been computed from a random permutation of the columns of the original data set. If a large number of simulated data sets have been created and for each one the index has been computed, one can see if the observed index value for the real data belongs, for instance, to the 5% "best" index values.
   b. The index value obtained for the real data set is considered as a population mean. It is then tested whether the index values obtained in the simulations can be regarded as drawn from a population with that mean index value. An approximate t test can be used for this purpose. This method is cruder but more practical, as it does not require as many simulations. It is implemented in the SIMULATE module of the SLEIPNER package and the corresponding t value with $df = s - 1$ is reported in the SIMULATE output (s = the number of simulations). The first type of test can also be carried out using SLEIPNER output. However, in our experience, it seldom makes much difference what test is used; they usually give the same result.
2. A small random error term can be added to each variable value. Then in a simulation study, a large number of new data sets are constructed based on the real data set but with the error "noise" added. The classifications derived from these new data sets are then compared to the original classification.
3. At various places in this volume, it has been pointed out that there are some reasons to believe that leaving a residue in the classification analysis (i.e., not classifying everyone) can improve the quality of a classification. We believe that sometimes this approach can reduce the effects of mea-

surement and sampling errors insofar as these errors are largely associated with outlier observations.

The sensitivity of the results to sampling variation (facet 4) is important to evaluate in situations in which the group studied is considered a sample and one wants to generalize to the larger population. This can be done in several different ways. For large samples, a simple procedure is to analyze random split halves separately and then compare the two classifications obtained. More elaborated procedures have been developed by Morey et al. (1983) and by Breckenridge (1989). However, for small samples, such types of replication procedures may be less attractive as there may be reasons to expect that half of a small sample will not provide a very reliable classification even though the whole sample may suffice to do so reasonably well. An alternative is to use data simulation and construct a large number of random samples drawn from the original sample, each comprising 90% of the original sample size. On each such sample, the original analysis is rerun and the results compared to the original classification (in particular, to the centroids and the relative frequencies of the observations in the clusters). For this purpose, SLEIPNER can be used, albeit awkwardly.

Concerning facet 5 and facet 6, we do not say more here about these difficult issues than that they should be taken seriously. Much has been written about them from a variable-oriented perspective, both within the survey research literature (e.g., Groves, 1989, for a discussion of survey errors) and within the literature on developmental methodology (e.g., Bergman, 1993; Nesselroade & Reese, 1973). See also Breckenridge (1989) for methods for comparing the results obtained from different samples, which relates to facet 5.

Facet 7 concerns the generalizability of the results to those that would have been obtained had the value profile been constituted of another set of variables similar to those studied. It is well known in the cluster analysis literature that adding/deleting/changing even a single variable that is part of a value profile can substantially alter the results produced by many clustering algorithms (Milligan, 1980). We believe that in this context, the following considerations are important (given in order of importance):

1. The fundament for carrying out a person approach studying Gestalts or profiles is a theoretically relevant definition of what variables should be included in the value profile and sound measurements of these variables. There is no room for casualness; for instance, including some extra variables in the profile because they "might be useful" or using two measures of the same theoretical concept as separate variables in the profile just because they are available.
2. Sometimes it is possible to construct an alternative variable profile to the original one that is based on slightly different variables but that can be assumed to be equivalent. The different classifications that are produced us-

ing the original profile and the alternative profile can then be compared using the methods described for facet 1, if the same sample was used. If different samples are compared, the situation is more difficult. After standardization of the involved variables, it might be possible to use the pairwise matching strategy just described to compare the cluster centroids between the two cluster solutions.

In this presentation we have, of course, not touched upon all aspects of validity. For example, predictions can be made of expected mean differences between the classes in some variable external to the classification (see Milligan, 1996). Cluster comparisons can be made for a validation variable using standard methods like ANOVA or by using stochastic comparative procedures (Vargha, 2001). Sometimes a classification is "validated" by establishing significant mean differences between the clusters in variables used for producing the classification. This is not a useful procedure, as any good clustering algorithm will most often produce mean differences between the clusters in the variables used in the classification, even for random data. To give a simple example: Assume one variable is measured and that its values are random numbers. Assume a cluster analysis carried out using this variable, dividing the sample into two clusters. The analysis will result in all observations smaller than a certain value being assigned to one cluster and all observations larger than this value assigned to the other cluster. It is clear there will be large mean differences between the clusters.

We would like to end this chapter with two comments. First, more elaborate procedures than those suggested here have been developed, especially within a cluster analytic framework, and the reader prepared to do thorough analyses along these lines is referred to the sources mentioned in this chapter. Second, the careful validation of results is at the heart of every serious research enterprise and cannot in any totality be captured by simple standardized procedures. In each special case, the researcher must also find his or her own method of establishing the generalizability and dependability of the results.

Chapter 8
SLEIPNER, A Statistical Package for Person-Oriented Analysis

1. INTRODUCTION

SLEIPNER is a set of computer programs forming a statistical package. It is a workbench for pattern-oriented analysis in the context of the person-oriented approach. It is structurally formulated to address classificatory questions that arise against a background of cluster analytic-oriented investigations of primarily longitudinal, but also cross-sectional data.

Historically, SLEIPNER was conceived of and conceptualized in the Stockholm Laboratory for Developmental Science by Lars Bergman and Bassam El Khouri. It has gradually evolved during the last 12 years with the program code written by El Khouri. The package is a collection of modules implementing methods of analysis that were carefully chosen to form a self-contained and empirically grounded toolbox for handling longitudinal data within the person-oriented paradigm. As the background concepts evolved and the need grew for special tailored tools for conducting the analysis, more modules were constructed. The version of SLEIPNER presented here (version 2.1) now comprises 16 distinct modules.

The majority of procedures are specifically constructed and implemented to answer specific questions in the classificatory setting advocated here. Some of the methods exist already implemented in other statistical packages, but as far as we know, SLEIPNER is the most comprehensive package available for person-oriented analysis in a developmental context.

1.1. Module Blocks Characterizing SLEIPNER

Four blocks of modules characterize, SLEIPNER specifically (a) data preprocessing modules, (b) modules for the analysis of patterns (mostly cluster analysis), (c) modules for the evaluation and comparison of classifications, and (d) special purpose modules for altering and creating data sets and files for subsequent use by other modules.

The data preprocessing modules comprise DESCRIBE, IMPUTE, and RESIDUE. The modules for pattern analysis comprise CLUSTER, CFA, RELOCATE, DENSE, and ISOA. The modules for the evaluation of classifications and comparison comprise EXACON, EVALUATE, CENTROID, and SIMULATE. Finally, the special purpose modules for altering data sets and files comprise CWRITE, RANDOM, SUBIND, and SHAKE.

Each module has its own distinct output, which in some cases can be used as input to other modules. Some modules produce two types of output[1]: a file reporting the details of the analysis and a data file that is the result of that analysis. For example, one output from the IMPUTE module (which produces both types of files) can be used as input to the RESIDUE module (which also produces both type of files) that, in turn, produces output that can be used as input to the CLUSTER module. Furthermore, one RESIDUE output (data file) needs to be merged with part of the CLUSTER output (by using the CWRITE module), before the result can be used as input to RELOCATE or EXACON, or DENSE and so on.

This characterization will be used throughout the chapter as a frame of reference around which the presentation of the modules is made.

1.2. SLEIPNER—The Program

The SLEIPNER program is similar in nature to most other large programs that have many subprograms. There are technical specifications that define the framework in which the programs operate (e.g., type of machine, operating system, memory requirements, and so forth). The source code consists of more than 17,000 lines of instructions the majority of which is written in FORTRAN 77. The program is structured into 16 modules that can be employed from within the program (once it is started) or act as stand-alone subprograms. There are descriptions of the type of analysis and results that each module can produce and there are schemes that define the type and the form of the input required by each module whether the module is run interactively or in a batch mode.

These descriptions, requirements, and constraints, are outside the scope of this chapter and are not presented here. Instead, they can be found detailed together with the SLEIPNER package on the SLEIPNER website: http://www.psychology.su.se/SLEIPNER Much work has been directed toward insuring that the manual is as complete, error free, self-contained, and easy to use as possible. By following the instructions and the examples presented in the manual, the researcher should find no difficulty in performing his or her intended analysis. SLEIPNER is given to other researches for free.

However, we ask all users to register at the website.

---

[1]Details of the types of output produced are given in the presentation of each module.

1.3. The Organization of the Chapter

Working with SLEIPNER comprises a series of more or less interwoven steps that can most easily be understood in the context of an empirical study. First, however, brief and general introductions to the individual steps are in order and these are presented in the following sections. In these introductions, some general methodological justifications for undertaking these steps are provided, and brief presentations of the corresponding modules in SLEPINER are given. A detailed empirical presentation is deferred to chapter 9 where a coherent methodological approach is highlighted against a sequence of analyses performed with the SLEPINER package. Strategies for performing longitudinal classification conforming to the person-oriented approach, which are presented and discussed elsewhere in this book, are illustrated using data from the Individual Development and Adaptation (IDA) project and the results are analyzed and discussed.

The presentation of the individual modules is made within the context of the module blocks discussed at the beginning of this chapter, and in such a way as to create a correspondence between the ideas discussed in the previous chapters and their associated data-related activities. These activities form a sequence that may be discerned in the empirical study in chapter 9. They reflect a general strategy that can be adopted for performing classificatory analysis in similar settings. Note, however, that the modules are "stand-alone modules" and, as such, many of them provide a way of analyzing data in contexts other than the longitudinal or even the classificatory.

A subset of the SLEPINER modules are handled here, specifically the DESCRIBE, IMPUTE, RESIDUE, CLUSTER, RELOCATE, ISOA, CFA, EXACON, SIMULATE, and CENTROID. The other modules, CWRITE, DENSE, RANDOM, EVALUATE, SUBIND, and SHAKE are presented only briefly. As mentioned earlier, complete input and output specifications and example runs for all the modules can be located in the SLEIPNER manual which, together with the program, can be found on the SLEIPNER website.

It is assumed that the reader has fair knowledge of the statistical and classificatory terms, concepts, and methods employed and referred to in this chapter, which is most easily obtained by reading the preceding chapters. Whenever appropriate, relevant references to detailed sources are made.

2. SLEIPNER—A WORKBENCH

As already mentioned, the modules in SLEIPNER can be organized conceptually into four blocks: data preprocessing modules, classificatory modules, modules for classificatory evaluations and comparisons, and special purpose modules for altering and creating data sets and files for subsequent use by other modules.

Because of the pattern-oriented nature of the analysis that is of interest here, it is useful to roughly delineate three phases in the classificatory process:

1. The preprocessing phase: an iterative phase in which variables are chosen, data are collected, coded, registered, scrutinized for errors, and edited, data missingness is analyzed, imputations performed, and residue analysis is conducted;
2. the analytical phase: an iterative phase in which classes and/or configurations are formed, and class membership identified; and
3. the evaluation phase in which the results are evaluated and/or compared to other results by appropriate methods.

At each step and in each phase, there are many choices to be made (e.g., choice of variables, methods, parameters, and so on). It should be kept in mind that the boundaries between these phases are permeable. Results in one phase may bring into focus a necessary change in the choices made in an earlier phase. Thus, the iteration aspect of the whole process is not confined to within a certain phase but may also involve elements from different phases.

2.1. Data Preprocessing

2.1.1. Data Description. When the data are collected, inspecting the statistical characteristics of each variable (e.g., mean, frequency, standard deviation, missingness, etc.) often yields valuable information for decision making about what variables to choose in constructing the unit of analysis (here a variable vector that optimally represents the system under focus) or whether the variables have the required scaling properties necessary for the analysis. Rescaling the data was discussed in chapter 3 where it was shown how applying quasiabsolute scaling methods can help establish comparative scales for the variables in the study.

Inquiring about the statistical properties of variables also involves examining their linear relationships. It is usually not recommended to have extremely highly correlated variables in a variable vector under analysis. As in a number of multivariate analysis methods, in cluster analysis this high linearity will unduly amplify the effects of these variables and is reflected in the computations of proximities between two distinct units.

Missingness is also of particular interest. Because the unit of investigation here is a pattern of values on a measurement vector, any missing value in one particular variable would render the individual case useless in the subsequent analysis unless certain actions are taken. Large missingness in one arbitrary variable implies a large loss in cases; something that the analyst usually would like to avoid. Sometimes, a straightforward solution might be to remove the variable altogether (reduce the dimensionality of the measurement vector by one) provided that the variable is somewhat expendable (i.e., the psychological dimension that the variable represents can be accounted for somewhat by another variable or set of variables), and the increase in the number of complete cases is substantial. When missingness is also multidimensional, a pair of variables may be removed that would result in the largest increase in complete cases. In short, the analyst may ask: (a) In a large set of variables, which should be removed to optimally increase the sample of cases with complete data? (b) What is the degree of partial dropout in the data set at hand?

The DESCRIBE module provides the basis for answering these questions.

The DESCRIBE Module

DESCRIBE provides descriptive information for multivariate data sets focusing on the configurations of missing values. For each variable, the module provides the mean, standard deviation, maximum value, minimum value, number of cases with missing values, and the increase in valid cases following the removal of that particular variable. The number of complete cases and the number of cases with missing values in one or more variables are also given. Moreover, the pair of variables that results in the largest increase in valid cases were this pair to be removed is specified, and the Pearson correlations are computed for all pairs of variables, and the results are printed in a table. An illustration of how the output is organized in DESCRIBE is given in Fig. 8.1.

2.1.2. Handling Missingness With Imputation. The results from DESCRIBE may lead the analyst to exclude variables for different reasons, one of which may be extensive missingness in one or more expendable variables. Moderate missingness in variables that are judged essential to the intended analysis may be handled without discarding these variables. The intention is then to reduce missingness on that variable, so that the information on other variables for the cases where that variable is missing is taken advantage of for making an intelligent guess of the missing value (known as *imputation*). Care should be taken not to treat these partly artificial cases as complete cases in settings other than those to be described, and unduly univariate analysis on variables with imputed values should be avoided. The imputed data file should not become the real data file; it is only a temporary file for a specific analysis.

Several imputation methods exist and can be used in a variety of situations depending on the purpose of the analysis and the assumptions made about the data. One relevant purpose in the present context is to discover common patterns in a data set. To this end, we use cluster analytic techniques, which in the present approach, exclusively rely on the average squared Euclidean distance as the proximity measure between two units, with the variables defining the measurement vector measured on at least an interval scale. With this purpose in mind, it is natural to employ a "hot deck" approach for imputation. In short, this means identifying, for each case with missing value(s) on some variable(s), the closest neighbor: a complete case whose values on the variable(s) in question are used for imputing the missing values. The proximity between an incomplete case and a complete one is, of course, computed using the variables for which imputation is not required.

In SLEIPNER, the IMPUTE module can be employed for performing close-neighbor imputations. It also possible to perform mean imputations, in which the

```
|============|============|============|============|============|
|  Variable  |    Mean    |     SD     |  Maximum   |  Minimum   |
|============|============|============|============|============|
|      1     |    1.491   |    .500    |      2     |      1     |
|      2     |    4.722   |   1.694    |      7     |      1     |
|      3     |    4.664   |   1.823    |      7     |      1     |
|      4     |    4.640   |   1.777    |      7     |      1     |
|      5     |    3.424   |    .917    |      5     |      1     |
|      6     |    3.491   |    .821    |      5     |      1     |
|      7     |    3.447   |    .883    |      5     |      1     |
|      8     |    3.529   |    .881    |      5     |      1     |
|    ETC...  |            |            |            |            |
|============|============|============|============|============|
```

```
|============|============|============|============|============|
|  Variable  |  Missing   |   No. of   |Valid cases | Increase in|
|            | value code |missing cases|           | valid cases|
|            |            |            |            | if removed |
|============|============|============|============|============|
|      1     |     9      |      0     |    908     |      0     |
|      2     |     9      |    285     |    623     |     12     |
|      3     |     9      |    248     |    660     |      7     |
|      4     |     9      |    291     |    617     |     51     |
|      5     |     9      |    280     |    628     |      0     |
|      6     |     9      |    236     |    672     |      0     |
|      7     |     9      |    223     |    685     |      0     |
|      8     |     9      |    280     |    628     |      0     |
|    ETC...  |            |            |            |            |
|============|============|============|============|============|
```

```
| Number of cases with missing values in EXACTLY K variables:     |
|=================================================================|
|  No. of cases    |    K                                         |
|==================|==============================================|
|      392         |    0                                         |
|       96         |    1                                         |
|        8         |    2                                         |
|        6         |    3                                         |
|      ETC...      |                                              |
|==================|==============================================|
```

```
| NOTE: No case have missing values in more than  12 variables    |
|=================================================================|
| Pair of variables giving the largest  |  Increase in valid cases|
| increase in valid cases if removed    |                         |
|=======================================|=========================|
|       5        |       8              |         280             |
```

FIG. 8.1. A snapshot showing part of the output of DESCRIBE. The output is altered to fit the screen.

missing values on a certain variable are imputed with the mean of the nonmissing values of that variable.

IMPUTE offers both a standard method of imputation and a user-tailored method of imputation in which either the close neighbor approach or mean imputation can be chosen.

If the nonstandard method is used, standardizing the data or not, type of proximity, threshold level of proximity, and weighting variables are all choices left for the user to make. Decisions of this sort depend partly on the statistical properties of the variables involved and partly on the type of subsequent analysis to be conducted. For instance, it is natural to use the same type of proximity measure in the imputation procedure as that intended for use in a subsequent residue analysis or cluster analysis. Moreover, standardizing the data is usually a wise step prior to the analysis if the variables have different scales and have ranges that vary considerably. Weighting the variables must also be considered in light of subsequent classificatory activities and must be properly justified. Also, the required level of proximity necessary for two cases to be labeled close neighbors must be decided against the background of these previous choices.

The IMPUTE module is described next.

The IMPUTE Module

IMPUTE performs imputation analysis on a data set with incomplete cases by replacing the missing values of an incomplete case with values taken from a "close neighbor" case. If the procedure is run with the standard option, the data are standardized prior to imputation, the squared Euclidean distance is used as a measure of proximity between cases, and the corresponding threshold for two cases to be considered close neighbors is set to .5. If the nonstandard routine is selected, the user is allowed to choose between performing the analysis on the original raw data or alternatively on the data after it is standardized, to choose as the measure of proximity the squared Euclidean distance or the correlation coefficient, to assign weights to the different variables, and to decide the threshold for considering two cases to be close neighbors. The imputed cases are reported together with their respective close neighbors, and a new data file is created in which the complete cases and the imputed cases are included and the cases with too many missing values and cases for whom no close neighbor was found are excluded. An illustration of how the output in IMPUTE is organized is given in Fig. 8.2.

2.1.3. Residue Analysis. So far we examined characteristics of the data set focusing on missingness. The data set is now well defined both in terms of the variables that are to be included in the analysis and in terms of having complete units for analysis. What is not yet known is whether all of these units are suitable for subsequent classificatory analysis given that (a) the data set may be of moderate size; (b) cluster analytic techniques are to be used for classification; and (c) error of mea-

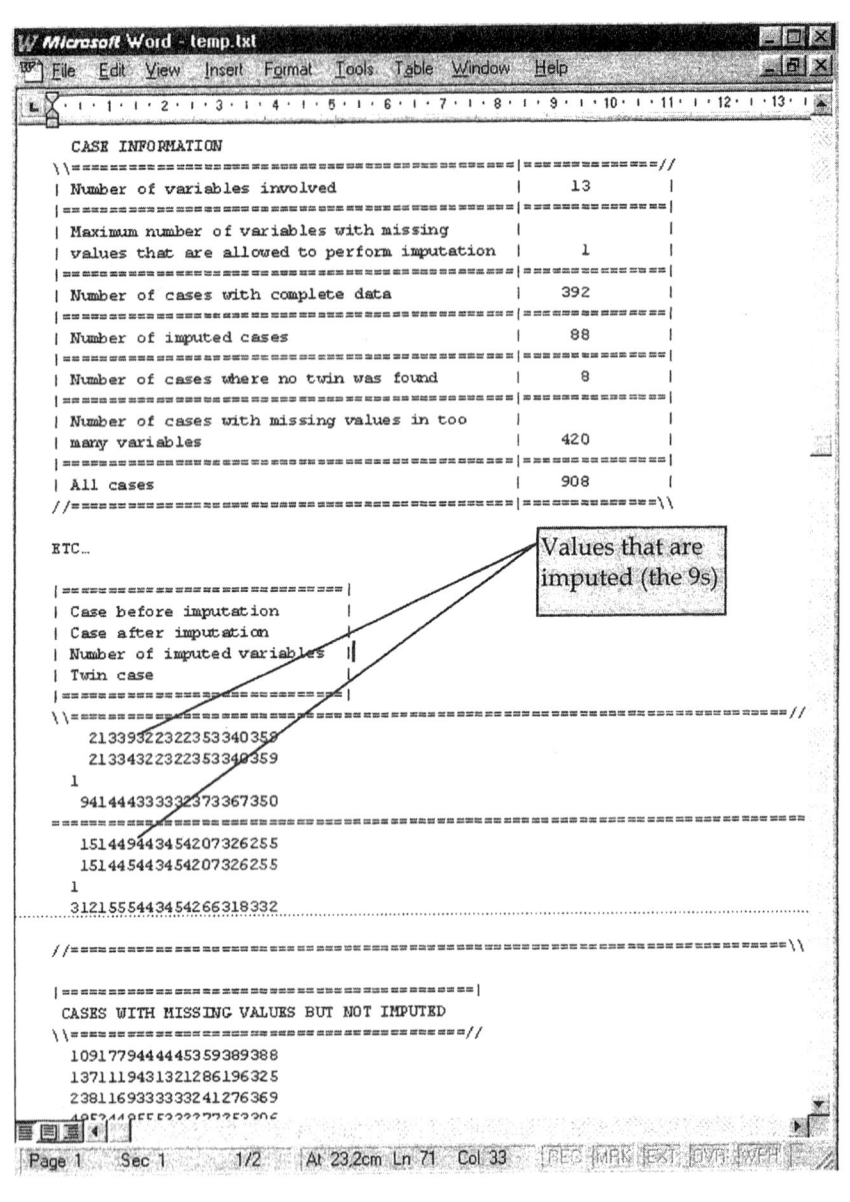

```
CASE INFORMATION
\\================================================|=============//
| Number of variables involved                    |     13      |
|=================================================|=============|
| Maximum number of variables with missing        |             |
| values that are allowed to perform imputation   |     1       |
|=================================================|=============|
| Number of cases with complete data              |    392      |
|=================================================|=============|
| Number of imputed cases                         |     88      |
|=================================================|=============|
| Number of cases where no twin was found         |      8      |
|=================================================|=============|
| Number of cases with missing values in too      |             |
| many variables                                  |    420      |
|=================================================|=============|
| All cases                                       |    908      |
//================================================|=============\\

ETC...

|=================================|
| Case before imputation          |
| Case after imputation           |
| Number of imputed variables     |
| Twin case                       |
|=================================|
\\================================================================//
   2133932232235334035̶8̶
   2133432232235334̶0̶359
 1
   941444333332̶373367350
==================================================================
   1514494434542073262̶55
   1514454434542073262̶55
 1
   312155544345426631833̶2̶
..................................................................

//================================================================\\

|============================================|
 CASES WITH MISSING VALUES BUT NOT IMPUTED
\\===========================================//
   10917794444453593893̶88
   13711194313212861963̶25
   2381693333332̶41276369
```

Values that are imputed (the 9s)

FIG. 8.2. A snapshot showing part of the output of IMPUTE. The output is altered to fit the screen.

surements are bound to exist in the data set, and there may be theoretical reasons not to expect some units to fall into any one common pattern.

If the purpose is to identify common patterns in the data set, then it can be crucial that units that are unique be identified and separated from the more common units. Whether these singletons arise because of one or a combination of the reasons already mentioned does not influence the fact that the singletons can be inspected on their own terms and indeed sometimes be subjected to a more thorough analysis. Normally, only a very small number of cases are removed in that way.

The same type of reasoning that justified the use of the close neighbor approach when discussing the IMPUTE module can also be used here. In a "normal" setting, a unit that bears no resemblance to any other unit is simply removed from the data set. It is required that a unit has at least one close neighbor; if this requirement is satisfied, the case is kept; otherwise it is removed to a residue set. Depending on the application and the type of classification expected in subsequent analysis, this requirement can be made more stringent by demanding that the number of close neighbors be larger than one, by requiring that the similarity between two cases be more pronounced, or both. Resemblance is then defined as a threshold of proximity beyond which, in a sense, two cases are no longer similar.

The RESIDUE module in SLEIPNER assists in conducting this kind of analysis. It offers a standard way of analysis, in which most parameters are set by the program, and a nonstandard way in which the analyst is required to set the parameters. In the nonstandard way, the analyst is required to choose as the indicator of proximity between the average squared Euclidean distance and the correlation coefficient. He or she is required to decide whether the data is to be standardized or not, to determine the threshold of similarity that identifies close neighbors, to decide the number of close neighbors required for a case to be retained in the analysis (and not moved to the set of residue cases), and to assign weights for the different variables. The same type of considerations regarding these choices and those made for the IMPUTE module can be applied here.

The RESIDUE module is described in the following.

The RESIDUE Module

RESIDUE identifies residual objects, creates a pruned data file from which residual objects have been removed, and reports the results of the residue analysis in another file. In the results, RESIDUE reports for each residue case the five most similar cases together with the respective proximity between each of these cases and the residue case. RESIDUE also reports summary statistics for the residue cases. An illustration of how the output is organized in RESIDUE is given in Fig. 8.3.

2.2. Classificatory Analysis

The three steps just described, describing, imputing, and removing outlying objects from the data sets, were asserted to be essential for "understanding" the nature of

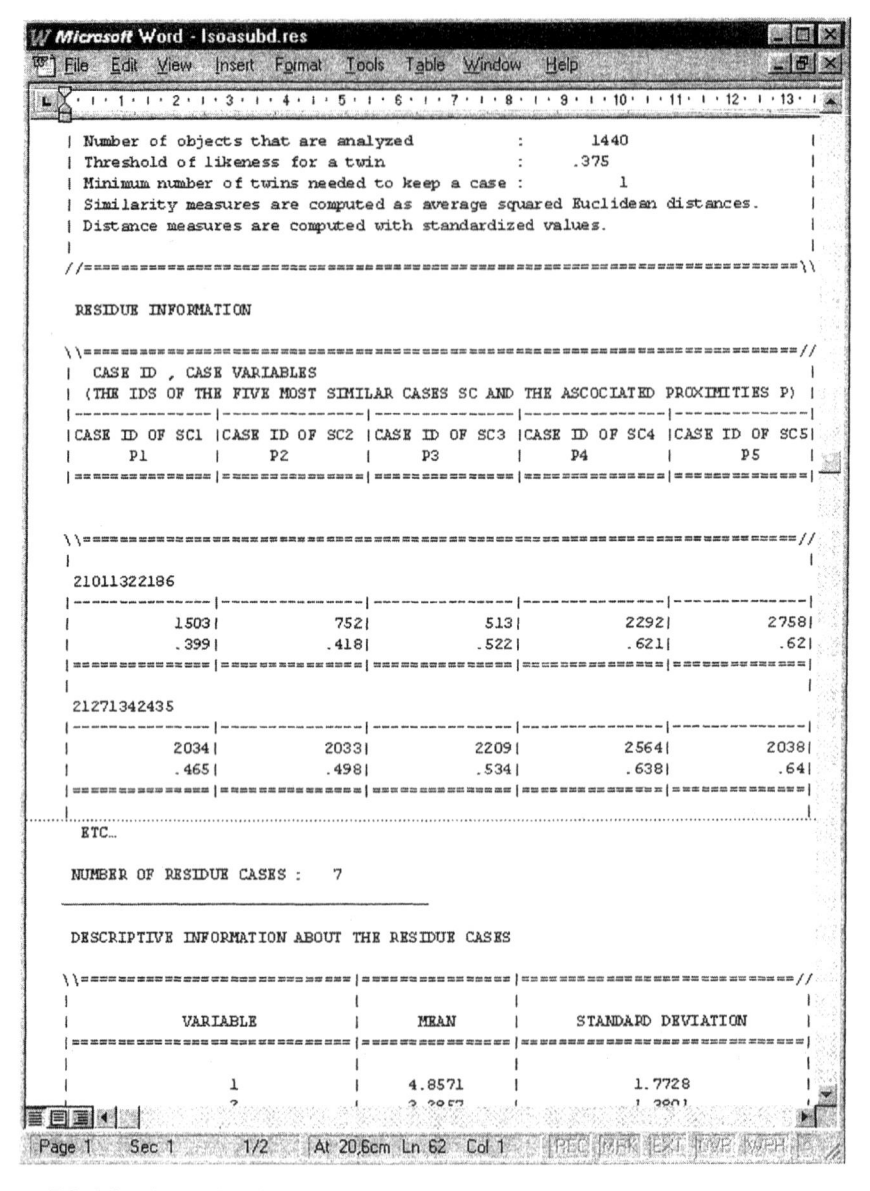

```
| Number of objects that are analyzed        :    1440
| Threshold of likeness for a twin           :    .375
| Minimum number of twins needed to keep a case :   1
| Similarity measures are computed as average squared Euclidean distances.
| Distance measures are computed with standardized values.
|
//=============================================================\\

   RESIDUE INFORMATION

\\=============================================================//
| CASE ID , CASE VARIABLES
| (THE IDS OF THE FIVE MOST SIMILAR CASES SC AND THE ASSOCIATED PROXIMITIES P)
|---------------|---------------|---------------|---------------|---------------|
|CASE ID OF SC1 |CASE ID OF SC2 |CASE ID OF SC3 |CASE ID OF SC4 |CASE ID OF SC5|
|      P1       |      P2       |      P3       |      P4       |      P5      |
|===============|===============|===============|===============|==============|


\\=============================================================//
|
  21011322186
|---------------|---------------|---------------|---------------|---------------|
|          1503 |           752 |           513 |          2292 |          2758|
|          .399 |          .418 |          .522 |          .621 |           .62|
|===============|===============|===============|===============|==============|
|
  21271342435
|---------------|---------------|---------------|---------------|---------------|
|          2034 |          2033 |          2209 |          2564 |          2038|
|          .465 |          .498 |          .534 |          .638 |           .64|
|===============|===============|===============|===============|==============|
|
   ETC...

   NUMBER OF RESIDUE CASES :    7
   _____

   DESCRIPTIVE INFORMATION ABOUT THE RESIDUE CASES

\\==============================|================|==============================//
|                               |                |                              |
|          VARIABLE             |      MEAN      |     STANDARD DEVIATION       |
|===============================|================|==============================|
|                               |                |                              |
|            1                  |    4.8571      |         1.7728               |
```

FIG. 8.3. A snapshot showing part of the output of RESIDUE. The output is altered to fit the screen.

the data and for strengthening the quality of the data prior to subsequent analysis. There are certainly other considerations that should be addressed at the design stage of the study and that touch on the choice of domain of interest (i.e., choosing the subsystem to study, establishing a theoretical background against which the study is conducted, deciding on an appropriate way of modeling that subsystem as reflected in the choice of variables, and if the study is not exploratory, the setting of relevant hypotheses that can be tested). However, we now turn to the classification analysis using cluster analysis.

2.2.1. Clustering the Data. The subject of cluster analysis was introduced and discussed in chapter 4. For more comprehensive reviews, readers are also referred to Blashfield and Aldenderfer (1988) and Arabie and Hubert (1996). In the present context, only hierarchical agglomerative methods are used and briefly emphasized as they form the bulk of the CLUSTER module introduced later in this section. Also, because an elaborate formal description cannot be provided due to lack of space, the terminology and the discussion is rather informal.

Several agglomerative methods are grouped under hierarchical cluster analysis. Common to all is that when cluster fusion is involved, the methods start by assuming each individual object to be a cluster, and at each step, those two clusters that are most similar, in some defined sense, are fused. The process continues until there is only one cluster left, at which point the process stops. The different methods that fall under this heading differ mainly in the way that similarities between entities in the analysis are handled and computed. In addition, some methods are well defined only with one type of proximity, usually distance measures satisfying particular metric properties; other methods accept different types of proximity measures. Different methods for cluster analysis vary in noise tolerance and may yield more or less different results depending on the choice, type, and quality of measurement of the chosen variables, as well as on the form of clusters assumed in the structure. A consequence of these differences is that some methods are more biased than others toward forming clusters of particular shapes (e.g., clusters in single linkage tend to be elongated, in Ward's method, spherical, and so on). Agglomerative hierarchical methods include the nearest neighbor or single-link method, the furthest neighbor or complete linkage method, the centroid method, the median method, group average clustering, Lance and Williams Beta-flexible method, and Ward's method.

In light of the aforementioned, the choice of method and of proximity must be considered carefully. The characteristics of the method must be well understood and the chosen proximity measure well suited for the method if the resulting classification is to be meaningful. However, the analysis is often explorative in nature and the proper choices are not always clear. Therefore, it is sometimes advantageous to cluster analyze the data set in a variety of ways using different methods in order to "get the feel" for the emerging structures. Analyzing and evaluating these different structures may then give hints as to what choices to make regarding method, proximity, and so forth. Another benefit from repeated application of different methods with the same data set may be gained in discovering stable structures that are moderately invariant across different methods. In other words, structures that are stable across methods are less likely to be by-products of the methods and thus may be more generally meaningful.

Because the clustering process is sequential, merging two clusters at each stage, it can be depicted as a tree with the root being one cluster containing all the units and the leaves as cluster singletons, each containing one distinct unit of analysis. In between the root and the leaves are the different cluster structures corresponding to the fusions made at each step (iteration). In order to visualize or summarize the clustering process, the tree is sometimes shown graphically or sometimes transformed in the form of a dendogram. The important point here is for the analyst to decide a cut-off point that determines the desired solution in the context of the analysis. Different factors may act independently or together to determine this cut-off point. Sometimes, one or more indices thought to measure the "quality" of a solution are employed at the narrower end of the clustering process where the number of clusters is manageable. These indices assume different values for solutions with different numbers of clusters and the solution, for which these indices are optimal given a parsimonious number of clusters, is chosen (see also chapter 6 where the LICUR approach is described). In other instances, the number of clusters is determined a priori and these indices can then be used for comparing the corresponding clustering solution with other solutions obtained by other means.

One way of characterizing a cluster is by enumerating all the units belonging to it or by choosing the most typical unit as a representative (this is not included in the CLUSTER module). Another way to characterize a cluster is by representing it with its vector of means of the variables in the study (centroid) taken over the units in that cluster, and by the vector of variances associated with the centroid. Ideally, the variances are small, indicating homogenous units in the cluster. In this case, the centroid is a good description of that cluster and may be used in subsequent analysis. The methods, indices, and characterizations already mentioned are part of the CLUSTER module.

The CLUSTER Module

CLUSTER performs hierarchical cluster analysis with either of the following methods: Single Linkage, Complete Linkage, Average Linkage, Median, Weighted-Average Linkage, Beta-flexible, and Ward. It reports at each iteration the identity of the clusters fused, the size of the clusters, the merging coefficient, and the error sum of squares explained by the solution corresponding to that iteration. CLUSTER also reports for the last 20 iterations at the final stages of clustering, the cluster membership of every unit in the data set and some statistics about the formed clusters (e.g., the size of each cluster, the means and standard deviations of the variables in each cluster, and the homogeneity coefficient, which here is the average within cluster proximity for that cluster). As explained in chapter 7, the output labeled *explained error sum of squares* should be interpreted as follows:

$$\textit{Explained ESS} = 100 \times \frac{\textit{Total ESS} - \textit{ESS of the given cluster solution}}{\textit{Total ESS}}$$

where ESS stands for error sum of squares.

An illustration of how the output is organized in CLUSTER is given in Fig. 8.4.

2.2.2. Relocating Cases in Clusters. Hierarchical methods are attractive because they conserve the history of the formed clusters. In other words, the parents of each formed cluster are identifiable by tracing back the history of the fusion process. This quality offers the researcher flexibility to analyze and present the results at different levels of detail. Sometimes, however, the interest is in one specific solution and the analyst wants to maximize the clustering quality of that particular solution regardless of how the partition came about. One way of achieving this is by analyzing a certain solution by focusing on the cluster membership of the units that form the clusters in that solution. For each unit it is asked, with respect to some optimizing criterion, whether the unit really belongs to the cluster or whether it can be relocated to a different cluster. Thus, one employs some optimizing criterion believed to reflect some aspect of the quality of a given solution. For example, if the explained error sum of squares is such a criterion, a unit is relocated if its relocation reduces that criterion. When all the units are exhausted, the process iterates until it either converges on a given solution (i.e., the final iteration results in no unit relocations at all), or when the number of iterations requested by the user is exceeded.

The RELOCATE module performs the already mentioned analysis.

The RELOCATE Module

RELOCATE starts from an initial classification and moves cases from one cluster to another, depending on whether their movement leads to a reduction in the total error sum of squares of the cluster solution. In this way, ill-fitting objects are moved to a more suitable cluster and more homogeneous clusters can be obtained. Before undertaking RELOCATE, cluster membership according to the initial classification has to be written to a new data file together with the ID number and the variable values. If the procedure CLUSTER in SLEIPNER is used to find the initial classification, the input file to RELOCATE can be prepared easily with the help of the CWRITE module presented in section 2.4.3.

RELOCATE reports information about the initial, the intermediate, and the final classification. The information reported for each classification comprises the error sum of squares explained by the classification, and the point biserial corresponding to that classification. Thus, changes in these indices can be inspected across the evolution of the relocation process. RELOCATE also reports statistics about the initial as well as the final clusters, specifically: the size of each cluster, the means and standard deviations of the variables in each cluster, and the homogeneity coefficient (this being the average within cluster proximity for that cluster). The output

```
|===========================================================================|
| ITERATION  |    CLUSTERS MERGED      | INCREASE IN ERROR SUM OF SQUARES   |
|===========================================================================|
|            |                         |                                    |
|   1413     |  24( 32) (+)  21( 25)   |            10.81872                |
|                                                                           |
|         20-CLUSTER SOLUTION:                                              |
|         ===================                                               |
|                                                                           |
|         CASE ID( CLUSTER MEMBERSHIP)                                      |
|         ============================                                      |
|              1(  1)    2(  2)    4(  3)    5(  4)    6(  5)               |
|              7(  5)    9(  2)   10(  2)   11(  9)   12( 10)               |
|         ETC...                                                            |
|                                                                           |
|         20-CLUSTER CENTROIDS:                                             |
|         ====================                                              |
|                                                                           |
|         CLUSTER   1  (n =  55) ,    Homogeneity Coef:    .1339835         |
|         ======================      ==================                    |
|                                                                           |
|         MEANS                                                             |
|                                                                           |
|            3.6000    4.0000    4.0000    3.0856                           |
|                                                                           |
|         STANDARD DEVIATIONS                                               |
|            .4944      .0000     .0000     .1986                           |
|                                                                           |
|         ETC...                                                            |
|                                                                           |
|         CLUSTER 149  (n =  25) ,    Homogeneity Coef:    .6657969         |
|         ======================      ==================                    |
|                                                                           |
|         MEANS                                                             |
|                                                                           |
|            5.8000    1.7600    1.9200    3.5320                           |
|                                                                           |
|         STANDARD DEVIATIONS                                               |
|            1.0801     .4359     .2769     .3464                           |
|                                                                           |
|                                         |=========================|       |
|                                         | EXPLAINED          ESS  |       |
|                                         |          75.1815        |       |
|===========================================================================|
| ITERATION  |    CLUSTERS MERGED      | INCREASE IN ERROR SUM OF SQUARES   |
```

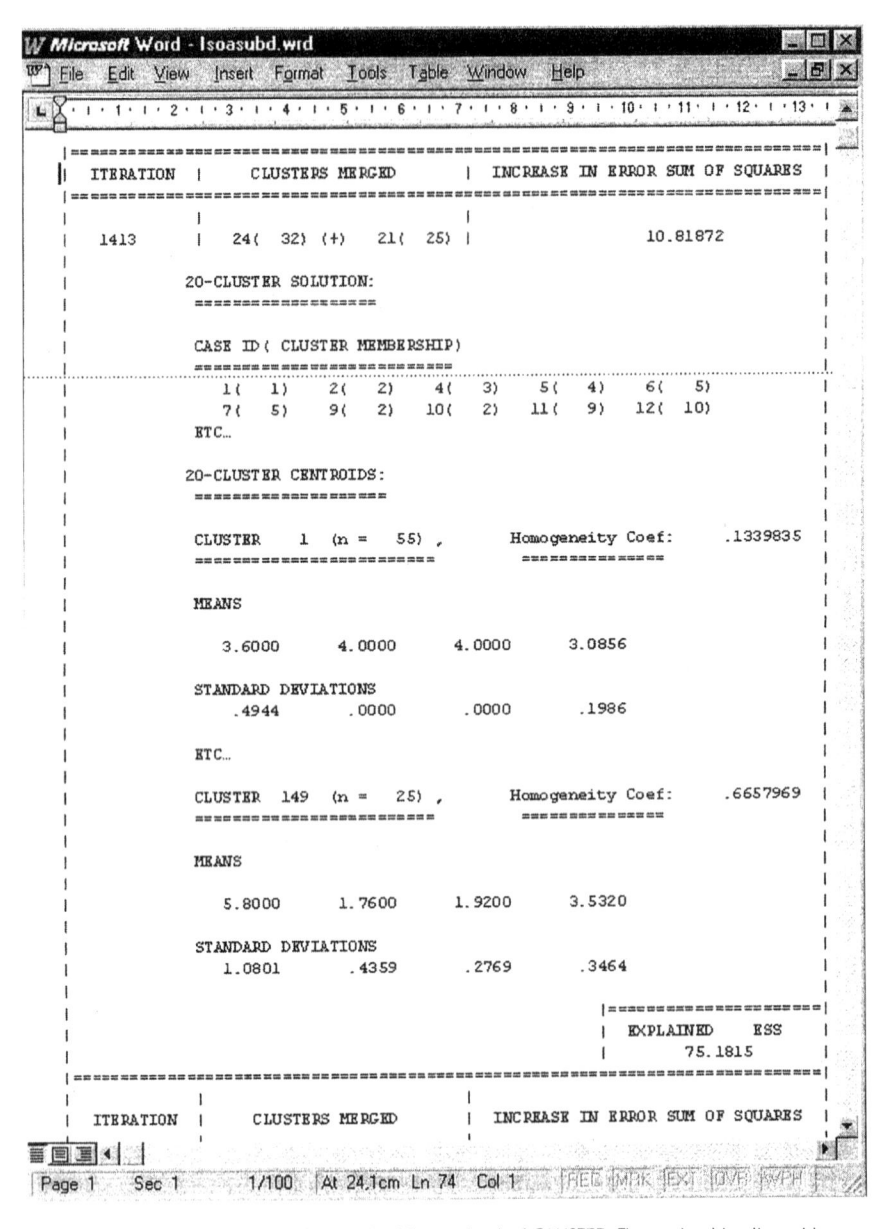

FIG. 8.4. A snapshot showing part of the output of CLUSTER. The output is altered to fit the screen.

labeled *explained error sum of squares* should be interpreted in the same way as in the CLUSTER procedure.

RELOCATE also reports the cluster membership of every unit in the data set according to the final solution, as well as the number of relocated objects for each intermediate solution.

An illustration of how the output is organized in RELOCATE is given in Fig. 8.5.

2.2.3. Searching for Types and Antitypes.

Configural frequency analysis (CFA), presented and discussed in chapter 5, can be used in the present context in at least two different ways. Consider first the cross-sectional situation in which units are measured on a variable vector and the variables are discrete. Each unit is then represented by a configuration of variable values and these configurations are more or less abundant in the data set. A classificatory approach could focus on the statistical characteristics of this state of affairs by probing the typicality and antitypicality of certain configurations. Thus, for each configuration, we can compute its observed and expected frequency of occurrence, and derive a probability for the deviance of the expected frequency from the observed one. Types are then configural patterns occurring more than would be expected by chance and antitypes are patterns occurring less frequently than would be expected by chance. In an exploratory setting in which no prior hypotheses are formed with regard to which configuration to test, all possible configurations are analyzed. Because the number of configurations is a function of the number of variables and the number of the categories in each variable, the number of tests may be huge. Therefore, care should be taken to correct for mass significance as emphasized in chapter 5.

In a longitudinal setting, the variables are classification variables formed by, for example, cluster analysis. Each variable refers to a classification obtained from a different measurement occasion, and the purpose is to study developmental sequences as they are reflected in the configurations. Using reasoning analogous to the cross-sectional case, a type is then an overrepresentation of a certain developmental sequence that can be tested a priori, or searched for in the data set. Antitypes are similarly underrepresentations of sequences occurring less frequently than one would expect by chance.

The CFA module provides the means to conduct configural frequency analysis. CFA requires the variables to be dichotomized or trichotomized. This is not a consequence of the method itself but a computational constraint imposed by the implementation. When the starting point is a variable vector, where some or all of the variables are either continuous or possess more categories than is allowed by CFA, then some recoding procedure is required.

Sometimes the information contained in the values coded for the variables in the study can be reduced to a dichotomy (e.g., *high* or *low*) or to a trichotomy (e.g., *high, medium,* or *low*). If, instead, the variables are classification variables (e.g., representing different cluster solutions at different points in time or different cross-sectional classifications of the same entities), then one may want to limit the

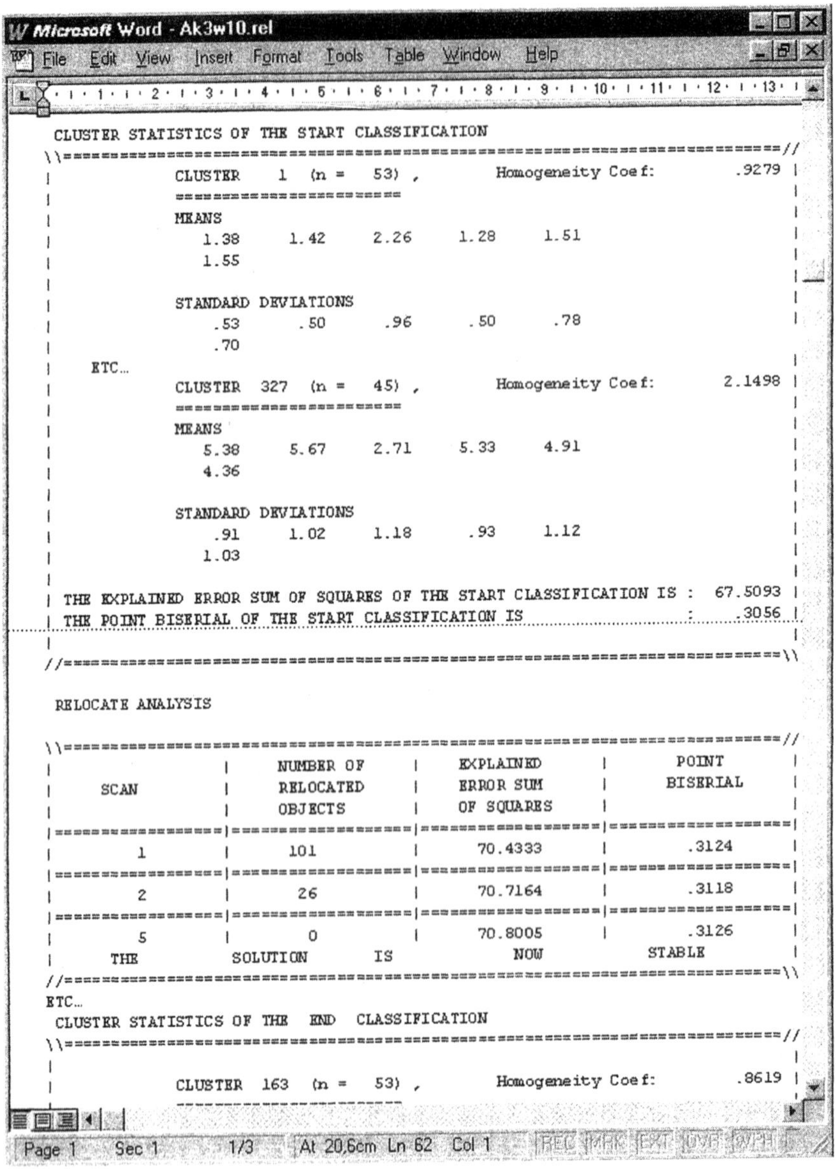

```
CLUSTER STATISTICS OF THE START CLASSIFICATION
\\===========================================================//
|           CLUSTER    1  (n =    53) ,    Homogeneity Coef:    .9279  |
|           ===================                                        |
|           MEANS                                                      |
|              1.38    1.42    2.26    1.28    1.51                    |
|              1.55                                                    |
|                                                                      |
|           STANDARD DEVIATIONS                                        |
|               .53     .50     .96     .50     .78                    |
|               .70                                                    |
|   ETC...                                                             |
|           CLUSTER  327  (n =    45) ,    Homogeneity Coef:   2.1498  |
|           ===================                                        |
|           MEANS                                                      |
|              5.38    5.67    2.71    5.33    4.91                    |
|              4.36                                                    |
|                                                                      |
|           STANDARD DEVIATIONS                                        |
|               .91    1.02    1.18     .93    1.12                    |
|              1.03                                                    |
|                                                                      |
| THE EXPLAINED ERROR SUM OF SQUARES OF THE START CLASSIFICATION IS :  67.5093 |
| THE POINT BISERIAL OF THE START CLASSIFICATION IS               :     .3056  |
|                                                                              |
//===========================================================\\

  RELOCATE ANALYSIS

\\===========================================================//
|           |  NUMBER OF   |  EXPLAINED   |    POINT    |
|   SCAN    |  RELOCATED   |  ERROR SUM   |  BISERIAL   |
|           |   OBJECTS    |  OF SQUARES  |             |
|===========|==============|==============|=============|
|     1     |     101      |   70.4333    |    .3124    |
|===========|==============|==============|=============|
|     2     |      26      |   70.7164    |    .3118    |
|===========|==============|==============|=============|
|     5     |       0      |   70.8005    |    .3126    |
|   THE        SOLUTION       IS    NOW       STABLE    |
//===========================================================\\
ETC...
  CLUSTER STATISTICS OF THE END CLASSIFICATION
\\===========================================================//
|                                                                      |
|           CLUSTER  163  (n =    53) ,    Homogeneity Coef:    .8619  |
```

FIG. 8.5. A snapshot showing part of the output of RELOCATE. The output is altered to fit the screen.

number of clusters in each solution to two or three clusters, presuming that this limitation can be justified for each solution.

The CFA Module

The CFA module performs configural frequency analysis using the exact binomial test. CFA handles both dichotomous and trichotomous variables or patterns of variables that are of a mixed type. Tests are made for both types and antitypes.

CFA reports (in a tabular form) the following for each possible configuration: the observed frequency, the expected frequency, The Chi-square component, the binomial probability, and the adjusted binomial probability. CFA also reports the probability (marginal frequency) of each category. An illustration of how the output is organized in CFA is given in Fig. 8.6.

2.2.4. Using I-States as Objects of Analysis. The rationale and the methodology underlying ISOA is presented in chapter 6 in this volume and more extensively in Bergman and El Khouri (1999). Briefly, if only short term development is the focus of the study, then it is reasonable to believe that, within this constrained time period, an individual may be described at a certain measurement occasion with one of a finite set of states. The setting is one of a multivariate repeated measures design for a set of individuals, and the available variable value profiles from all time points are used collectively to define a finite set of states. Because each profile (belonging to a distinct individual and to a distinct time point) is included in the analysis, it can then be replaced with its corresponding state. After replacement, the researcher has a set of longitudinal profiles expressed in terms of state sequences (instead of the original repeated measurements multivariate data set).

The researcher typically starts with one file in which the individual values for the set of domain variables are recorded for each case. Preliminary, one has to create a new file where the n individuals (with each individual described k times on L variables) are replaced with N subindividuals described on L variables and where $N = nxk$. This can be accomplished with the help of the module SUBIND.

The file resulting from SUBIND is a data file that can be input to IMPUTE and RESIDUE for further analysis. The output data file from RESIDUE can then be input to the procedure CLUSTER, the result examined, and a suitable cluster solution chosen that reflects the number and the profile of states with which the individuals are ultimately described.

The module ISOA uses the results from the cluster analysis step and creates two files: one new data file with state sequences constituting individuals and one result file in which the analyses are reported. Longitudinally, the result for each individual is a state sequence. For all individuals, the result is a data file that can be input for further analysis (e.g., with EXACON where states from adjacent time periods are cross tabulated). Individuals whose value profiles on any measurement occasion happen to fall into a residue (when RESIDUE is used) are separated into a different file.

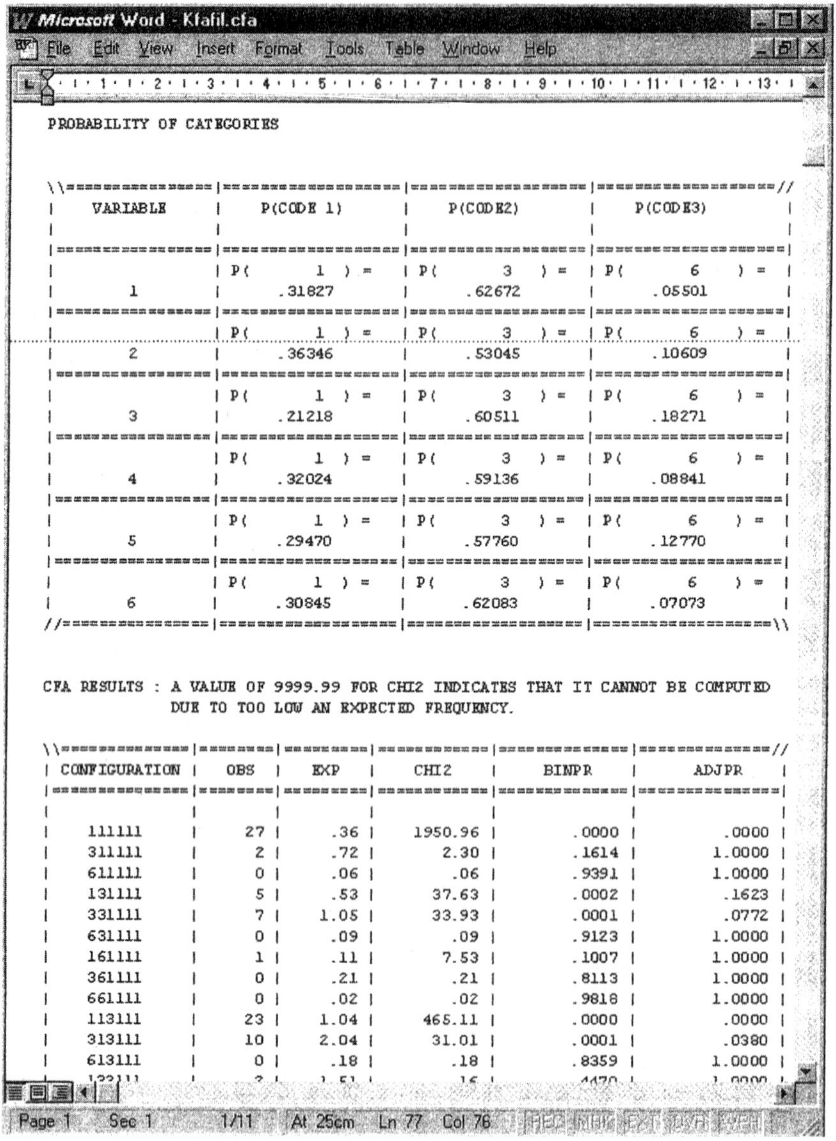

```
PROBABILITY OF CATEGORIES

\\===============|==============|==============|==============//
|   VARIABLE     |   P(CODE 1)  |   P(CODE2)   |   P(CODE3)   |
|================|==============|==============|==============|
|                | P(   1  ) =  | P(   3  ) =  | P(   6  ) =  |
|       1        |    .31827    |    .62672    |    .05501    |
|================|==============|==============|==============|
|                | P(   1  ) =  | P(   3  ) =  | P(   6  ) =  |
|       2        |    .36346    |    .53045    |    .10609    |
|================|==============|==============|==============|
|                | P(   1  ) =  | P(   3  ) =  | P(   6  ) =  |
|       3        |    .21218    |    .60511    |    .18271    |
|================|==============|==============|==============|
|                | P(   1  ) =  | P(   3  ) =  | P(   6  ) =  |
|       4        |    .32024    |    .59136    |    .08841    |
|================|==============|==============|==============|
|                | P(   1  ) =  | P(   3  ) =  | P(   6  ) =  |
|       5        |    .29470    |    .57760    |    .12770    |
|================|==============|==============|==============|
|                | P(   1  ) =  | P(   3  ) =  | P(   6  ) =  |
|       6        |    .30845    |    .62083    |    .07073    |
//===============|==============|==============|==============\\


CFA RESULTS : A VALUE OF 9999.99 FOR CHI2 INDICATES THAT IT CANNOT BE COMPUTED
              DUE TO TOO LOW AN EXPECTED FREQUENCY.

\\==============|========|========|===========|==========|==========//
| CONFIGURATION |  OBS   |  EXP   |   CHI2    |  BINPR   |  ADJPR   |
|===============|========|========|===========|==========|==========|
|    111111     |   27   |   .36  |  1950.96  |   .0000  |   .0000  |
|    311111     |    2   |   .72  |     2.30  |   .1614  |  1.0000  |
|    611111     |    0   |   .06  |      .06  |   .9391  |  1.0000  |
|    131111     |    5   |   .53  |    37.63  |   .0002  |   .1623  |
|    331111     |    7   |  1.05  |    33.93  |   .0001  |   .0772  |
|    631111     |    0   |   .09  |      .09  |   .9123  |  1.0000  |
|    161111     |    1   |   .11  |     7.53  |   .1007  |  1.0000  |
|    361111     |    0   |   .21  |      .21  |   .8113  |  1.0000  |
|    661111     |    0   |   .02  |      .02  |   .9818  |  1.0000  |
|    113111     |   23   |  1.04  |   465.11  |   .0000  |   .0000  |
|    313111     |   10   |  2.04  |    31.01  |   .0001  |   .0380  |
|    613111     |    0   |   .18  |      .18  |   .8359  |  1.0000  |
```

FIG. 8.6. A snapshot showing part of the output of CFA. The output is altered to fit the screen.

The ISOA Module

The ISOA module creates, based on a data file and a result file from the CLUSTER module, a new data file, in which each individual whose state sequence contains no residue states is represented.

ISOA also creates an analysis file where basic descriptives of state sequences are presented together with state sequences comprising residue states. ISOA lists in the analysis file the frequencies of patterns occurring in the resulting data file and reports percentages of individuals characterized by different typical states at different occasions. An illustration of how the output is organized in ISOA is given in Fig. 8.7.

2.3. Classificatory Simulation and Evaluation

Once a cluster analysis is conducted and a solution is chosen, often the analyst would like to determine if the revealed structure is a "real" one. Clustering methods will impose structure on any type of data. What guarantee is there that the chosen solution did not arise at random as an artifact of the method itself or as a reflection of noisy or random data? How do we strengthen the belief that the clusters are real clusters and not arbitrary ones? Sometimes the answer is easy, in particular in cases in which the newly found structure replicates earlier valid findings on other data sets, can be operationally validated in the given domain, and/or conforms to or can be derived from theory, and so forth. When these situations do not occur, other measures have to employed.

2.3.1. Simulation Analysis. One approach is to employ simulation. First, the solution using the original data set is evaluated on a number of indices. Second, the original data set is altered in a random fashion. Third, the same type of cluster analysis initially performed on the original data set is conducted for the randomly altered data set. The same cluster solution, that is, the same number of clusters, is chosen and then evaluated on the same type of indices as in step 1. Steps 2 to 3 are repeated a number of times, where each time a new set of evaluating indices is generated. Finally, each of the indices from step 1 is compared to its corresponding set computed from the randomly altered data sets. A statistically significant deviance of the indices in step 1 from the ones corresponding to the analyses made on random data strengthen the belief that the original solution is, in a sense, real, and that the data giving rise to that solution are not random. This issue is discussed in chapter 7. The procedure SIMULATE in SLEIPNER performs the 3-steps analysis just described. Two issues in the implementation in SIMULATE deserve special comments. First, evaluation proceeds by computing the explained error sum of squares and five other internal criteria that measure the goodness-of-fit between the input data and the resulting data partition (Milligan, 1981a). Second, the original data set is randomly altered by performing permutations over the values of a variable. Thus, for each variable the frequencies corresponding to the initial values for that variable are preserved. Chaos mathematics is used to generate random numbers used in the permutation procedure and the clock in the PC gives a start value. Hence, different "shakings" can be regarded as independent.

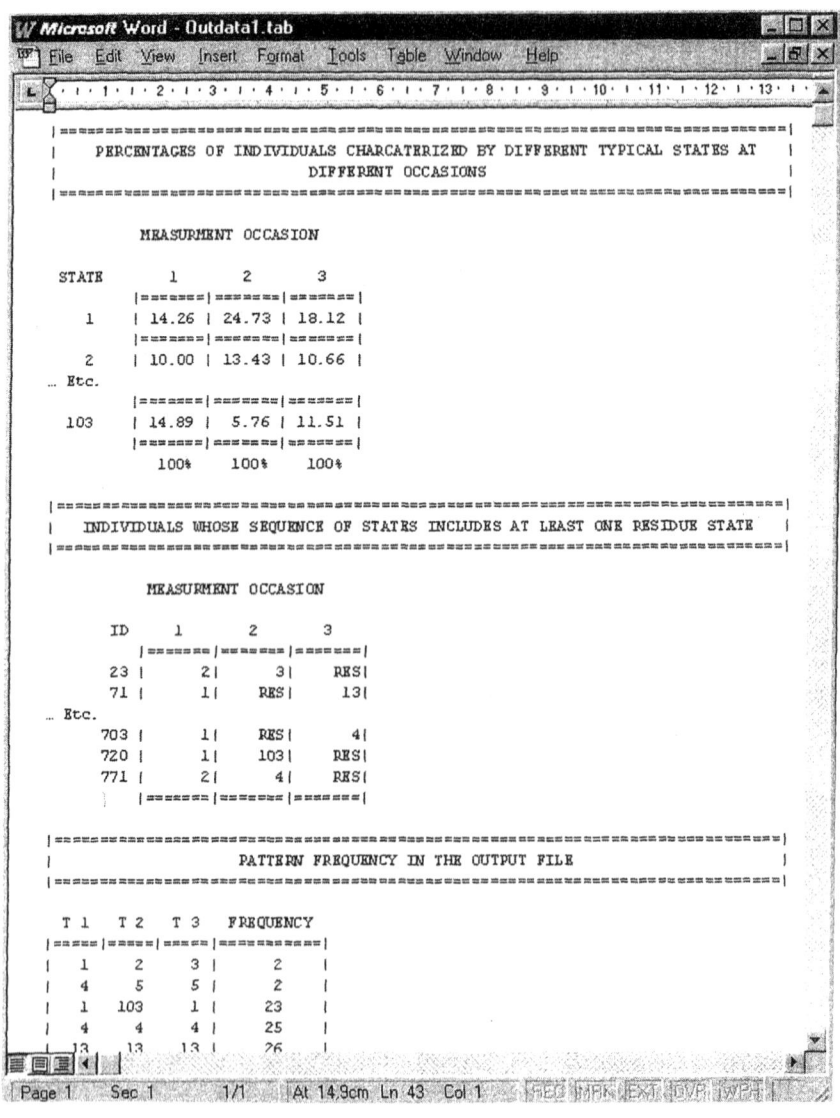

```
PERCENTAGES OF INDIVIDUALS CHARCATERIZED BY DIFFERENT TYPICAL STATES AT
                           DIFFERENT OCCASIONS

               MEASUREMENT OCCASION

    STATE          1      2      3
                |======|======|======|
      1         | 14.26 | 24.73 | 18.12 |
                |======|======|======|
      2         | 10.00 | 13.43 | 10.66 |
    ... Etc.
                |======|======|======|
     103        | 14.89 |  5.76 | 11.51 |
                |======|======|======|
                  100%   100%   100%


    INDIVIDUALS WHOSE SEQUENCE OF STATES INCLUDES AT LEAST ONE RESIDUE STATE

               MEASUREMENT OCCASION

           ID       1       2       3
                |=======|=======|=======|
          23  |     2|      3|    RES|
          71  |     1|    RES|     13|
    ... Etc.
         703  |     1|    RES|      4|
         720  |     1|    103|    RES|
         771  |     2|      4|    RES|
                |=======|=======|=======|


                     PATTERN FREQUENCY IN THE OUTPUT FILE

      T 1    T 2    T 3    FREQUENCY
    |=====|=====|=====|==========|
    |  1     2     3  |    2     |
    |  4     5     5  |    2     |
    |  1    103    1  |   23     |
    |  4     4     4  |   25     |
    | 13    13    13  |   26     |
```

FIG. 8.7. A snapshot showing part of the output of ISOA. The output is altered to fit the screen.

The SIMULATE Module

The SIMULATE procedure does the following:

1. Performs a cluster analysis on a set of data;
2. computes the error sum of squares explained by that solution as well as five internal indices measuring the extent of cluster recovery by the proposed solution. The five indices are the Gamma index, the C index, the point biserial, the W/B index, and the G(+) index;
3. reports these measures in a separate output file;
4. repeats these analyses n times (where n is user-specified parameter) for n artificial data sets created from the original one by permutations over the values of the variables;
5. reports these measures in the output file;
6. computes for each index a t value relating the index value found for the original data set to the distribution of those found for the n artificial data sets; and
7. computes for each index the mean and the standard deviation.

An illustration of how the output is organized in SIMULATE is given in Fig. 8.8.

2.3.2. Structural Stability and Change. Theoretical considerations for studying individuals over time have been treated in earlier chapters. There are several ways of linking (longitudinally) one classification of data corresponding to one point in time to another classification corresponding to another point in time. For instance, if the same variables are used at both occasions to measure some underlying psychological dimensions, one could examine the structural stability of the given classifications across time, that is, to what extent clusters in one classification at one time are reproduced in the other classification at the next time; what clusters are similar and to what extent, and so on. To this end, the CENTROID procedure in SLEIPNER may be used.

The CENTROID procedure provides descriptive information of two sets of clusters focusing on the similarities between the centroids. In this context, each centroid is represented by the means of the variables computed across the units that form the cluster. Other ways of representing a cluster exist (e.g., using the cluster's most typical unit). Here, however, we use the former representation and define similarity between clusters in terms of the squared average Euclidean distance between the centroids of those clusters. Similarities between centroids belonging to the same set are reported and a similarity-based pairwise matching between centroids of different sets is conducted. The matching is performed so that the two most similar centroids from each set are coupled together, the second most similar pair are coupled together, and so on (see also chap. 7).

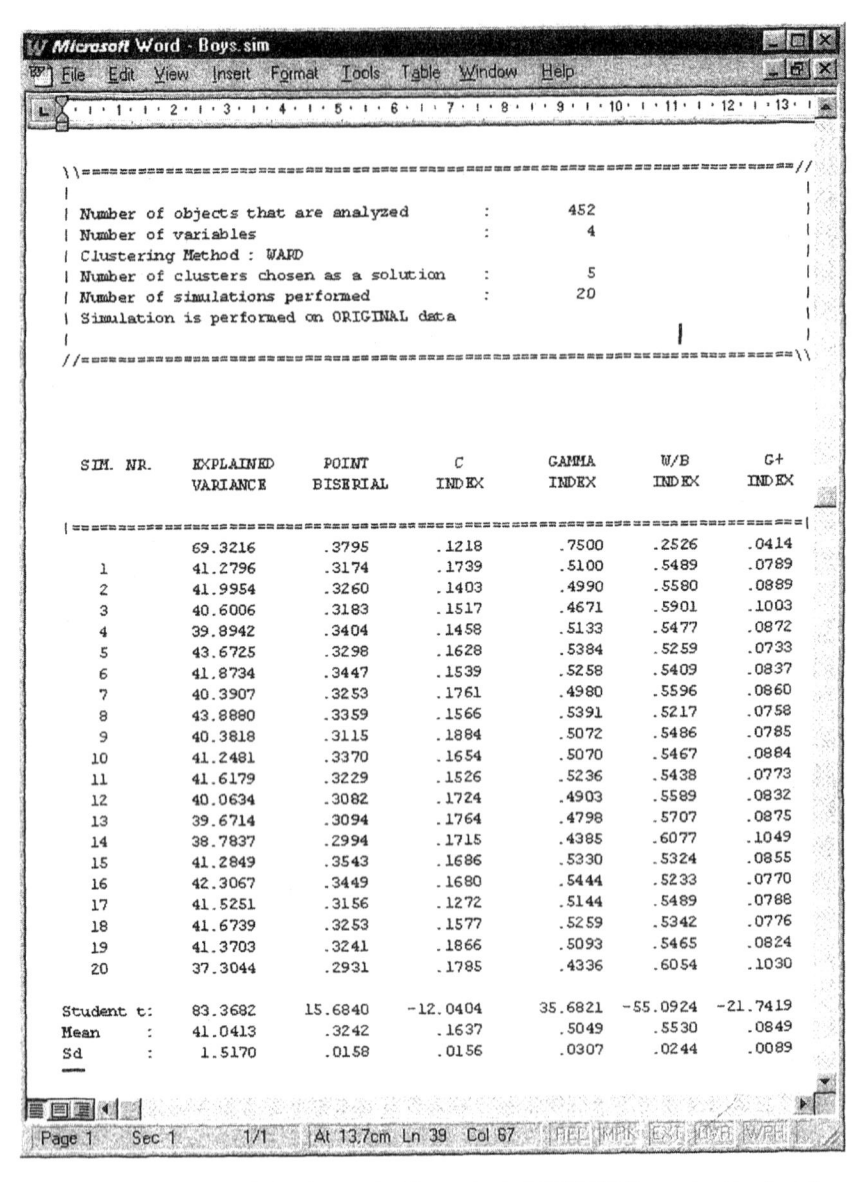

```
\\=================================================================//
|                                                                   |
| Number of objects that are analyzed      :     452                |
| Number of variables                      :       4                |
| Clustering Method : WARD                                          |
| Number of clusters chosen as a solution  :       5                |
| Number of simulations performed          :      20                |
| Simulation is performed on ORIGINAL data                          |
|                                                                   |
//=================================================================\\
```

SIM. NR.	EXPLAINED VARIANCE	POINT BISERIAL	C INDEX	GAMMA INDEX	W/B INDEX	G+ INDEX
	69.3216	.3795	.1218	.7500	.2526	.0414
1	41.2796	.3174	.1739	.5100	.5489	.0789
2	41.9954	.3260	.1403	.4990	.5580	.0889
3	40.6006	.3183	.1517	.4671	.5901	.1003
4	39.8942	.3404	.1458	.5133	.5477	.0872
5	43.6725	.3298	.1628	.5384	.5259	.0733
6	41.8734	.3447	.1539	.5258	.5409	.0837
7	40.3907	.3253	.1761	.4980	.5596	.0860
8	43.8880	.3359	.1566	.5391	.5217	.0758
9	40.3818	.3115	.1884	.5072	.5486	.0785
10	41.2481	.3370	.1654	.5070	.5467	.0884
11	41.6179	.3229	.1526	.5236	.5438	.0773
12	40.0634	.3082	.1724	.4903	.5589	.0832
13	39.6714	.3094	.1764	.4798	.5707	.0875
14	38.7837	.2994	.1715	.4385	.6077	.1049
15	41.2849	.3543	.1686	.5330	.5324	.0855
16	42.3067	.3449	.1680	.5444	.5233	.0770
17	41.5251	.3156	.1272	.5144	.5489	.0788
18	41.6739	.3253	.1577	.5259	.5342	.0776
19	41.3703	.3241	.1866	.5093	.5465	.0824
20	37.3044	.2931	.1785	.4336	.6054	.1030
Student t:	83.3682	15.6840	-12.0404	35.6821	-55.0924	-21.7419
Mean :	41.0413	.3242	.1637	.5049	.5530	.0849
Sd :	1.5170	.0158	.0156	.0307	.0244	.0089

FIG. 8.8. A snapshot showing part of the output of SIMULATE. The output is altered to fit the screen.

The CENTROID Module

CENTROID compares two clustering solutions with one other by matching each cluster centroid in one solution to the most similar cluster centroid in the other solution. Thus, the outcome is a set of pairs of centroids each belonging to one solution and in which the pairs are given in order of decreasing similarity.

CENTROID also reports basic statistics for each centroid set such as the average squared Euclidean distances computed for centroids pairs within a set, variable means, and variances. An illustration of how the output is organized in CENTROID is given in Fig. 8.9.

2.3.3. Individual Stability and Change. Regardless of whether the variables are believed to be the "same" at the two different occasions or not, the two classifications are still based on the same underlying units. Thus, it can be informative to examine how individual cluster membership is related over time. If the same variables are measured at both occasions, individual stability and change can also be studied. In a contingency table formed between the two classifications, each cell represents a set of units belonging to two clusters, one taken from each classification (at each time point). Of special interest are cells that are overfrequented or underfrequented (see chap. 5). This examination may have exploratory value for generating hypotheses about the relation of one classification to the other, or have its main focus on testing hypotheses about specific relations among clusters in the two different classifications. Thus, a "type" (an overrepresentation of units in a cell), or an "antitype" (an underrepresentation of units in a cell) highlights a relation between the two parent clusters of that cell.

Indeed, the arguments already presented are not confined to longitudinal analyses but also to cross-sectional analyses as well. The two classifications pertaining to two different measurement occasions are simply exchanged for two cross-sectional classifications pertaining to one measurement occasion but focusing on different domains of interest. Thus, different aspects of the same "subsystem" are contrasted cross-sectionally. The EXACON procedure in SLEIPNER is also a tool for performing this type of analysis.

The EXACON Module

EXACON produces a contingency table for two categorical variables and examines it with a focus on cell-wise analysis of types or antitypes based on exact tests. For each cell, the module computes the observed frequency, the expected frequency, the CHI-2 component, the one-tailed probability of the observed cell frequency according to the binomial model, and the one-tailed probability of the observed cell frequency according to the hypergeometric model. In addition, the overall CHI-2 and the contingency coefficient are reported. An illustration of how the output is organized in EXACON is given in Fig. 8.10.

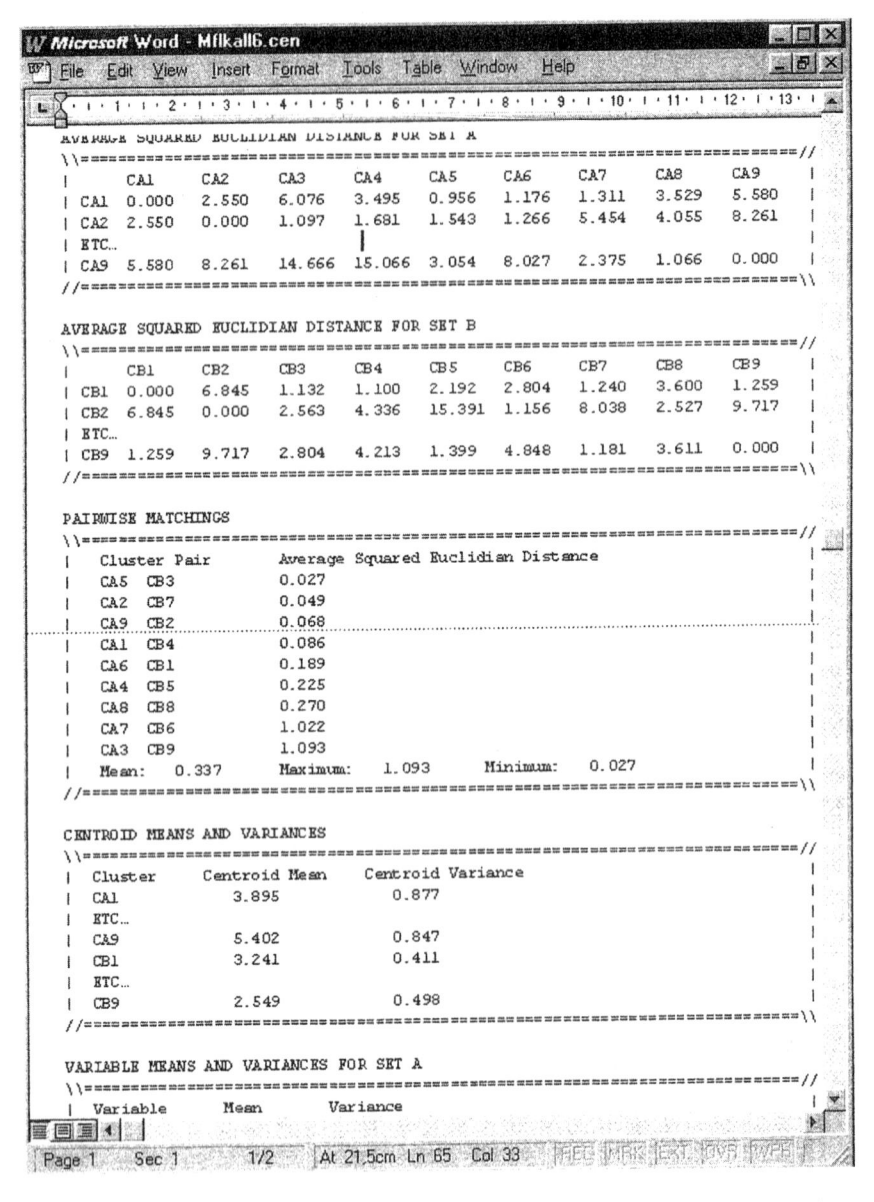

```
 W Microsoft Word - Mflkall6.cen                                    _ □ X
   File  Edit  View  Insert  Format  Tools  Table  Window  Help      _ 8 X
 · 1 · 1 · 1 · 2 · 1 · 3 · 1 · 4 · 1 · 5 · 1 · 6 · 1 · 7 · 1 · 8 · 1 · 9 · 1 · 10 · 1 · 11 · 1 · 12 · 1 · 13 · 1 ·

     AVERAGE SQUARED EUCLIDIAN DISTANCE FOR SET A
     \\=====================================================//
     |        CA1     CA2     CA3     CA4     CA5     CA6     CA7     CA8     CA9      |
     | CA1   0.000   2.550   6.076   3.495   0.956   1.176   1.311   3.529   5.580    |
     | CA2   2.550   0.000   1.097   1.681   1.543   1.266   5.454   4.055   8.261    |
     | ETC..                                                                            |
     | CA9   5.580   8.261  14.666  15.066   3.054   8.027   2.375   1.066   0.000    |
     //=====================================================\\

     AVERAGE SQUARED EUCLIDIAN DISTANCE FOR SET B
     \\=====================================================//
     |        CB1     CB2     CB3     CB4     CB5     CB6     CB7     CB8     CB9      |
     | CB1   0.000   6.845   1.132   1.100   2.192   2.804   1.240   3.600   1.259    |
     | CB2   6.845   0.000   2.563   4.336  15.391   1.156   8.038   2.527   9.717    |
     | ETC..                                                                            |
     | CB9   1.259   9.717   2.804   4.213   1.399   4.848   1.181   3.611   0.000    |
     //=====================================================\\

     PAIRWISE MATCHINGS
     \\=====================================================//
     |  Cluster Pair        Average Squared Euclidian Distance                          |
     |  CA5  CB3            0.027                                                       |
     |  CA2  CB7            0.049                                                       |
     |  CA9  CB2            0.068                                                       |
     |  CA1  CB4            0.086                                                       |
     |  CA6  CB1            0.189                                                       |
     |  CA4  CB5            0.225                                                       |
     |  CA8  CB8            0.270                                                       |
     |  CA7  CB6            1.022                                                       |
     |  CA3  CB9            1.093                                                       |
     |  Mean:   0.337    Maximum:   1.093    Minimum:   0.027                          |
     //=====================================================\\

     CENTROID MEANS AND VARIANCES
     \\=====================================================//
     |  Cluster   Centroid Mean    Centroid Variance                                    |
     |  CA1          3.895             0.877                                            |
     |  ETC..                                                                           |
     |  CA9          5.402             0.847                                            |
     |  CB1          3.241             0.411                                            |
     |  ETC..                                                                           |
     |  CB9          2.549             0.498                                            |
     //=====================================================\\

     VARIABLE MEANS AND VARIANCES FOR SET A
     \\=====================================================//
     |  Variable       Mean         Variance                                            |

 Page 1    Sec 1      1/2     At 21.5cm  Ln 65  Col 33
```

FIG. 8.9. A snapshot showing part of the output of CENTROID. The output is altered to fit the screen.

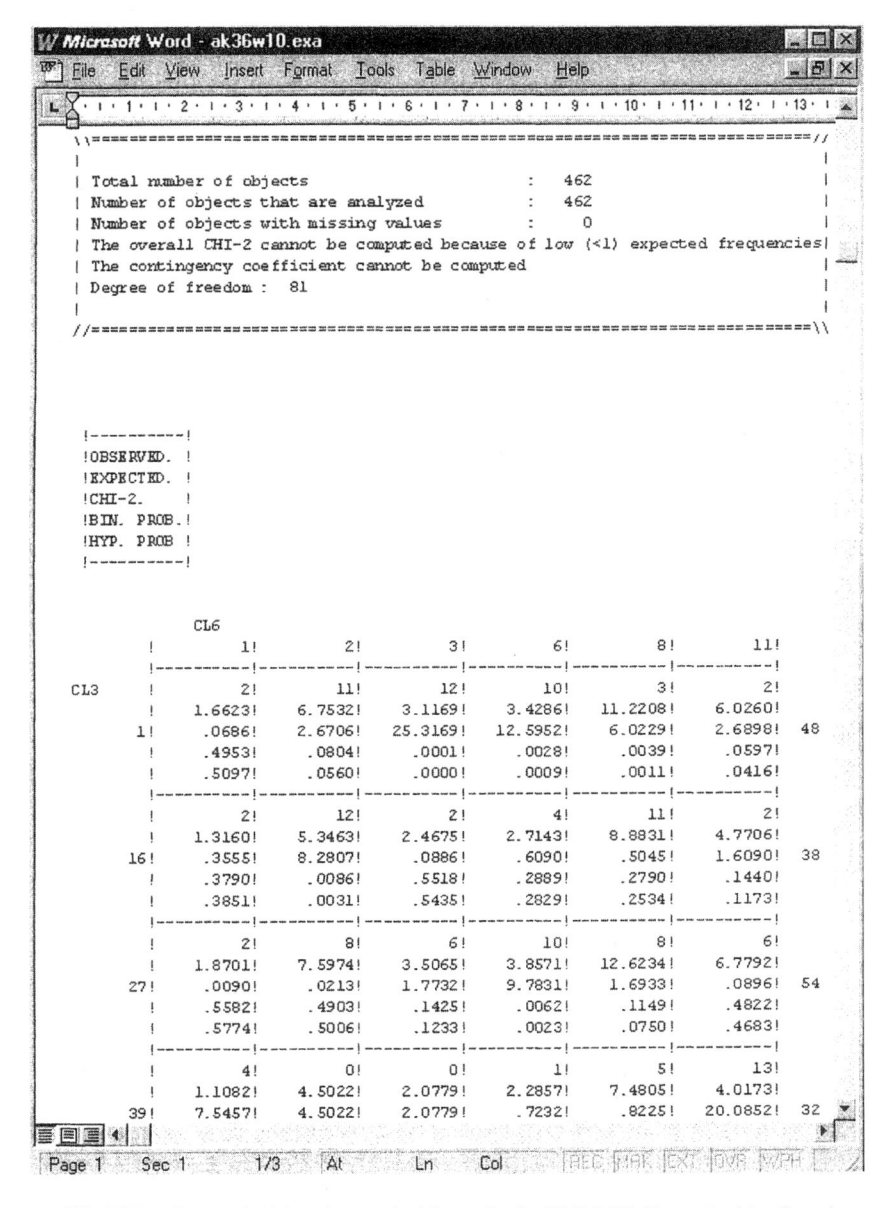

```
W Microsoft Word - ak36w10.exa

 File  Edit  View  Insert  Format  Tools  Table  Window  Help

\\================================================================//
|                                                                  |
| Total number of objects                    :   462               |
| Number of objects that are analyzed        :   462               |
| Number of objects with missing values      :     0               |
| The overall CHI-2 cannot be computed because of low (<1) expected frequencies|
| The contingency coefficient cannot be computed                   |
| Degree of freedom :  81                                          |
|                                                                  |
//================================================================\\




        !----------!
        !OBSERVED. !
        !EXPECTED. !
        !CHI-2.    !
        !BIN. PROB.!
        !HYP. PROB !
        !----------!


             CL6
         !    1!       2!        3!       6!        8!       11!
         !-----!--------!---------!--------!---------!---------!
   CL3   !    2!      11!       12!      10!        3!        2!
         ! 1.6623!  6.7532!  3.1169!  3.4286! 11.2208!   6.0260!
       1!  .0686!  2.6706! 25.3169! 12.5952!  6.0229!   2.6898!  48
         !  .4953!  .0804!   .0001!   .0028!   .0039!    .0597!
         !  .5097!  .0560!   .0000!   .0009!   .0011!    .0416!
         !-------!--------!---------!--------!---------!---------!
         !    2!      12!        2!       4!       11!        2!
         ! 1.3160!  5.3463!  2.4675!  2.7143!  8.8831!   4.7706!
      16!  .3555!  8.2807!   .0886!   .6090!   .5045!   1.6090!  38
         !  .3790!  .0086!   .5518!   .2889!   .2790!    .1440!
         !  .3851!  .0031!   .5435!   .2829!   .2534!    .1173!
         !-------!--------!---------!--------!---------!---------!
         !    2!       8!        6!      10!        8!        6!
         ! 1.8701!  7.5974!  3.5065!  3.8571! 12.6234!   6.7792!
      27!  .0090!  .0213!  1.7732!  9.7831!  1.6933!    .0896!  54
         !  .5582!  .4903!   .1425!   .0062!   .1149!    .4822!
         !  .5774!  .5006!   .1233!   .0023!   .0750!    .4683!
         !-------!--------!---------!--------!---------!---------!
         !    4!       0!        0!       1!        5!       13!
         ! 1.1082!  4.5022!  2.0779!  2.2857!  7.4805!   4.0173!
      39!  7.5457!  4.5022! 2.0779!   .7232!   .8225!  20.0852!  32
```

FIG. 8.10. A snapshot showing part of the output of EXACON. The output is altered to fit the screen.

2.4. Special Purpose Modules in SLEIPNER

2.4.1. Random Samples. A crude way of getting some idea of the sensitivity of one's results to sampling variation would be to draw a sample (e.g., 2/3 of the original sample) of the group one has analyzed, and repeat the main analyses to verify that the core results replicate. To randomly select cases for the analysis and create a new data file, one could use the RANDOM module.

The RANDOM Module

RANDOM draws a random sample without replacement from a population. Chaos mathematics is used to generate random numbers used in the drawing procedure and the clock in the PC provides a start value. Hence, different drawings could be regarded as independent samples. The output from RANDOM is a new data file similar to the original input data file but with fewer cases. The number of cases to include is specified by the user.

2.4.2. Artificial Data Sets. SHAKE can be used to alter the structure of a data set in a random fashion while preserving the variable frequencies in the original data set. The result is a new data file that can be used for comparative analysis similar to those performed in connection with SIMULATE module.

The SHAKE Module

SHAKE creates an artificial data set from an existing one by performing permutations across the values of a variable. Thus, for each variable, the frequencies corresponding to the initial values for that variable are preserved. Chaos mathematics is used to generate random numbers used in the permutation procedure and the clock in the PC gives a start value. Hence, different shakings could be regarded as independent.

2.4.3. Including Classification Variables in the Data Set. Some of the analysis conducted with SLEIPNER require as input the class membership of the units in the data set. These analyses are usually done with RELOCATE, EXACON, or EVALUATE but sometimes also with DENSE or CFA. Within the context of SLEIPNER, the class (or cluster) membership is determined and written in the output files reported by CLUSTER and RELOCATE. The cluster membership could also have originated by other means. To add this information for each unit so that it can be used in subsequent analysis, the CWRITE module is used.

The CWRITE Module

The CWRITE module adds to the original data file the value for a classification variable by writing the corresponding values for each unit in a new data file. The values for the classification variable are the cluster-memberships retrieved from the output of either CLUSTER, RELOCATE, or a user-constructed file.

2.4.4. Mapping the Neighborhood of a Unit. It is sometimes of interest to identify dense regions in the variable space in which subjects are close neighbors, but without necessarily undertaking a complete classification.

This type of analysis can be performed by DENSE.

The DENSE Module

DENSE reports for each case its nearest neighbors and furthest neighbors using the average squared Euclidean distance as the dissimilarity measure. This can be done using either raw scores or standardized scores. When DENSE starts from a classification, the output lists for each unit the two most similar cases in the same cluster, the two most similar cases in the data set, and the average distance to the cases in the cluster. Otherwise, if no prior classification is used, the output lists the five furthest cases, the five closest cases, and the average distance to all the cases. An illustration of how the output is organized in DENSE when it starts with a classification is given in Fig. 8.11.

2.4.5. Evaluating and Comparing Partitions. In the context of the module SIMULATE, it was noted that evaluation may be conducted by computing the explained error sum of squares and five other internal criteria measuring the goodness-of-fit between the input data and the resulting data partition. This can be done for the original data as well as for a set of artificial data sets. The module EVALUATE computes these indices for a solution and also provides a mean of comparing two solutions to one another.

The EVALUATE module

The EVALUATE module has two primary functions.

1. It evaluates a given cluster solution for a data set by computing the explained error sum of squares and five other internal criteria measuring the goodness-of-fit between the input data and the resulting data partition (Milligan 1981a). The five indices are: the Gamma index, the C index, the Point-biserial, the W/B index, and the G(+) index. EVALUATE also reports the centroids, the standard deviations associated with each centroid, and the homogeneity coefficient associated with each cluster. An illustration of how this type of output is organized in EVALUATE is given in Fig. 8.12.
2. Alternatively, it compares two cluster solutions for a data set and presents the comparison in a tabular form together with the corrected RAND index (Hubert & Arabie, 1985) that is associated with the two solutions.

2.4.6. Preparing a File Composed of Subindividuals. In the context of performing an ISOA analysis, it is necessary to prepare a data file for that analysis in a special manner. When performing a residue analysis to identify unique states and

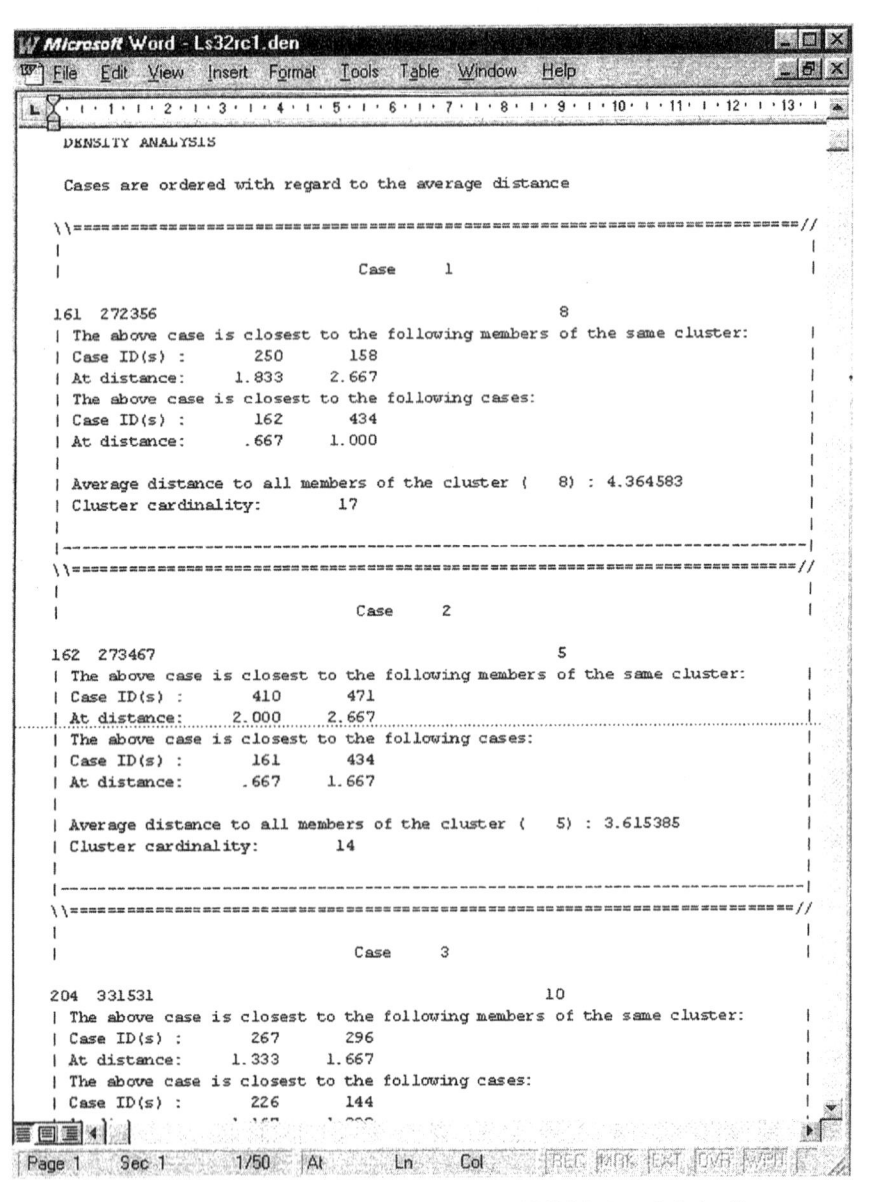

```
W Microsoft Word - Ls32rc1.den
 File  Edit  View  Insert  Format  Tools  Table  Window  Help

  DENSITY ANALYSIS

  Cases are ordered with regard to the average distance

\\=====================================================//
|                                                       |
|                       Case     1                      |
                                                        
 161   272356                                 8
| The above case is closest to the following members of the same cluster: |
| Case ID(s) :     250      158                         |
| At distance:     1.833    2.667                       |
| The above case is closest to the following cases:     |
| Case ID(s) :     162      434                         |
| At distance:     .667     1.000                       |
|                                                       |
| Average distance to all members of the cluster (  8) : 4.364583 |
| Cluster cardinality:        17                        |
|                                                       |
|-------------------------------------------------------|
\\=====================================================//
|                                                       |
|                       Case     2                      |

 162   273467                                 5
| The above case is closest to the following members of the same cluster: |
| Case ID(s) :     410      471                         |
| At distance:     2.000    2.667                       |
| The above case is closest to the following cases:     |
| Case ID(s) :     161      434                         |
| At distance:     .667     1.667                       |
|                                                       |
| Average distance to all members of the cluster (  5) : 3.615385 |
| Cluster cardinality:        14                        |
|                                                       |
|-------------------------------------------------------|
\\=====================================================//
|                                                       |
|                       Case     3                      |

 204   331531                                10
| The above case is closest to the following members of the same cluster: |
| Case ID(s) :     267      296                         |
| At distance:     1.333    1.667                       |
| The above case is closest to the following cases:     |
| Case ID(s) :     226      144                         |
```

FIG. 8.11. A snapshot showing part of the output of DENSE when it starts with a classification. The output is altered to fit the screen.

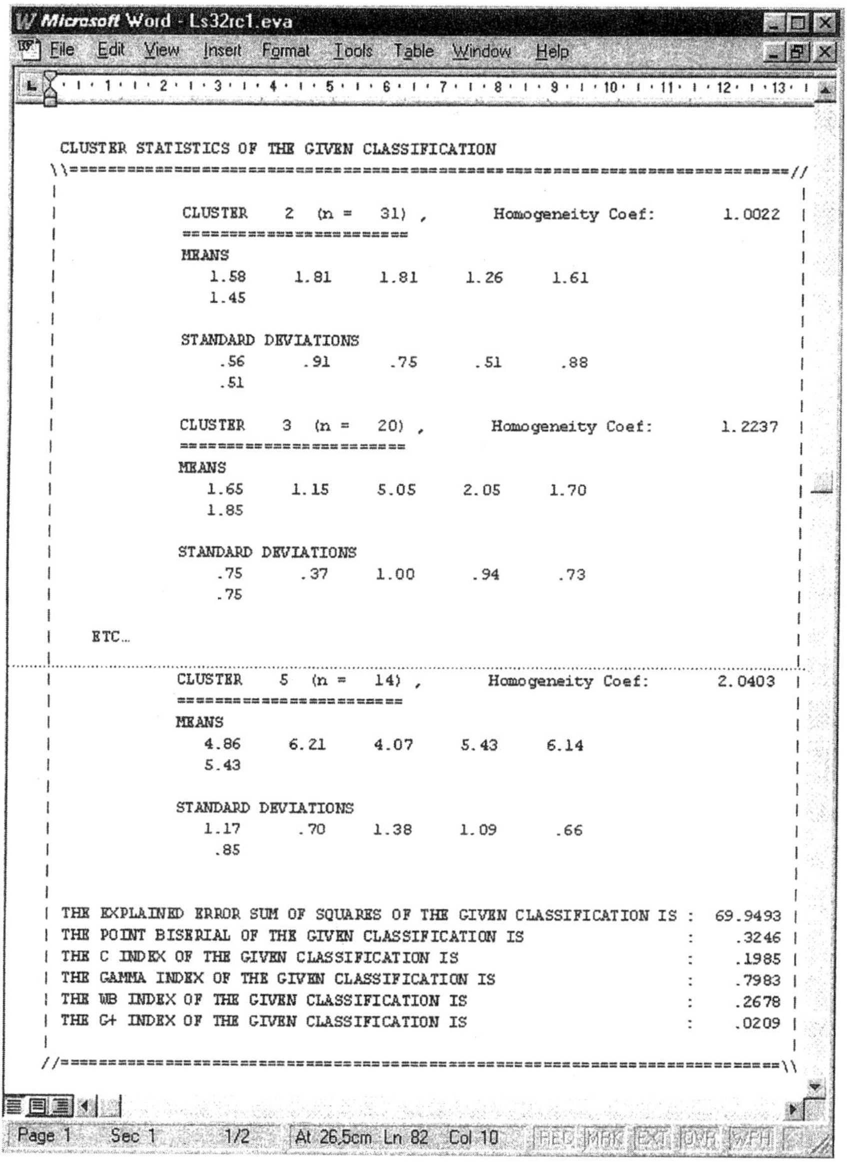

```
CLUSTER STATISTICS OF THE GIVEN CLASSIFICATION
\\====================================================//
|                                                              |
|           CLUSTER   2  (n =   31) ,    Homogeneity Coef:    1.0022  |
|           =========================                         |
|           MEANS                                              |
|             1.58      1.81      1.81      1.26      1.61    |
|             1.45                                             |
|                                                              |
|           STANDARD DEVIATIONS                                |
|              .56       .91       .75       .51       .88    |
|              .51                                             |
|                                                              |
|           CLUSTER   3  (n =   20) ,    Homogeneity Coef:    1.2237  |
|           =========================                         |
|           MEANS                                              |
|             1.65      1.15      5.05      2.05      1.70    |
|             1.85                                             |
|                                                              |
|           STANDARD DEVIATIONS                                |
|              .75       .37      1.00       .94       .73    |
|              .75                                             |
|                                                              |
|   ETC...                                                     |
|                                                              |
|           CLUSTER   5  (n =   14) ,    Homogeneity Coef:    2.0403  |
|           =========================                         |
|           MEANS                                              |
|             4.86      6.21      4.07      5.43      6.14    |
|             5.43                                             |
|                                                              |
|           STANDARD DEVIATIONS                                |
|             1.17       .70      1.38      1.09       .66    |
|              .85                                             |
|                                                              |
| THE EXPLAINED ERROR SUM OF SQUARES OF THE GIVEN CLASSIFICATION IS :  69.9493 |
| THE POINT BISERIAL OF THE GIVEN CLASSIFICATION IS            :    .3246 |
| THE C INDEX OF THE GIVEN CLASSIFICATION IS                   :    .1985 |
| THE GAMMA INDEX OF THE GIVEN CLASSIFICATION IS               :    .7983 |
| THE WB INDEX OF THE GIVEN CLASSIFICATION IS                  :    .2678 |
| THE G+ INDEX OF THE GIVEN CLASSIFICATION IS                  :    .0209 |
|                                                              |
//====================================================\\
```

FIG. 8.12. A snapshot showing part of the output of EVALUATE. The output is altered to fit the screen.

when performing cluster analysis to identify common states, the subindividuals are treated as if they were individuals themselves. When the ISOA module is used to reconstruct the original individuals as state sequences, a composite ID is needed that (a) identifies a subindividual in itself in both the residue analysis output file and the cluster analysis output file, (b) identifies the corresponding "whole" individual, and (c) identifies the measurement occasion corresponding to that subindividual within the corresponding individual.

The SUBIND Module

SUBIND takes as input a data file in which the record starts with a unique numeric ID that identifies the individual and that ranges between 1 and 9,999. The variable vectors corresponding to different measurement occasions are recorded relative to their positions on the time axis. That is, the variable vector corresponding to measurement occasion one is recorded first after the ID, followed by the variable vector for measurement occasion 2, and so on.

The output from SUBIND is a data file in which each record represents a subindividual and it contains an ID that takes up to 10 positions. The first 4 positions are occupied by a unique serial number that identifies the subindividual in the new file, the middle 2 positions are occupied by an ID that tells us which measurement occasion is concerned, and the last 4 positions are occupied by the original ID taken from the input file. This composite ID is then followed by the variable values corresponding to a distinct individual and to a distinct measurement occasion.

An input data file to SUBIND and the resulting output file are illustrated in Fig. 8.13.

2.5. Concluding Remarks

Some of the aspects of SLEIPNER and the methodological considerations that can be made when it is put into use have been presented briefly here. The presentation is by no means preemptive and any omissions or summary descriptions are either because of space constraints or because they were not focal. SLEIPNER makes no pretension of mirroring all the diversity of methods that can be used in connection with person-oriented methodology. Instead, it offers a self-contained tool box that in many classificatory settings, is sufficient (e.g., when applying the LICUR or the RESIDAN approach discussed in earlier chapters). In chapter 9, an empirical study, illustrating the functionality of SLEIPNER and its output, is presented.

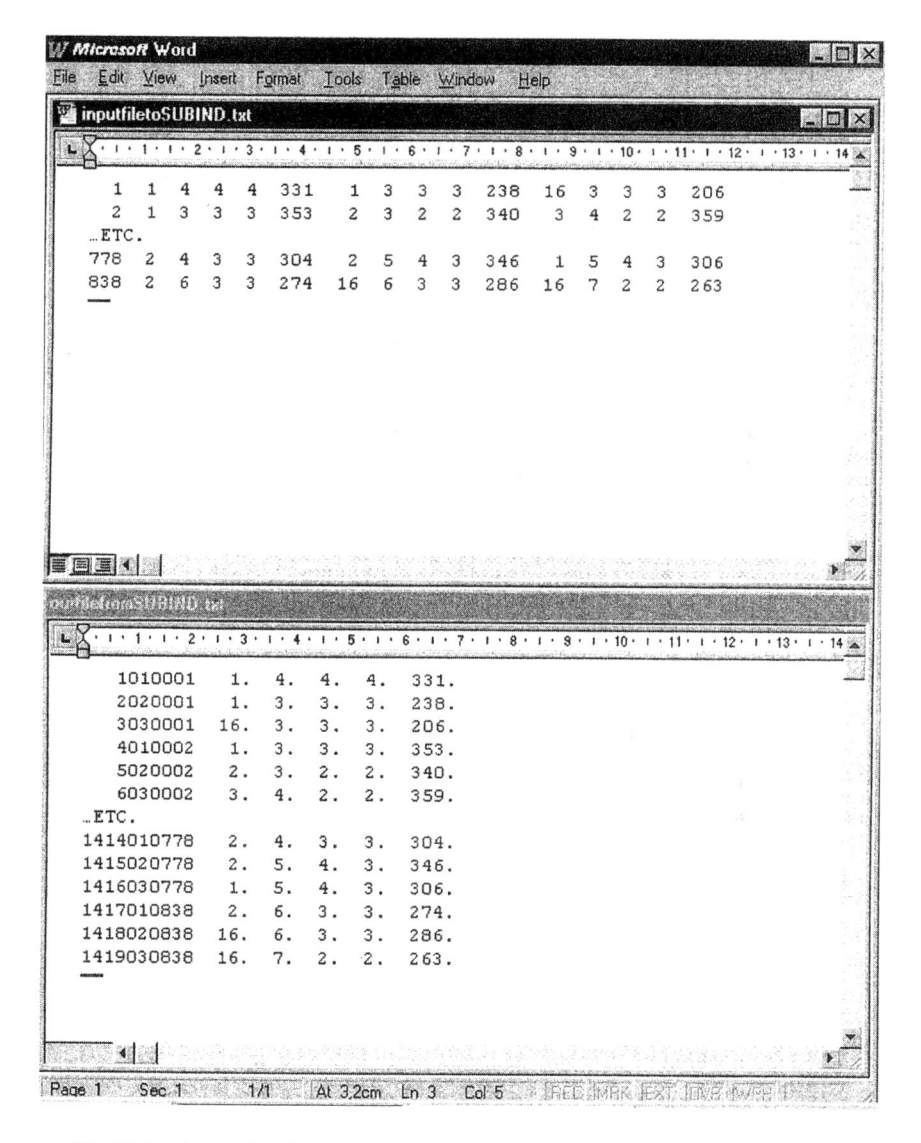

```
inputfiletoSUBIND.txt

  1   1   4   4   4   331    1   3   3   3   238   16   3   3   3   206
  2   1   3   3   3   353    2   3   2   2   340    3   4   2   2   359
...ETC.
778   2   4   3   3   304    2   5   4   3   346    1   5   4   3   306
838   2   6   3   3   274   16   6   3   3   286   16   7   2   2   263
```

```
outfilefromSUBIND.txt

1010001         1.   4.   4.   4.   331.
2020001         1.   3.   3.   3.   238.
3030001        16.   3.   3.   3.   206.
4010002         1.   3.   3.   3.   353.
5020002         2.   3.   2.   2.   340.
6030002         3.   4.   2.   2.   359.
...ETC.
1414010778      2.   4.   3.   3.   304.
1415020778      2.   5.   4.   3.   346.
1416030778      1.   5.   4.   3.   306.
1417010838      2.   6.   3.   3.   274.
1418020838     16.   6.   3.   3.   286.
1419030838     16.   7.   2.   2.   263.
```

FIG. 8.13. A snapshot showing part of the output of SUBIND. The output is altered to fit the screen.

Chapter 9
STABILITY AND CHANGE IN PATTERNS OF SCHOOL ADJUSTMENT: AN EMPIRICAL STUDY

1. INTRODUCTION

The presentation of results in this chapter is detailed with different types of analyses. The reader who quickly wants to know the essential empirical findings could, after reading section 1, go directly to section 5.

1.1. Theoretical Background

The purpose of this chapter is to examine, using a bird's-eye perspective, the growth of boys' school adjustment as seen through the eyes of their teachers. Of course, this area has been studied intensively, especially with regard to negative adjustment. This is also the case within the research program from which the data analyzed here were drawn (see, e.g., Magnusson, Dunér & Zetterblom, 1975). Traditionally, the perspective has almost always been variable oriented and the interest focused on either risk or resilience research (Coie et al., 1993) or on stability and change in indicators of bad adjustment (e.g., Olweus, 1979). During the last 10 years, the degree of sophistication in theory formation and empirical analysis in this vast area has increased in the way the complex phenomenon of risk and protective factors are addressed (Luthar, 1993), in the recognition of the need to study risk mechanisms, not just risk factors (Rutter, 1994), and in the approaches used to study co-morbidity issues (see Stattin & Magnusson, 1996, for a partly person-oriented approach to the study of antisocial development). From the perspective presented in this volume, it seems obvious that these phenomena need to also be studied using a person-oriented approach as has been advocated by Bergman and Magnusson (1987, 1991) and Magnusson (1985,

1988). A judicious use of pattern-based methods may offer greater possibilities of, for instance, mirroring a risk mechanism that may have as an essential feature operating factors configured in specific characteristic patterns. Additionally, questions about co-morbidity are sometimes most naturally answered using an approach that allows the direct analysis of multivariate co-morbidity through profiles of adjustment problems rather than through a more indirect variable-based approach. It is a limitation of the latter approach that it is often based on a model of pairwise linear relationships that are assumed to contain all information about co-morbidity.

Far less effort has been devoted to studying positive adaptation (Seligman, 1998). There are several reasons for this state of affairs, the main one probably being that resources tend to be concentrated on solving problems in society. Positive adjustment is studied most frequently in the context of resilience or protective factors and then the absence of a bad outcome is interpreted as a good outcome (Durlak, 1997). A discussion of the lack of attention given to the positive side is provided by Cowen (1991) in which he points out that the word "wellness" does not even exist. It seems obvious that the negative-centered approach is too limited a perspective; the positive side merits its own study (see Ryff & Singer, 1998, for a discussion of this issue within the health area). A major portion of the work to date on positive adaptation has related to subjective well-being and its concomitants (DeNeve & Cooper, 1998; Diener, Suh, Lucas, & Smith, 1999). Naturally, it can be difficult to decide what constitutes positive adaptation both with regard to cut-off points in a particular dimension and with regard to which dimensions should or could be included (cf. Allport, 1961; Vaillant, 1977).

From a person-oriented perspective, one would like to see how positive adjustment is organized within the individual, that is whether there are clear-cut typical patterns as there are for negative adjustment, or whether the picture is more complex. In fact, there are reasons to believe that the situation is different when the positive side is considered. For instance, there may exist greater stability for typical patterns characterized by a single good adjustment indicator (see Mahoney & Bergman, 2002, for further discussion of this issue). Very little research has been carried out along these lines.

Equally important to what has already been said is to simultaneously consider good and bad sides in a person's total adjustment. To what extent can these two sides be combined in the same person? It seems clear that the agenda outlined briefly here is beyond the capacity of any single research team, and may be most naturally carried out using a person-oriented perspective. From a practical viewpoint, a complication encountered when undertaking the suggested approach is that most of the measures of adjustment factors in current use are focused on discriminating on the negative side and may be less useful for discriminating on the positive side.

It is our aim to make a contribution to the field just introduced by concentrating on one aspect, namely boys' school adjustment as seen through their teachers' eyes. This admittedly limited focus was employed because it made it possible to obtain measures that could be used for studying both the positive and negative side in a developmental context and because a coherent frame of reference for adjustment was achieved in that way.

1.2. Description of the Data Set

1.2.1. Sample. The sample includes boys who are studied at the age of 10 and then again at the age of 13. Data were drawn from the longitudinal Individual Development and Adaptation (IDA) program, initiated in 1964 and led until 1996 by David Magnusson (Magnusson, 1988). Almost all the boys were born in 1955 in the Swedish town of Örebro and were in grade 3 at the time of the first data collection. This cohort consisted of 517 boys. To this group were added those boys who, by moving into Örebro, became their classmates at age 13. The Örebro cohort was found to be reasonably representative of other Swedish urban populations (Bergman, 1973). About 2% to 3% of the children at those ages living in Örebro were not included in the sample because they were in other institutions or received special schooling. At each data collection point, there is almost no dropout in the teachers' ratings (less than 1%), but due to migration, there is a sizable dropout in the longitudinal analyses amounting to 13.2% of the original sample.

1.2.2. Variables. Only data from teachers' ratings were used at both age 10 and age 13. Ratings were made for the following dimensions: *aggression, motor restlessness, timidity, disharmony, lack of concentration,* and *low school motivation*. They are measured on a 7-point scale (1 to 7). Descriptions of them are provided in Table 9.1.

The ratings were made by the teacher for one variable at a time for all the boys in his or her class. The order in which the pupils were rated was changed between variables. The teachers were instructed to expect that most of the children would be between the extremes and to strive for a normal distribution. In spite of this, large differences were found between the mean ratings for different classes, indicating that a more absolute scale was used and perhaps also that different teachers had different standards. The teachers' ratings have been used extensively within the IDA program and have been shown to exhibit high reliability and validity as evidenced by, for instance, fairly high correlations among ratings made by different teachers for children of different ages (Backteman & Magnusson, 1981) and by strong relations between the teachers' ratings and subsequent adult adjustment (Bergman & Magnusson, 1991; Magnusson, 1988; Magnusson & Bergman, 1988; Stattin & Magnusson, 1996).

1.3. Note on the Presentation of SLEIPNER Results

Most of the analyses in this chapter were performed using SLEIPNER, which was presented in the previous chapter. We will, as far as it is possible, present the results in a form that corresponds to the output from the different modules in SLEIPNER. We believe that this is a welcome redundancy as it helps to present SLEIPNER as a

TABLE 9.1
Descriptions of the Teachers' Ratings Used in the Study

Variable Name	Description of "7"	Description of "1"
Aggression	They are aggressive against teachers and classmates. They may, for example, be impertinent and impudent, actively obstructive, or incite to rebellion. They like disturbing and quarreling with classmates.	They work in harmony with the teacher and have positive contacts with classmates. Their relations to others easily become warm and affectionate.
Motor Restlessness	They find it very difficult to sit still during lessons. They fidget uneasily in their seats or wish to move about in the classroom, even during lessons. They may also be talkative and noisy.	They have no difficulties at all in satisfying even great demands on silence and quietness.
Timidity	The behavior of such children is characterized by bashfulness and shyness. They seem to have poor self-esteem. They are inhibited and afraid to express themselves.	Characteristic of these pupils is that they are always open and frank.
Disharmony	They seem very disharmonious and unhappy. They are often in restrained or open conflict with their surroundings or themselves.	They seem to be very harmonious and well balanced, and are seldom involved in serious conflicts with their surroundings or themselves. They seem to be emotionally "at home" in school.
Lack of Concentration	They cannot concentrate on their work, but are occupied with irrelevant things, or sit day-dreaming. For a few moments they may work but are soon lost in other thoughts again. They usually give up quickly, even when the work is suited to their level of intelligence.	They have a marked ability to concentrate on a task and persevere with it. They never allow themselves to be distracted, and do not give up as long as a task suits their level of intelligence.
Low School Motivation	They give an impression of feeling averse to learning and to the subject, and they seem to experience a general feeling of discomfort in the school, a feeling of being "fed up" with school. They are uninterested and it is very difficult to get them to take part in ordinary school work.	Their school motivation is strong and they feel at home in the school environment.

From Magnusson, Dunér & Zetterblom (1975)

working tool, exemplifies some of the issues discussed earlier, and provides a convenient way of summarizing information. Sometimes we use tables to summarize SLEIPNER output, especially when the output is too large to be accommodated within the boundaries of this chapter. However, when a module's output is presented, the output is, whenever necessary and without loss of important details, often altered or shortened for reasons of space.

Several different types of cluster analysis were undertaken. The cluster solution in each analysis has its own denotation to indicate the clusters. The cluster labels differ between the computer output and the text, which uses more informative labels. To help the reader identify the different cluster labels, an overview of these labels in the context (section names) in which they were produced, is given in Table 9.2. Please note that not all the sections in which these labels are cited are mentioned in the tables, only those that are most relevant to the origin of those labels.

2. CROSS-SECTIONAL CLASSIFICATIONS OF PATTERNS OF SCHOOL ADJUSTMENT FOLLOWED BY LINKING

2.1. Introduction

In chapter 6, we presented the LICUR procedure as a tool for carrying out cross-sectional classification analysis with linking. Applying the LICUR method to the data set just introduced amounts to the following: (a) For each age separately we conducted preparatory analyses that included imputing for missing values if and when that was feasible, and conducting a residue analysis to search for residual ob-

TABLE 9.2
An Overview for Each Age Group (Complete Samples), of Different Cluster Labels Referring to the Same Set of Clusters*

Basic Analysis on the Total Sample Excluding Residue Cases					
Age 10			Age 13		
Output from CLUSTER (2.3.1)	Renamed (2.4)	From CENTROID (2.4)	Output from CLUSTER (2.3.1)	Renamed (2.4)	From CENTROID (2.4)
1	A3L1	CA1	1	A6L1	CB1
5	A3L5	CA2	3	A6L3	CB2
10	A3L10	CA3	8	A6L8	CB3
12	A3L12	CA4	10	A6L10	CB4
13	A3L13	CA5	11	A6L11	CB5
17	A3L17	CA6	13	A6L13	CB6
18	A3L18	CA7	14	A6L14	CB7
			15	A6L15	CB8
			25	A6L25	CB9

continued

TABLE 9.2 (continued)

Replication Analysis of Basic Analysis on Random Half Excluding Residue Cases

Age 10	Age 13
Output from CLUSTER (renamed) (Section 2.6.1)	Output from CLUSTER (renamed) (Section 2.6.1)
H3L1	H6L1
H3L2	H6L3
H3L4	H6L4
H3L5	H6L5
H3L10	H6L6
H3L13	H6L7
H3L19	H6L13
	H6L14
	H6L33

Basic ISOA Analysis Excluding Residue Cases

Total Sample		Random Half
ISOA Output (Section 3.3)	Renamed (Section 3.2)	Renamed (Section 3.7)
1	I1	IH1
3	I3	IH2
6	I6	IH4
9	I9	IH8
19	I19	IH11
23	I23	IH13
24	I24	IH23
25	I25	IH24
33	I33	IH32

*Also given are the section numbers in which these labels first occur.

jects (outliers; see also Bergman, 1988b; Bergman and El Khouri, 1986); (b) We performed cluster analysis separately at each age and chose a suitable cluster solution according to the LICUR evaluation criteria (discussed in chap. 4); (c) We linked the solutions between age 10 and age 13 and looked for structural and individual stability in the resulting classifications.

Notice that we conducted the analysis on each set separately. Thus, decisions made for the analysis of one set did not influence decisions made for the other set. That is, we did not set the criteria for choosing a solution at one point in time based on findings at the other point in time. For instance, we did not demand the same number of clusters at both measurement occasions. Thus, in being less conservative, one allows, for instance, for more profiles to emerge at the later age in domains where differentiation occurs, and conversely, we may have fewer profiles at a later age in domains where convergence of early profiles occurs.

The procedures and parameters involved in the analysis already summarized were then reapplied to a randomly chosen subset of the original data set for purposes of replication. As mentioned before, the variables included in the analyses were *aggression, motor restlessness, timidity, disharmony, lack of concentration,* and *low school motivation*. It is to be understood that they will appear in that order in all subsequent analyses and presentations.

Finally, the results were tested against a null hypothesis of no relationships in the data.

2.2. Preparatory Analyses

The results from running DESCRIBE on the combined age 10 and 13 data set are presented in Fig. 9.1 and Fig. 9.2. At each age, and of the six variables included in the analysis, only *timidity* shows a weak to no correlation with the other variables, whereas the remaining five variables show moderate to high intercorrelations. The figures also indicate that 517 individuals have complete data at age 10, and 193 have missing values on all six variables at that age. The corresponding figures for age 13 are 540 individuals with complete data and 169 individuals with missing values on all six variables. Distributional analyses shows that all six variables are approximately normally distributed at each time point.

Because all the individuals with missing values at age 10 have these missing values across all the six variables, none of them is eligible for imputation.[1] The same applies for age 13 except for one individual who had a missing value for only one variable. The standard procedure for imputation in the module IMPUTE[2] was used and the results are shown in Fig. 9.3 in which it can be seen that the one individual with missing value on exactly one variable was successfully imputed with regard to the variable, *low school motivation*.

In Fig. 9.4 and Fig. 9.5, the results of performing residue analysis using the RESIDUE module separately at each age are presented. In these analyses, we look for residue cases that do not conform to our chosen set of criteria for retaining a case; there should exist at least one other case in the data set to which the average squared Euclidean distance (henceforth denoted ASED) computed with raw values is less than 1.34. In other words, a case is considered a residue case if all its ASEDs to the other cases are larger than 1.34.

---

[1] The procedure IMPUTE could still be used to clean the original file from these individuals. Certain modules in SLEIPNER, for example, CLUSTER, require files with no missing cases. It is then sufficient to specify 0 (null) as the number of allowed missing values per case when using IMPUTE.

[2] See chapter 8 for details.

```
DESCRIPTIVE INFORMATION

|============|==============|==============|==============|==============|
| Variable   | Mean         | SD           | Maximum      | Minimum      |
|============|==============|==============|==============|==============|
|            |              |              |              |              |
|     1      |   3.720      |   1.565      |      7       |      1       |
|     2      |   4.010      |   1.729      |      7       |      1       |
|     3      |   3.867      |   1.636      |      7       |      1       |
|     4      |   3.878      |   1.536      |      7       |      1       |
|     5      |   3.959      |   1.719      |      7       |      1       |
|     6      |   3.718      |   1.488      |      7       |      1       |
|            |              |              |              |              |
|============|==============|==============|==============|==============|


|============|==============|==============|==============|==============|
| Variable   | Missing      | No. of       | Valid cases  | Increase in  |
|            | value code   | missing cases|              | valid cases  |
|            |              |              |              | if removed   |
|============|==============|==============|==============|==============|
|            |              |              |              |              |
|     1      |      9       |     193      |     517      |      0       |
|     2      |      9       |     193      |     517      |      0       |
|     3      |      9       |     193      |     517      |      0       |
|     4      |      9       |     193      |     517      |      0       |
|     5      |      9       |     193      |     517      |      0       |
|     6      |      9       |     193      |     517      |      0       |
|            |              |              |              |              |
|============|==============|==============|==============|==============|


|================================================================|
| PRODUCT MOMENT CORRELATIONS (= PEARSON CORRELATIONS) computed using pairwise |
|                    deletion of missing data                    |
|================================================================|

CORRELATIONS:  VAR ( 1 - 6 ) / VAR ( 1 - 6 )

\\==================================================================//
|         | VAR  1 | VAR  2 | VAR  3 | VAR  4 | VAR  5 | VAR  6 |
|---------------------------------------------------------------|
| VAR  1  | 1.0000 |  .6332 | -.0078 |  .6637 |  .4986 |  .5383 |
|---------------------------------------------------------------|
| VAR  2  |  .6332 | 1.0000 | -.1536 |  .5579 |  .6411 |  .5327 |
|---------------------------------------------------------------|
| VAR  3  | -.0078 | -.1536 | 1.0000 |  .1948 |  .1524 |  .2487 |
|---------------------------------------------------------------|
| VAR  4  |  .6637 |  .5579 |  .1948 | 1.0000 |  .5649 |  .6250 |
|---------------------------------------------------------------|
| VAR  5  |  .4986 |  .6411 |  .1524 |  .5649 | 1.0000 |  .7358 |
|---------------------------------------------------------------|
| VAR  6  |  .5383 |  .5327 |  .2487 |  .6250 |  .7358 | 1.0000 |
//==================================================================\\
```

FIG. 9.1. Descriptive statistics of age 10 data resulting from the DESCRIBE module. The variables appear in the order listed in the text. Part of the output is here omitted.

```
DESCRIPTIVE INFORMATION
|===============|===============|===============|===============|===============|
| Variable      | Mean          | SD            | Maximum       | Minimum       |
|===============|===============|===============|===============|===============|
|               |               |               |               |               |
|       1       |     3.847     |     1.624     |       7       |       1       |
|       2       |     3.969     |     1.756     |       7       |       1       |
|       3       |     3.887     |     1.519     |       7       |       1       |
|       4       |     3.932     |     1.487     |       7       |       1       |
|       5       |     4.007     |     1.685     |       7       |       1       |
|       6       |     3.896     |     1.481     |       7       |       1       |
|               |               |               |               |               |
|===============|===============|===============|===============|===============|


|===============|===============|===============|===============|===============|
| Variable      | Missing       | No. of        | Valid cases   | Increase in   |
|               | value code    | missing cases |               | valid cases   |
|               |               |               |               | if removed    |
|===============|===============|===============|===============|===============|
|               |               |               |               |               |
|       1       |       9       |      169      |      541      |       0       |
|       2       |       9       |      169      |      541      |       0       |
|       3       |       9       |      169      |      541      |       0       |
|       4       |       9       |      169      |      541      |       0       |
|       5       |       9       |      169      |      541      |       0       |
|       6       |       9       |      170      |      540      |       1       |
|               |               |               |               |               |
|===============|===============|===============|===============|===============|


|=========================================================================|
| PRODUCT MOMENT CORRELATIONS (= PEARSON CORRELATIONS) computed using pairwise |
|                    deletion of missing data                             |
|=========================================================================|

CORRELATIONS: VAR ( 1 - 6 ) / VAR ( 1 - 6 )

\\=========================================================================//
|          | VAR 1  | VAR 2  | VAR 3  | VAR 4  | VAR 5  | VAR 6  |
|----------------------------------------------------------------|
| VAR 1    | 1.0000 |  .6686 | -.1061 |  .6113 |  .5417 |  .5708 |
|----------------------------------------------------------------|
| VAR 2    |  .6686 | 1.0000 | -.2777 |  .5119 |  .6804 |  .6105 |
|----------------------------------------------------------------|
| VAR 3    | -.1061 | -.2777 | 1.0000 |  .1744 |  .0669 |  .1457 |
|----------------------------------------------------------------|
| VAR 4    |  .6113 |  .5119 |  .1744 | 1.0000 |  .5853 |  .6482 |
|----------------------------------------------------------------|
| VAR 5    |  .5417 |  .6804 |  .0669 |  .5853 | 1.0000 |  .7938 |
|----------------------------------------------------------------|
| VAR 6    |  .5708 |  .6105 |  .1457 |  .6482 |  .7938 | 1.0000 |
//=========================================================================\\
```

FIG. 9.2. Descriptive statistics of age 13 data resulting from the DESCRIBE module. The variables appear in the order listed in the text. Part of the output is here omitted.

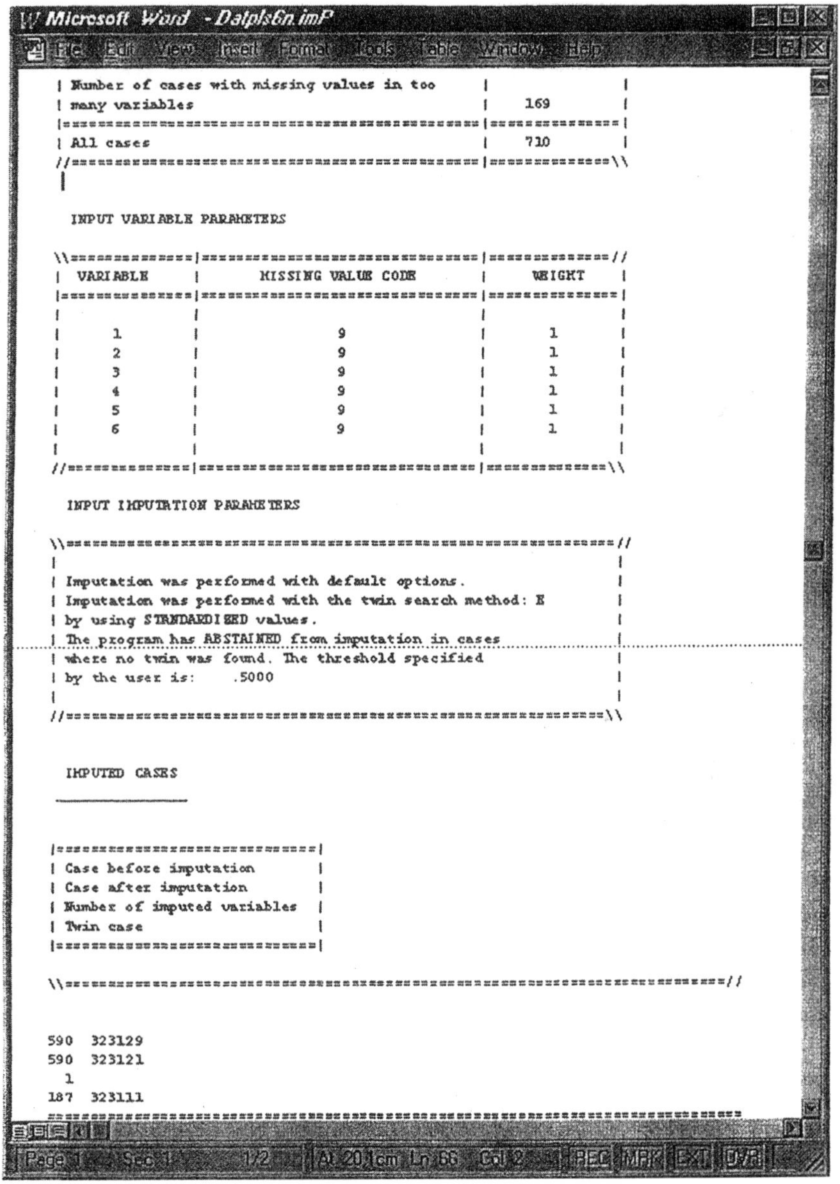

```
| Number of cases with missing values in too |       |
| many variables                             | 169   |
|============================================|=======|
| All cases                                  | 710   |


    INPUT VARIABLE PARAMETERS

| VARIABLE | MISSING VALUE CODE | WEIGHT |
|----------|--------------------|--------|
|    1     |         9          |   1    |
|    2     |         9          |   1    |
|    3     |         9          |   1    |
|    4     |         9          |   1    |
|    5     |         9          |   1    |
|    6     |         9          |   1    |


    INPUT IMPUTATION PARAMETERS

| Imputation was performed with default options.
| Imputation was performed with the twin search method: E
| by using STANDARDIZED values.
| The program has ABSTAINED from imputation in cases
| where no twin was found. The threshold specified
| by the user is:  .5000


    IMPUTED CASES
    _____

| Case before imputation     |
| Case after imputation      |
| Number of imputed variables|
| Twin case                  |


590  323129
590  323121
  1
187  323111
```

FIG. 9.3. The result of imputing the one individual with one missing value at age 13. The variables appear in the order listed in the text. Part of the output is here omitted.

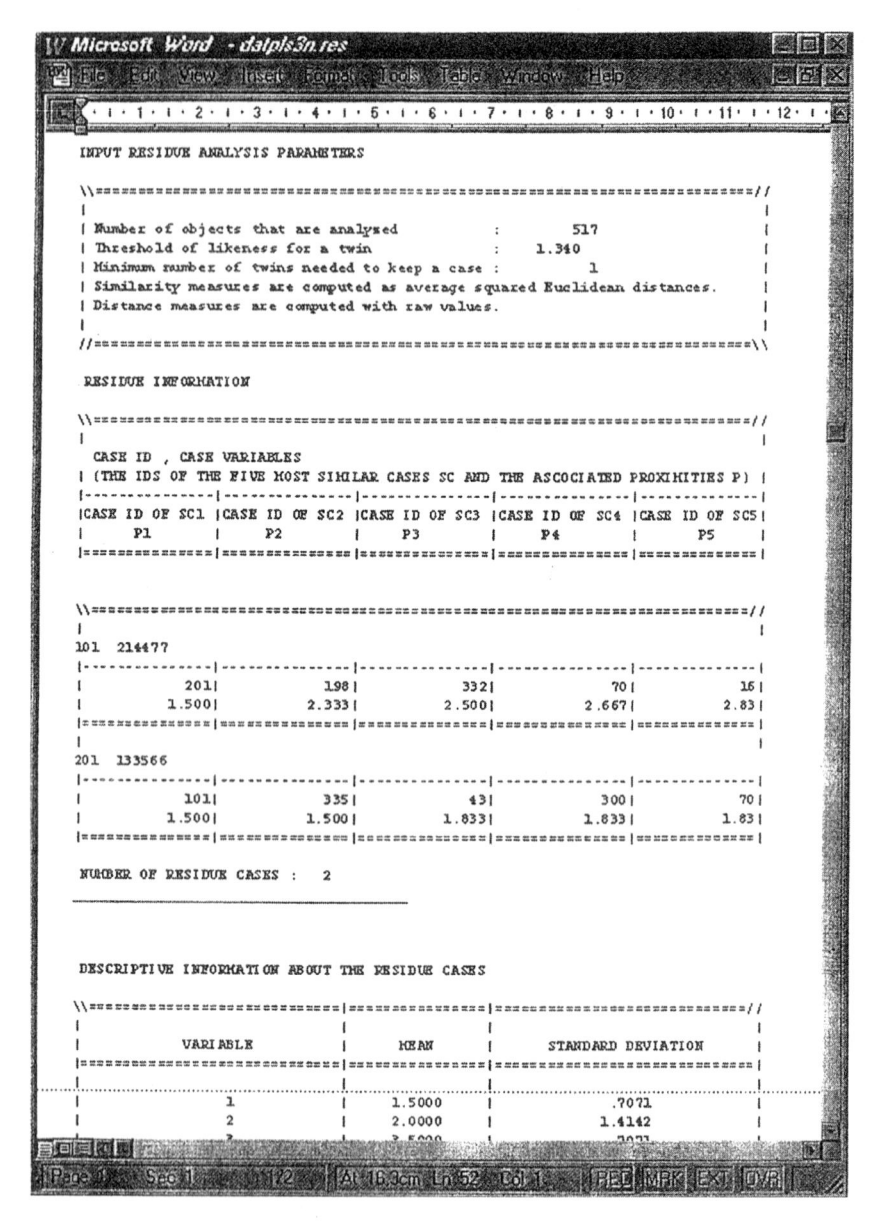

```
INPUT RESIDUE ANALYSIS PARAMETERS

\\==========================================================================//
|                                                                            |
| Number of objects that are analysed       :       517                      |
| Threshold of likeness for a twin          :     1.340                      |
| Minimum number of twins needed to keep a case :     1                      |
| Similarity measures are computed as average squared Euclidean distances.   |
| Distance measures are computed with raw values.                            |
|                                                                            |
//==========================================================================\\


RESIDUE INFORMATION

\\==========================================================================//
|                                                                            |
|    CASE ID , CASE VARIABLES                                                |
| (THE IDS OF THE FIVE MOST SIMILAR CASES SC AND THE ASCOCIATED PROXIMITIES P) |
|---------------|---------------|---------------|---------------|---------------|
|CASE ID OF SC1 |CASE ID OF SC2 |CASE ID OF SC3 |CASE ID OF SC4 |CASE ID OF SC5|
|      P1       |      P2       |      P3       |      P4       |      P5     |
|===============|===============|===============|===============|=============|


\\==========================================================================//
|                                                                            |
101  214477
|---------------|---------------|---------------|---------------|---------------|
|         201|          198|          332|           70|           16|
|        1.500|         2.333|        2.500|        2.667|         2.83|
|===============|===============|===============|===============|=============|
|                                                                            |
201  133566
|---------------|---------------|---------------|---------------|---------------|
|         101|          335|           43|          300|           70|
|        1.500|         1.500|        1.833|        1.833|         1.83|
|===============|===============|===============|===============|=============|

NUMBER OF RESIDUE CASES :    2
_____


DESCRIPTIVE INFORMATION ABOUT THE RESIDUE CASES

\\==========================|===============|================================//
|                           |               |                                |
|       VARIABLE            |     MEAN      |    STANDARD DEVIATION          |
|===========================|===============|================================|
|                           |               |                                |
|           1               |    1.5000     |        .7071                   |
|           2               |    2.0000     |       1.4142                   |
```

FIG. 9.4. Residue analysis on the data set from age 10 using the module RESIDUE . Part of the output is here omitted.

STABILITY AND CHANGE

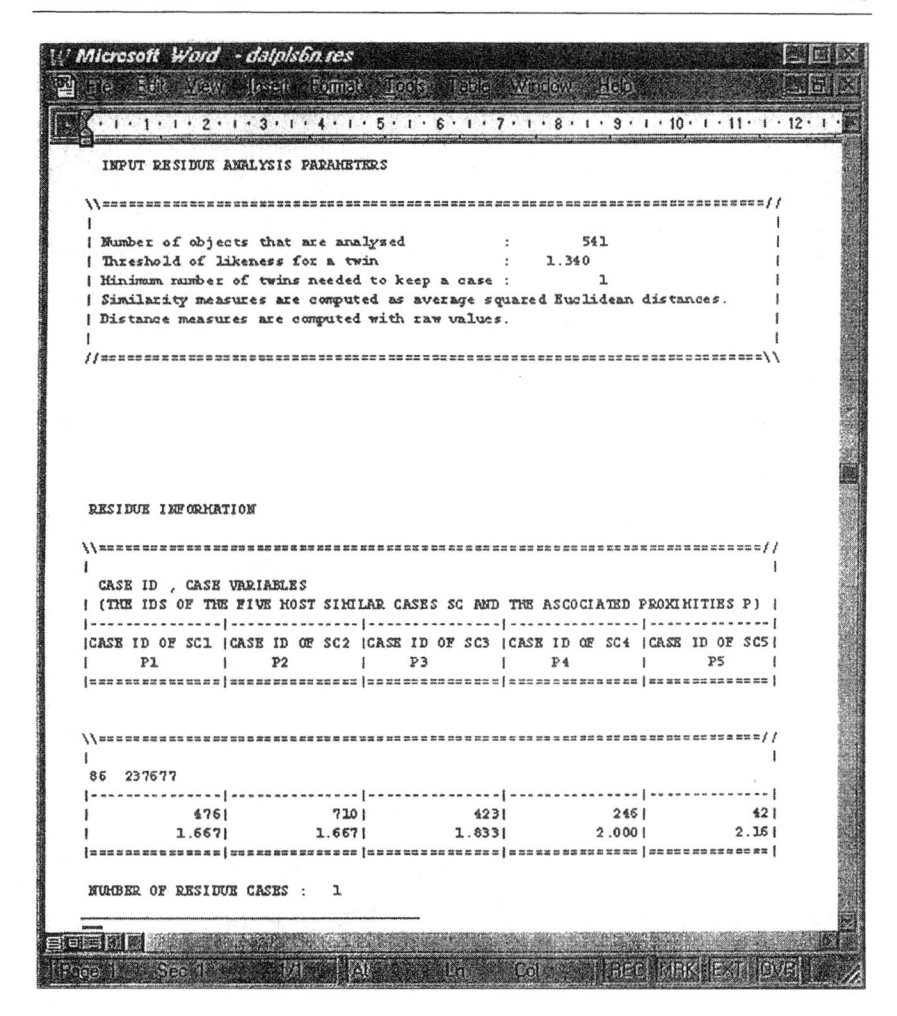

FIG. 9.5. Residue analysis on the data set from age 13 using the module RESIDUE. Part of the output is here omitted.

The choice of the threshold 1.34 demands some explanation. It is often the case that the scales of the variables included in the analysis have varying properties and it is natural to standardize them before further analyses are conducted. In this case, it might be reasonable to use the SLEIPNER default threshold value of .5 as the cut-off point for assigning a case to the residue set (i.e., a case is a residue case if all its ASEDs to other cases are larger than .5). However, for the present data sets, all the variables are on a comparable 1 to 7 scale and it was decided to retain that scale in the analysis so that information is preserved about level and scatter differences between the variables. Table 9.3 illustrates the types of deviations between two value profiles that correspond to different ASED values. Here, a case is kept for further analysis if it has a "twin" that corresponds to exactly one of the entries in Table 9.3 up to and including 1.334. After careful consideration, we decided that the threshold of 1.34 for regarding two cases as similar was reasonable and it was adopted in the residue analyses. It would have been conceivable to demand a higher degree of similarity to retain a case but in the present application, we settled for removing only those cases that were clearly dissimilar to all other cases.

As shown in Fig. 9.4 and Fig. 9.5, three residue cases were identified, two at age 10 and one at age 13. As it turned out, the two residue cases at age 10 were actually mutually similar albeit at a larger dissimilarity coefficient than was allowed, something that is not normally expected. The child with the ID number, 101 (with profile, 214477, on the six variables) had no conduct problems, was average on *timidity* and *disharmony*, but extremely high on *lack of concentration* and *low school motivation*. The child with the id-number, 201 (133566) was also low on conduct problems, average on *timidity*, but above average on *disharmony*, high on *lack of concentration*, and high on *low school motivation*.

TABLE 9.3
ASED Between Two Cases as a Function of Number of Units Deviation and Number of Variables That Deviate*

1 Unit Deviation on X Variables	2 Units Deviation on X Variables	3 Units Deviation on X Variables	ASED
			0
X = 1			.167
X = 2			.334
X = 3			0.5
X = 4			.667
	X = 1		.667
X = 5			.834
X = 1	X = 1		.834
X = 6			1.0
X = 2	X = 1		1.0
X = 3	X = 1		1.167
	X = 2		1.334
X = 4	X = 1		1.334
X = 5	X = 1		1.5
		X = 1	1.5

*Empty cells correspond to X = 0.

STABILITY AND CHANGE   147

Although these cases were odd cases in themselves one can still discern the same type of contrast in both profiles, which is the co-occurrence of no "pure" conduct problems together with school performance related problems. However, an examination of these individuals' profiles at age 13 shows that although their school maladjustment was still at the same level as at age 10, their level of conduct problems had worsened to well above average by age 13. *Timidity* also rose in both cases especially for child 101, whose score became extremely high. The value profiles associated with these individuals at age 13 were 557566 and 565656 respectively, and were not found in the residue at that age.

At age 13, only one residue case was observed. The child with the ID number 86 (237677) was characterized by being extremely high on *timidity, disharmony, lack of concentration,* and *low school motivation,* but below average on pure conduct problems. Hence, the opposing relation of conduct problems to school performance related problems is also present in this residue case as it was in the previous two cases at age 10. The exception is in this case that this is coupled with high levels on *timidity* as well as *disharmony*. Examining the profile of this child at age 10 (674476) reveals a profile that is very high on conduct problems as well as school adjustment but somewhat average on *timidity* and *disharmony*. In other words, the opposing relation of conduct problems to school performance related problems was not present at age 10 nor was the case found to be in the residue at that age. A further analysis of the residue cases would be interesting but was not carried out here.[3]

2.3. Cross-Sectional Classifications

2.3.1. Introduction. Some characteristics of the SLEIPNER output for the chosen solution from WARD cluster analysis on the data set from age 10 are shown in Fig. 9.6. Table 9.4 summarizes the same characteristics for the data set from age 13. Both analyses were performed on the original data without standardization of the variables. As mentioned before, the reason for this is that all variables are already on the same comparable scale from 1 to 7 and we wanted to retain the information contained in varying standard deviations. As is implied in Fig. 9.6 and Table 9.6, at age 10, the seven-clusters solution was chosen, and at age 13, the nine-clusters solution was chosen. For each solution, also shown are the centroids of the clusters and the standard deviations of the variables involved. The homogeneity coefficients are also presented, and are the average of all ASEDs computed separately between all possible pairs of individuals in each cluster. The percentage of explained error sums of squares for the solutions at age 10 and at age 13 are 61.26 and 67.18, respectively, which are here considered reasonably satisfactory, albeit not very high.

---

[3] For instance, using other information sources to try to ascertain whether the observed profiles were likely to have been influenced by error of measurement or whether they could be regarded as "true" outliers.

```
     CLUSTER   1 (n =  133) ,       Homogeneity Coef:   1.6409220
     ==========================      ================
     MEANS
        3.5038    3.9323    3.8647    3.7293    3.6767
        3.4962
     STANDARD DEVIATIONS
        1.0122     .7900    1.0645     .7989     .9338
         .7941


     CLUSTER   5 (n =   85) ,       Homogeneity Coef:   2.3736720
     ==========================      ================
     MEANS
        4.4353    4.4353    5.5412    5.1059    5.0706
        4.7059
     STANDARD DEVIATIONS
        1.0850    1.3043    1.0183     .9389    1.1628
         .9859
     CLUSTER  10 (n =   59) ,       Homogeneity Coef:   2.0424720
     ==========================      ================
     MEANS
        5.9153    6.2712    3.9322    5.6610    6.3559
        5.7627
     STANDARD DEVIATIONS
         .8364     .7151    1.3629    1.2678     .6889
         .9885
     CLUSTER  12 (n =   54) ,       Homogeneity Coef:   1.5534590
     ==========================      ================
     MEANS
        1.9259    1.7778    2.6481    1.8889    1.5185
        1.7222
     STANDARD DEVIATIONS
        1.0252     .7439    1.1016     .9248     .6063
         .7871
     CLUSTER  13 (n =   21) ,       Homogeneity Coef:   1.7984130
     ==========================      ================
     MEANS
        2.4286    4.3333    1.4286    2.0000    2.5714
        2.0952
     STANDARD DEVIATIONS
        1.2873    1.1106     .6761     .7746     .9258
         .7684
     CLUSTER  17 (n =   81) ,       Homogeneity Coef:   2.3339490
     ==========================      ================
     MEANS
        4.3951    5.4938    2.2099    4.3210    4.6790
        4.0494
     STANDARD DEVIATIONS
        1.1798     .9890     .8905    1.0586    1.2533
        1.0712
     CLUSTER  18 (n =   82) ,       Homogeneity Coef:   2.4209550
     ==========================      ================
     MEANS
        2.6463    2.0366    5.1585    2.9024    2.7317
        2.9146
     STANDARD DEVIATIONS
        1.1372     .8527    1.0940    1.2030    1.1659
```

FIG. 9.6. The 7-clusters solution from cluster analysis of the data set at age 10. The module CLUSTER, option Ward, was used. Between parentheses is the number of individuals in the corresponding cluster. Not shown for this solution is the cluster membership of the individuals, the increase in the ESS (19.65), and the explained ESS (61.27).

TABLE 9.4
The Nine-Clusters Solution of the Data Set at Age 13*

Cluster Name	Aggression		Motor Restlessness		Timidity		Disharmony		Lack of Concentration		Low School Motivation		N	HC
	M	SD	M	SD	M	SD	M	SD	M	SD	M	SD		
A6L1	3.8	0.76	3.9	.68	4.1	.64	3.9	.63	4.0	1.0	3.8	.79	146	1.19
A6L3	2.4	1.0	1.5	.57	5.3	.99	3.9	.95	2.8	1.1	3.4	.96	54	1.89
A6L8	2.5	1.2	3.4	1.1	2.8	1.1	2.2	.73	3.1	1.0	2.7	.79	74	2.20
A6L10	6.1	.83	6.2	.80	2.8	1.3	5.4	1.1	5.8	.94	5.5	.81	68	2.00
A6L11	3.7	.43	3.1	1.1	6.3	.59	4.4	1.1	4.4	.75	4.3	.79	36	1.41
A6L13	4.4	1.1	6.0	.73	4.4	1.4	5.2	.97	6.5	.49	6.2	.68	43	1.85
A6L14	1.6	.88	1.3	.75	3.3	1.6	1.5	.66	1.3	.52	1.5	.72	45	1.66
A6L15	5.3	.63	5.0	.72	4.1	.84	4.9	.99	4.8	.93	4.5	.81	35	1.39
A6L25	5.1	1.0	5.2	.99	2.3	.97	4.3	1.2	3.0	1.1	3.2	.83	39	2.16

*The means (M) and the standard deviations (SD) of the variables in each cluster are given together with homogeneity coefficient (HC) and the number of individuals in the cluster (N).

Later, in the course of comparing and linking the two solutions (i.e., when we investigate structural and individual stability and change over age) we say more about the interpretation of the clusters in each solution.

2.3.2. Deciding the Number of Clusters. Table 9.5 presents the increase in the error sum of squares, henceforth ESS, as well as the percentage explained ESS for the last 23 iterations in the Ward cluster analyses for the two data sets using SLEIPNER's module CLUSTER.

A few points need clarification at this point. There are no definitive rules that will automatically generate a logical cut-off point in cluster analysis. There are, however, procedures for determining the number of clusters and general recommendations about how to proceed on the issue (see, e.g., Milligan & Cooper, 1985). We also presented our set of guidelines in chapter 4. These are used as a basis for the line of reasoning we now present.

It is often preferred that a manageable number of clusters is obtained. If the level of description is too fine-grained, it may not be useful and some other type of analysis may be required. In addition, provided we are working with hierarchical cluster analysis and provided we preserve the hierarchical nature of the solution for future use, the decision about the number of clusters is not so critical as one could move up and down the hierarchy in different analyses or presentations depending on the level of detail that is most useful in the specific case. Having said that, there are almost always certain characteristics of the solution that may shed light on the question of where to place the cut-off point. For instance, an acceptable minimum level of the percentage explained ESS can be required, and in the spirit of factor analysis, one could look for a sharp increase (or decrease) in the value of the optimizing function; here the increase in the ESS; or inspect the resulting dendogram for a suitable cut-off point.

Other characteristics of the resulting solution may also be inspected, such as the means in a cluster, often denoted the centroid of the cluster, and the associated variances. Normally it is required that the variances of the incorporated variables be small and not increase much as a result of a previous merge. Also, with regard to the homogeneity coefficient, the result of a merge of two clusters with moderate homogeneity should not be a cluster with a much higher homogeneity coefficient[4] than the parent clusters. Furthermore, sometimes there may be theoretical reasons for why two clusters should not be joined.

Table 9.5 shows how considerations regarding the percentage of explained ESS and the increase in ESS come to bear on choice of a solution. Table 9.4 and Fig. 9.6 show the centroids, the associated standard deviations, and the homogeneity coefficients.

All these considerations, taken together, led to the choice of the seven-cluster solution at age 10, and the nine-cluster solution at age 13, as the primary solutions.

---

[4]The lower the coefficient, the better the homogeneity within a cluster.

STABILITY AND CHANGE

TABLE 9.5
Summary Table for the Last 23 Iterations in Ward Cluster Analysis
on the Data Set From Age 10 and Age 13*

Iteration	Increase in ESS	Explained ESS	Iteration	Increase in ESS	Explained ESS
492	6.68048	76.9654	517	6.09084	78.8058
493	7.33633	76.4166	518	6.41282	78.3376
494	7.66026	75.8436	519	6.41731	77.8690
495	8.78457	75.1865	520	6.76848	77.3747
496	9.11775	74.5045	521	7.16758	76.8513
497	9.48946	73.7947	522	8.61238	76.2224
498	10.20833	73.0311	523	9.34568	75.5400
499	12.71616	72.0799	524	9.91490	74.8160
500	12.88805	71.1158	525	10.47178	74.0514
501	13.21713	70.1272	526	13.37173	73.0749
502	13.73170	69.1001	527	13.66566	72.0771
503	14.19730	68.0381	528	15.28791	70.9607
504	16.00895	66.8406	529	16.66541	69.7438
505	17.26673	65.5490	530	17.14608	68.4918
506	18.30577	64.1797	**531**	**17.93664**	**67.1821**
507	19.25998	62.7391	532	22.63423	65.5293
508	**19.65078**	**61.2692**	533	27.50084	63.5212
509	24.01810	59.4726	534	30.38346	61.3026
510	64.03127	54.6829	535	50.55844	57.6108
511	65.16453	49.8085	536	58.59970	53.3318
512	76.18999	44.1094	537	75.97601	47.7840
513	56.63220	32.3932	538	88.98990	33.9838
514	33.05760	.0000	539	65.39950	.0000
	Age 10			Age 13	

*The bold entry corresponds to the chosen solutions at each age (7 clusters at age 10 and 9 clusters at age 13).

2.4. Structural Stability and Change

In the next step of the analysis, we focus on the stability over age of a clustering solution. There are several key issues that should be discussed and, if possible, verified at the onset of such an analysis. For brevity, we consider only the case of two measurement occasions as in the data set studied here. See also chapter 3 and chapter 7.

If the same variables have been measured at the two time points and can also be regarded as having the same meaning at these two different occasions, and if the two solutions are essentially identical at some descriptive level, we speak of perfect *structural stability*. If the two solutions are only partially identical, we speak of *partial structural stability*. Typically, this means that some clusters dissolve over time and new clusters may be formed, whereas other clusters remain stable. If the matching is poor, indicating that the solutions are largely different, the solution is then considered structurally unstable. Fortunately, the latter, although theoretically feasible, is not usually encountered in practice.

Individual stability and change, denoting the tendency for individuals in one cluster to reemerge in a similar or a new cluster at a higher age, is another stability/change issue that is closely related but not equivalent to structural stability as becomes apparent later on in the analysis.

In the following, we describe the clusters by their respective centroids. In studying structural stability, we compare two sets of centroids taken from different measurement occasions. The comparison uses a matching procedure, described in chapter 7, which pairs those centroids, each taken from a different occasion, which are most similar (provided that none of these candidate centroids is already paired with some other centroid in a previous matching). This procedure is intuitively attractive, as it provides a basis for considering the solutions from the two occasions as a total, that is, the clusters receive their meaning not only in relation to the other clusters present in the solution from the same age, but also in relation to the cluster solution from the other age studied. This does come out at a price however. If structural stability is not perfect, matching clusters becomes increasingly dependent on the matches already made. Poorly matched clusters may appear at the last stages of the matching procedure. These clusters may be more similar to another cluster that is not available because it has already been matched. This phenomenon must be identified and discussed in the interpretation of the results.

We matched the solutions from age 10 and age 13 using the CENTROID method in SLEIPNER. In Fig. 9.7, the rows numbered 1 to 9 under the headings "Allwage13" are the 9-clusters centroids obtained from the cluster analysis of the age 13 data set entered in the order in which they appear in the Ward solution. The centroids for age 10 are not shown (please note that two dummy rows had to be added to the age 10 centroids to make the number of centroids equal to that of age 13). For convenience, we sometimes refer to the clusters at age 10 by preceding the original name that appears in the ward solution by the prefix A3L. Thus, cluster 1 at age 10 is referred to as A3L1 and cluster 5 at age 10 is referred to as A3L5, and so on. Likewise, we prefix the clusters for age 13 by A6L.[5] Thus, cluster 1 at age 13 is referred to as A6L1 and cluster 3 at age 13 is now A6L3, and so on. The names given in Fig. 9.7 do not follow this rule because they are automatically named by SLEIPNER. For instance, CA1 equals A3L1, and so on.

---

[5]At age 10, the boys were in elementary school year 3, and at age 13, in elementary school year 6 in the Swedish school system. Hence the "A3" and the "A6" in "A3L" and "A6L," which are a shorthand way of depicting the Swedish names for those school years. The "L" in both expressions refers to the ratings being made by the teachers.

```
| allwage13
| 1:    3.801   3.904   4.116   3.959   4.048   3.808
| 2:    2.426   1.500   5.370   3.907   2.815   3.426
| 3:    2.595   3.460   2.811   2.243   3.135   2.730
| 4:    6.103   6.206   2.853   5.456   5.838   5.559
| 5:    3.750   3.111   6.361   4.417   4.444   4.333
| 6:    4.465   6.023   4.419   5.233   6.581   6.233
| 7:    1.600   1.378   3.311   1.511   1.333   1.511
| 8:    5.343   5.057   4.143   4.943   4.800   4.571
| 9:    5.128   5.256   2.308   4.359   3.026   3.205
```

AVERAGE SQUARED EUCLIDIAN DISTANCE FOR SET A

	CA1	CA2	CA3	CA4	CA5	CA6	CA7	CA8	CA9
CA1	0.000	1.539	4.556	3.301	2.238	1.272	1.320	39.710	39.710
CA2	1.539	0.000	1.871	8.933	7.277	2.237	3.773	26.348	26.348
CA3	4.556	1.871	0.000	15.285	10.559	2.237	9.830	19.577	19.577
CA4	3.301	8.933	15.285	0.000	1.588	6.903	1.801	65.514	65.514
CA5	2.238	7.277	10.559	1.588	0.000	3.245	3.458	57.428	57.428
CA6	1.272	2.237	2.237	6.903	3.245	0.000	5.133	34.729	34.729
CA7	1.320	3.773	9.830	1.801	3.458	5.133	0.000	49.055	49.055
CA8	39.710	26.348	19.577	65.514	57.428	34.729	49.055	0.000	0.000
CA9	39.710	26.348	19.577	65.514	57.428	34.729	49.055	0.000	0.000

AVERAGE SQUARED EUCLIDIAN DISTANCE FOR SET B

	CB1	CB2	CB3	CB4	CB5	CB6	CB7	CB8	CB9
CB1	0.000	1.819	1.383	3.450	1.052	3.157	5.086	0.970	1.405
CB2	1.819	0.000	2.296	9.682	1.511	8.224	2.757	4.832	5.182
CB3	1.383	2.296	0.000	7.581	3.845	7.623	1.807	4.222	2.436
CB4	3.450	9.682	7.581	0.000	5.324	1.037	16.006	0.980	2.800
CB5	1.052	1.511	3.845	5.324	0.000	3.601	7.169	1.951	4.370
CB6	3.157	8.224	7.623	1.037	3.601	0.000	15.783	1.299	4.676
CB7	5.086	2.757	1.807	16.006	7.169	15.783	0.000	10.233	7.057
CB8	0.970	4.832	4.222	0.980	1.951	1.299	10.233	0.000	1.468
CB9	1.405	5.182	2.436	2.800	4.370	4.676	7.057	1.468	0.000

PAIRWISE MATCHINGS

Cluster Pair	Average Squared Euclidian Distance
CA1 CB1	0.073
CA4 CB7	0.155
CA3 CB4	0.259
CA7 CB2	0.277
CA2 CB8	0.547
CA5 CB3	0.580
CA6 CB9	0.675
CA8 CB6	21.034
CA9 CB5	32.317
Mean: 6.213 Maximum: 32.317   Minimum: 0.073

FIG. 9.7. Modified output from the module CENTROID when run on the seven-clusters solution at age 10 (CA1 to CA7 in the figure) and the nine-clusters solution at age 13 (CB1 to CB9 in the figure). CA8 and CA9 in the figure are dummy entries. Not shown are the centroids at age 10. CA1 to CA7 and CB1 to CB9 appear in the same order found in the Ward solutions.

As shown in Fig. 9.7, the correspondence between the two solutions is quite high as judged by the average squared Euclidean distances between the seven centroids from age 10, and seven (out of nine) centroids from age 13: the best match having an ASED of .073 and the worst match having an ASED of .675. Please note that CA8 and CA9 indicate dummy centroids for age 10 and should not be interpreted. Table 9.6 presents the matching together with the names and sizes associated with each cluster. A graphical depiction of this state of affair is shown in Fig. 9.8.

It can be seen in Fig. 9.8 that the largest clusters in each solution namely, A3L1 and A6L1, are also those that match best. These clusters exhibit average levels in all six variables. Clusters A3L12 and A6L14 are very low on all variables except for *timidity* indicating a generally good adjustment that is more pronounced at age 13 than at age 10. A mirror image of this profile can be found in A3L10 and A6L10. These clusters show a high degree of adjustment problems in all variables except for *timidity*. Again it seems that this profile is more pronounced at age 13 than it is at age 10. Clusters A3L18 and A6L3 are characterized by moderately low levels of *aggression, disharmony, lack of concentration,* and *low school motivation*, but low on *motor restlessness,* and high on *timidity*. Clusters A3L5 and A6L15 are above average on most variables. Clusters A3L13 and A6L8 are low in all variables except *motor restlessness,* which is more pronounced at age 10 than at age 13. Clusters A3L17 and A6L25 are above average on *aggression* and *motor restlessness* but low on *timidity*.

The two remaining clusters in the nine-clusters solution from age 13 (from which seven were employed in the previous matching) are depicted in Fig. 9.9. The clusters are matched with the best fitting clusters from age 10 without any consideration of previous matches. It can be seen that A6L13 has a good match at age 10. Only Cluster A6L11 at age 13 remains unique, characterized by high levels of *tim-*

TABLE 9.6
The Output Shown in Fig. 9.7 is Recaptured, Showing the Names and Sizes of the Clusters and the ASEDs Between the Matched Clusters

Seven-Clusters Solution of Age 10 Data Set	N	ASED	N	Nine-Clusters Solution of Age 13 Data Set
A3L1	133	.073	146	A6L1
A3L12	54	.155	45	A6L14
A3L10	59	.259	68	A6L10
A3L18	82	.277	54	A6L3
A3L5	85	.547	35	A6L15
A3L13	21	.580	74	A6L8
A3L17	81	.675	39	A6L25
			36	A6L11
			43	A6L13
SUM	515		540	SUM

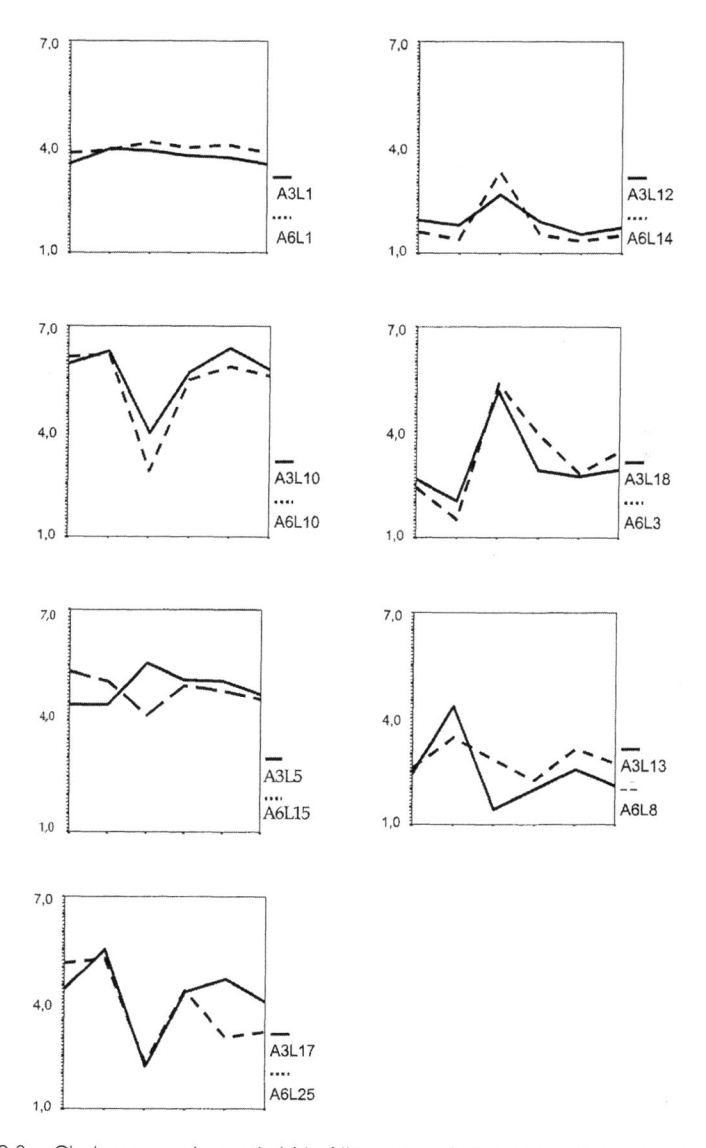

FIG. 9.8. Cluster means (= centroids) of the seven-cluster solution from age 10 graphically captured when matched against the seven best fitting centroids from the nine-cluster solution of age 13. The six presented variables in the figure are ordered as follows: Aggression, Motor Restlessness, Timidity, Disharmony, Lack of Concentration, and Lack of School Motivation.

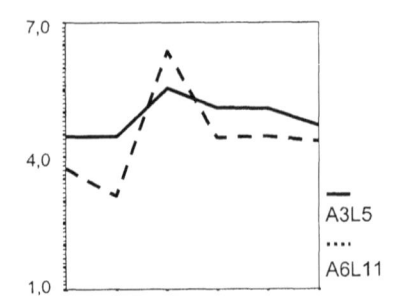

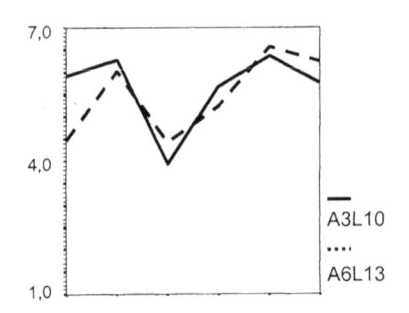

FIG. 9.9. The two age 13 clusters that were not used in the seven-clusters match depicted together with the best matching clusters from age 10. The six presented variables in the figure are ordered as follows: Aggression, Motor Restlessness, Timidity, Disharmony, Lack of Concentration, and Lack of School Motivation.

idity and normal ranges for the other variables. It is interesting to note that when inspecting the hierarchy of classification at age 13, we find that the seven-clusters solution is reached by merging A6L13 and A6L10, both of which were found closest to A3L10 but under different matching conditions. Cluster A6L11, however, is found intact in the seven-cluster solution at age 13.

2.5. Individual Stability and Change

To study individual movements between clusters at different ages, we used the EXACON module in SLEIPNER for the exact analysis of single cells in a contingency table (chap. 8, this volume; Bergman & El Khouri, 1987). Fig. 9.10 shows the results from such an analysis, in which the rows correspond to the seven-clusters solution at age 10 and the columns correspond to the nine-clusters solution at age 13. The first row in a cell is the observed frequency in that cell, the second row is the expected frequency and the fifth row is the hypergeometrical probability associated with the discrepancy between the first and the second rows. A type is said to occur in a cell if the observed frequency is so much larger than the expected one that the associated hypergeometrical probability is *low*. That is, we observe a significantly larger frequency than we expect to observe by chance alone. In the reverse setting, when we observe less than we expect by chance alone, we say that we have an *antitype*.

2.5.1. Looking for Types. As shown in Fig. 9.10, four of the seven primary matches presented previously are indeed types, indicating partial individual stability. These four matches are cell (1,1), cell (10,10), cell (18,3), and cell (12,14), with the highest associated probability being .0006 for cell (1,1). Thus, a larger proportion of

FIG. 9.10. A cross-tabulation of the solution at age 10 and the solution at age 13 with the exact analysis of the cells in the table. The output is produced by EXACON, in SLEIPNER, but modified to fit the page. The entries in each cell are as follows: First is given the observed frequency, which is followed by the expected frequency, the CHI-2 component, the binomial probability, and the hypergeometrical probability, in that order. Not shown in the figure is the overall CHI-2, which is 255.2339, and the contingency coefficient, which is .6020.

individuals than expected by chance belong to clusters 1, 10, 12 and 18 at age 10 and retain their profiles at age 13. These individuals are those who show moderate values on all variables (the largest cluster in both solutions), those who are normal with a slight expression of *timidity*, those with a multiple problem profile but who are somewhat moderate with respect to *timidity,* and those with no *motor restlessness* but who are above average on *timidity* and below average on the rest of the variables.

It can also be seen from Fig. 9.10 that the two secondary matches (shown in Fig. 9.9) are also types. The first match corresponds to cell (10,13), with patterns at both ages characterized by severe problems on all variables except for *timidity*, which is in the normal range, and *aggression,* which gets moderated with age. The second match corresponds to cell (5,11) with patterns characterized by high to moderate adjustment problems and high to very high expressions of *timidity*, as one moves from age 10 to age 13. The probabilities associated with those two cells are well below .01. Fig. 9.11 shows pictorially the six longitudinal streams described.

2.5.2. Looking for Antitypes. Next we look for the most infrequent individual movements between the two ages. We assume that these occur for the most dissimilar clusters. Table 9.7 contains a dissimilarity matrix between the seven clusters at age 10 and the nine clusters at age 13. Seven cells corresponding to the seven highest ASEDs dissimilarities between clusters, one from each age, were selected for analysis. It can be seen in Fig. 9.10 that as anticipated, six probabilities out of seven confirm the existence of antitypes, with the probabilities ranging between .0009 and .0126. Fig. 9.12 shows pictorially the six "dry-streams" described here.

2.5.3. Exploring the Remaining Cells. Exploring the contingency table in Fig. 9.10 further, we had to adjust for the mass significance problem as discussed by Krauth and Lienert (1973) and von Eye (1990b). We used a conservative test and

TABLE 9.7
The Dissimilarity Matrix Computed Between the Centroids at Age 10 and Those of Age 13, the Dissimilarity Coefficient Being the Average Squared Euclidean Distance*

		Age 13								
		A6L1	A6L3	A6L8	A6L10	A6L11	A6L13	A6L14	A6L15	A6L25
A	A3L1	0.073	1.687	0.875	4.143	1.455	3.965	4.135	1.436	1.287
g	A3L5	0.980	3.474	4.607	2.430	0.650	1.402	**9.910**	0.547	3.100
e	A3L10	3.692	**9.681**	8.574	0.259	4.637	0.476	**17.24**	1.034	3.936
	A3L12	4.205	2.733	1.176	**13.86**	6.777	**14.12**	0.155	8.813	5.507
1	A3L13	3.041	4.839	0.580	8.941	6.988	**9.932**	2.513	6.024	2.653
0	A3L17	1.184	5.642	2.697	1.458	3.912	2.397	8.583	0.917	0.675
	A3L18	1.592	0.277	1.362	**9.635**	1.843	8.501	1.800	4.769	4.491

*The bold entries in the table are the seven highest dissimilarity coefficients.

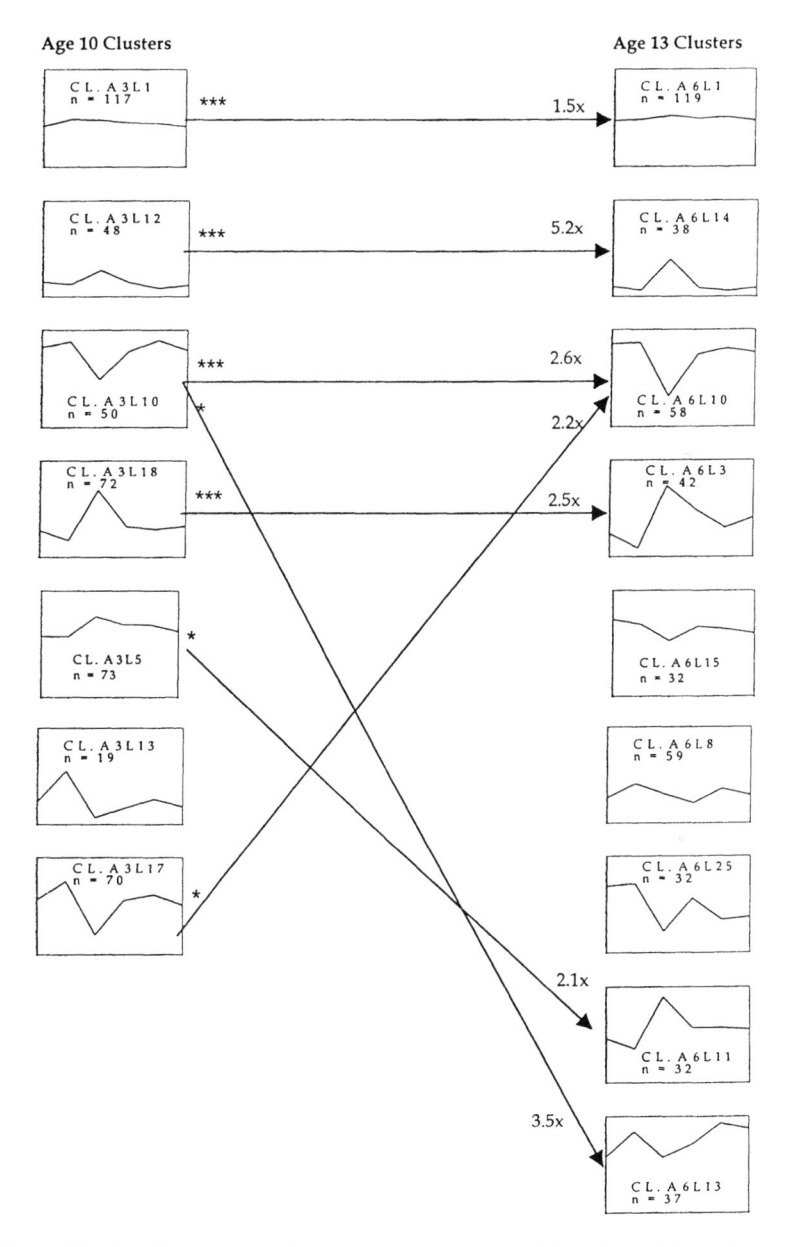

FIG. 9.11. Significant longitudinal streams between age 10 and age 13. Numbers attached to the end of the arrows indicate how many more times the flow was observed as compared to what would be expected from chance alone. Only significant streams are presented and an exact 1-tailed hypergeometric test was used. *p < .01, **p < .001, and ***p < .0001.

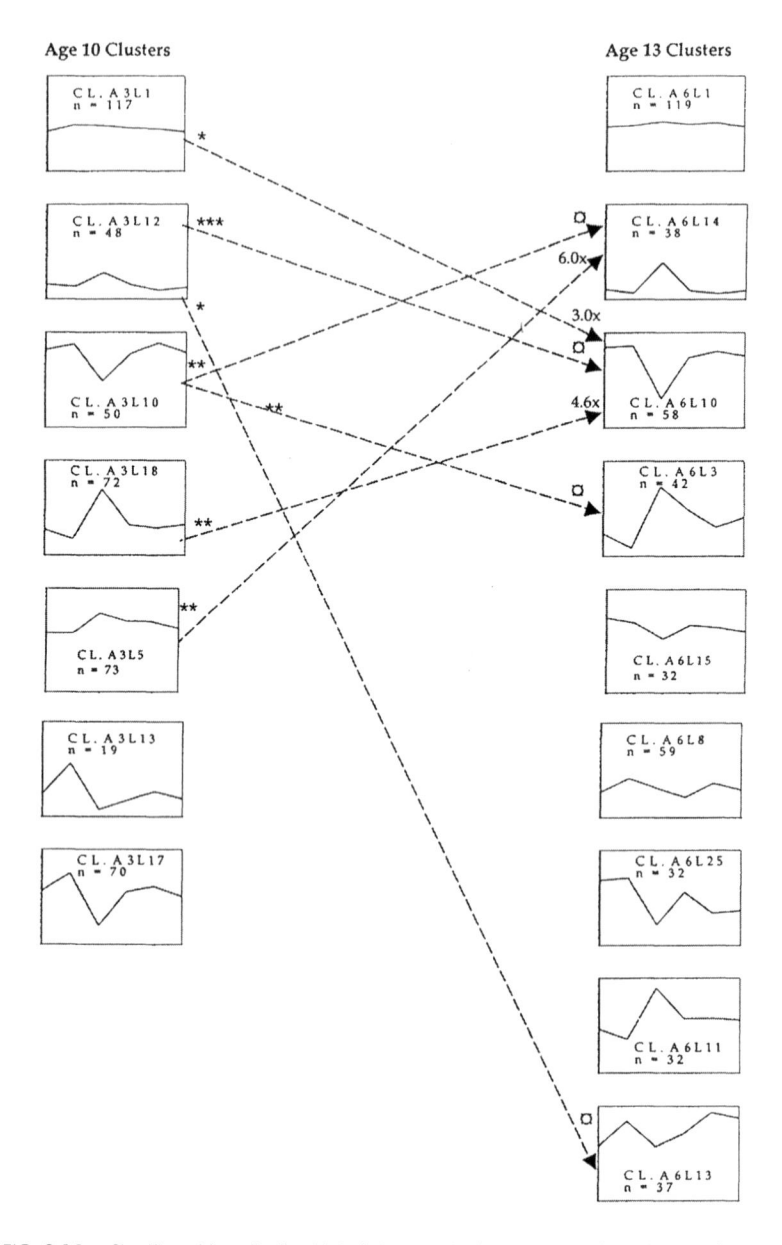

FIG. 9.12. Significant longitudinal "dry" streams between age 10 and age 13. Numbers attached to the arrows indicate how many times less the flow was observed as compared to what would be expected from chance alone. A "¤" indicates that no individuals moved in the direction of the arrow. Only significant dry streams are presented and an exact 1-tailed hypergeometric test was used. *p < .05, **p < .01, and ***p < .001.

multiplied the resulting probability in each cell by 94, which is twice the number of cells remaining in the table following the tests for types and antitypes previously made (see sections 2.5.1 and 5.2.2). After adjusting the probabilities, it can be seen that cell (1,10) is an antitype with $p < .05$ and that cell (17,10) is a type with $p < .01$. It can be seen in Fig. 9.11 that the type we find corresponds to individuals with a profile of slightly above average scores on all variables except *timidity,* and who move to another cluster with the same shape but with the problems more pronounced. Fig. 9.13 shows the pairs of clusters already mentioned.

2.6. Replicating Results on a Random Half

At each age, a randomly chosen subset of one half of the total data set was selected and analyzed in the same fashion as the total sample had been analyzed at each age, with the choice of parameters dictated by the choices that were made for the total sample at each age.

As may be expected due to the smaller sample size, the residue analysis yielded more residue cases than obtained when analyzing the total sample. Some of the individuals who barely met the conditions to be retained in the analysis on the total sample appeared here in the residue because the cases to which they were most similar were not selected to be in this subset. In total, four individuals at age 10 appeared in the residue analysis of which two were those found in the analysis of the total sample, and five individuals appeared in the residue at age 13, none of whom were found in the total sample.

2.6.1. Replicating the Cross-sectional Cluster Structure. Using CENTROID in SLEIPNER, we compared the seven-clusters solution for the random half with the seven-clusters solution for the total sample at age 10, and we compared the nine-clusters solution for the random half at age 13 with that of the total sample. The ASEDs associated with these matches ranged for age 10 from .05 to .369 with a mean

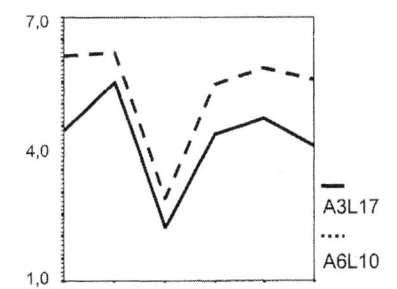

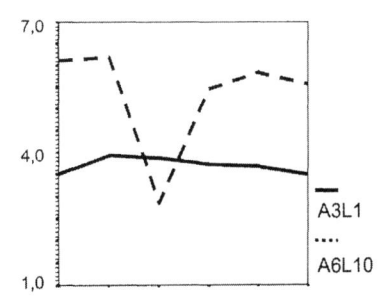

FIG. 9.13. One type and one antitype not hypothesized but found in the matched and cross-tabulated solutions.

of .223, and for age 13, the ASEDs ranged between .035 and .543 with a mean of .260. This represents a good agreement between the solutions. The percentage of ESS explained in the new analysis was 61.85 for the age 10 random half, and 71.04 for the age 13 random half. These percentages can be compared to the corresponding figures for the total samples, namely 61.27 for age 10, and 67.18 for age 13. The result from multidimensional scaling analysis using the Euclidean distance model in SPSS is shown in Fig. 9.14. There, the centroids for both the total sample and the random half at age 10 are the scaled objects. The figure captures well the intended replication. A similar analysis for age 13 is shown in Fig. 9.15. The results of these analyses show that the results concerning the cluster structure replicate well on a random half.

2.6.2. Replicating the Cross-Sectional Classification With Regard to Individual Cluster Membership. Because cluster analysis is sensitive to sampling variation, a relevant question concerns whether the resulting classification can be generalized to a larger population. We now focus the interest on individual class membership, not on cluster centroids as were just discussed. In the absence of data from the larger population, we addressed the question indirectly. Instead of measuring the degree of recovery of cluster structure between the solution obtained for the main sample and that of

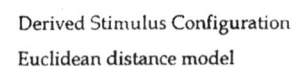

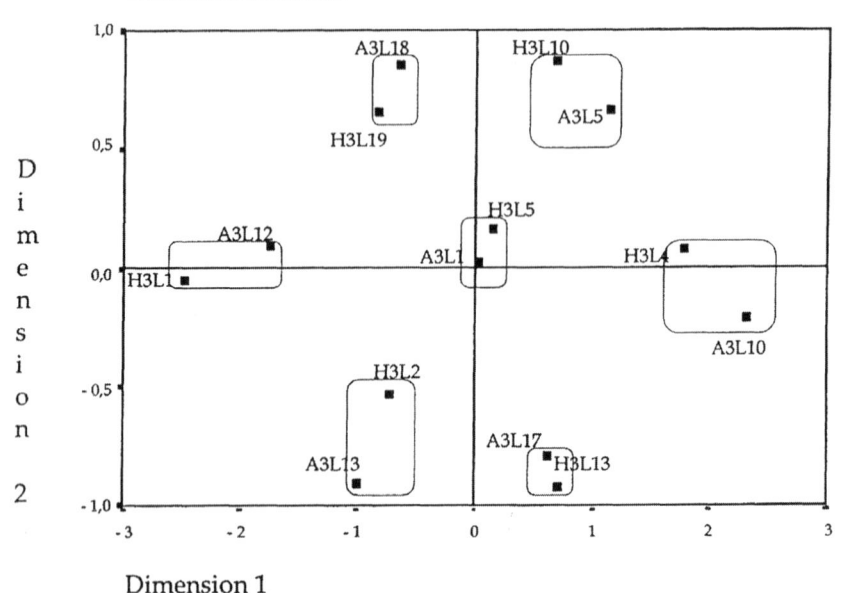

FIG. 9.14. Multidimensional scaling of the centroids obtained from the total sample (A3L1–A3L18) and from a randomly chosen half (H3L1–H3L19) at age 10. Matched centroids are bounded with a black line.

STABILITY AND CHANGE

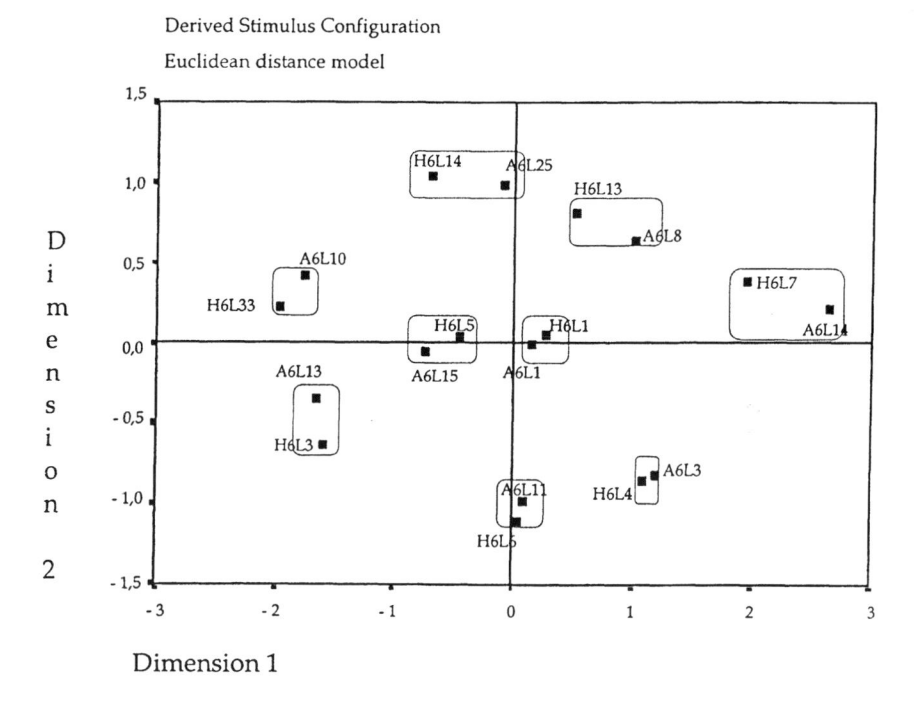

Derived Stimulus Configuration
Euclidean distance model

[Scatter plot with Dimension 1 on x-axis (ranging from -3 to 3) and Dimension 2 on y-axis (ranging from -1.5 to 1.5). Points labeled include H6L14, A6L25, H6L13, A6L10, A6L8, H6L33, H6L7, H6L5, H6L1, A6L14, A6L13, A6L15, A6L1, H6L3, A6L11, A6L3, H6L4, H6L6. Matched centroids are bounded with black lines.]

FIG. 9.15. Multidimensional scaling of the centroids obtained from the total sample (A6L1–A6L25) and from a randomly chosen half (H6L1–H6L33) at age 13. Matched centroids are bounded with a black line.

a larger population, we proceeded to measure the agreement between the solution for the main sample and the solution obtained for a set of 20 random halves. Thus, in each analysis, the main sample plays the role of a population for which a clustering solution is known, and a random half plays the role of a sample whose solution is to be validated. It is believed that a measure obtained based on this line of reasoning would reflect a conservative approximation of the degree of generalizability of the classification results for the main sample to the real population.

At each age, the adjusted Rand index (Hubert & Arabie, 1985) was computed between the solution obtained for the main sample and a corresponding solution obtained from a similar analysis on a random half. A set of 20 random halves was drawn for each age group, and the index was computed between each of them and the main solution. The indices ranged between .31 and .50, with a median of .37 at age 10, and between .37 and .57, with a median of .45 at age 13. The ranges and medians of the indices reported here can be regarded as fairly acceptable, at least with regard to age 13. The seven-clusters solution at age 10, with a moderate but acceptable percentage of explained ESS, may have been too fuzzy a solution to allow for good replications on reduced data sets.

2.6.3. Replicating the Linking Over Time. To test the replicability of the longitudinal analysis of types and antitypes presented earlier, we proceeded as follows. We first linked the two clustering solutions (one from age 10 and one from age 13) obtained for the random half using EXACON, yielding a contingency table similar to that presented in Fig. 9.10. Next, for the cells for which types were determined in the original analysis based on the whole sample, we found the corresponding cells in the new table based on the random half. The correspondence was established, based on the matches that were done between the centroids of the total set and the centroids of the random half at different ages. We found, for these original "type cells," that in the new analysis of the random half, four cells out of seven showed significant types with probabilities ranging from .0001 to .05, and two cells showed tendencies with exact probabilities of .08 and .09. Only one cell completely failed to show a type. Three cells out of six showed significant antitypes. Overall, the replicability of the LICUR linking results on a random half appears to be fairly good.

In summary, the structure of the solutions obtained for the total sample seems to hold even when a random subset is analyzed. The analyses that were conducted to link the results across age were also shown to be replicable to a reasonable extent.

There is, of course, a multitude of ways for conducting replication and validation analysis. For a discussion of these issues, the reader is referred to chapter 7.

2.7. Testing the Results Against a Null Hypothesis of No Relationships in the Data

It is of some interest to find out whether the obtained cluster solution is of a comparable "quality" with what could be expected to be found in similar data sets in which all the relationships have been removed.[6] If this is the case, the results can be regarded as "uninteresting" in the sense that they are only what could be expected to result from analyzing a random data set.

The quality of the structure can be summarized by some index (e.g., the percentage explained ESS). And for the purpose of comparison, two tests were indicated in chapter 7 making different assumptions.

Using SIMULATE, we generated 20 random data sets and computed for each one the relevant indices of the "quality" of the cluster solution. As shown in Fig. 9.16, for age 10, the first test is significant for most indices, indicating that the quality of the original solution is higher than for any of the solutions based on random data. For instance, the percent of explained variance in the original data set (61.3%) is higher than in any of the 20 "shaken" samples. The t values generated by the second test are also highly significant.

---

[6]This issue was discussed in chapter 7.

STABILITY AND CHANGE 165

The same procedure was then applied for the age 13 data set yielding similar results. The results show that the cluster structure found cannot be regarded as originating from an analysis of a random data set in which there are no relationships between the variables in the value profile.

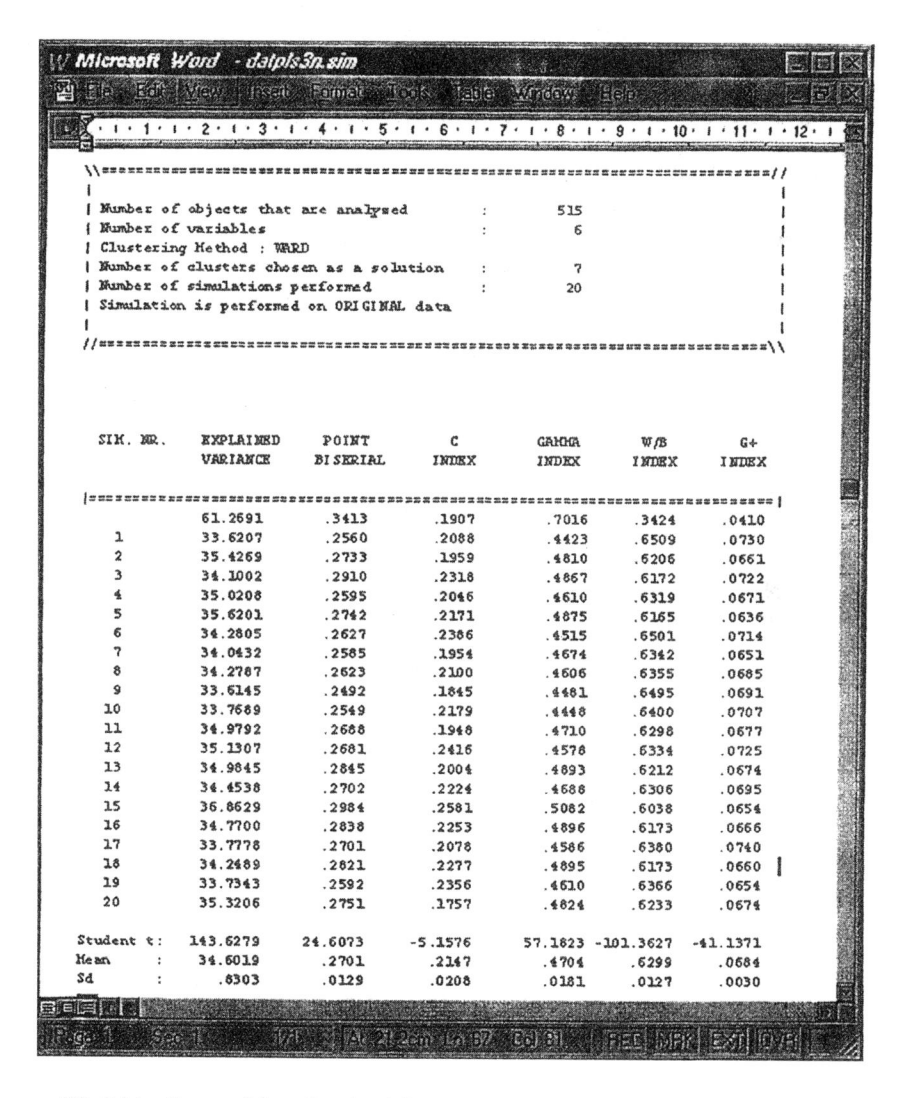

```
Number of objects that are analysed    : 515
Number of variables                    : 6
Clustering Method : WARD
Number of clusters chosen as a solution: 7
Number of simulations performed        : 20
Simulation is performed on ORIGINAL data
```

SIM. NR.	EXPLAINED VARIANCE	POINT BISERIAL	C INDEX	GAMMA INDEX	W/B INDEX	G+ INDEX
	61.2691	.3413	.1907	.7016	.3424	.0410
1	33.6207	.2560	.2088	.4423	.6509	.0730
2	35.4269	.2733	.1959	.4810	.6206	.0661
3	34.1002	.2910	.2318	.4867	.6172	.0722
4	35.0208	.2595	.2046	.4610	.6319	.0671
5	35.6201	.2742	.2171	.4875	.6165	.0636
6	34.2805	.2627	.2386	.4515	.6501	.0714
7	34.0432	.2585	.1954	.4674	.6342	.0651
8	34.2787	.2623	.2100	.4606	.6355	.0685
9	33.6145	.2492	.1845	.4481	.6495	.0691
10	33.7669	.2549	.2179	.4448	.6400	.0707
11	34.9792	.2688	.1948	.4710	.6298	.0677
12	35.1307	.2681	.2416	.4578	.6334	.0725
13	34.9845	.2845	.2004	.4893	.6212	.0674
14	34.4538	.2702	.2224	.4688	.6306	.0695
15	36.8629	.2984	.2581	.5082	.6038	.0654
16	34.7700	.2838	.2253	.4896	.6173	.0666
17	33.7778	.2701	.2078	.4586	.6380	.0740
18	34.2489	.2821	.2277	.4895	.6173	.0660
19	33.7343	.2592	.2356	.4610	.6366	.0654
20	35.3206	.2751	.1757	.4824	.6233	.0674
Student t:	143.6279	24.6073	-5.1576	57.1823	-101.3627	-41.1371
Mean :	34.6019	.2701	.2147	.4704	.6299	.0684
Sd :	.8303	.0129	.0208	.0181	.0127	.0030

FIG. 9.16. The result from the simulation procedure using SIMULATE in SLEIPNER. The first row in the table evaluates the original seven-cluster solution for age 10. The next numbered 20 rows refers to evaluating the seven-cluster solution for 20 "shaken" samples.

3. ANALYZING PATTERNS OF SCHOOL ADJUSTMENT WITHIN AN AGE-INVARIANT CLASSIFICATION STRUCTURE

3.1. Introduction

If the assumption can be made that the variables under investigation do not differ in meaning from one point to another, and if the developmental span under study is short enough to allow an interspersion of value patterns across the time span, we can then postulate that a finite number of patterns, common to both points in time, are sufficient to classify the patterns independent of which point in time they belong to. In other words, we assume that a common classificatory grid can be used at both points in time. We call this approach the ISOA approach, which has been addressed in chapter 6 and more thoroughly discussed in Bergman and El Khouri (1999).

In the context of this study, ISOA amounts to the following: First, create a new data set that comprises the observed variable profiles regardless of which age they come from. Because each individual occurs twice in the new data set, each time with a measurement vector from a different time point, the elements of the new data set are referred to as subindividuals. Second, perform a preparatory analysis including imputation and residue analysis and proceed with a cluster analysis on the new data set with subindividuals as the objects. Third, apply a relevant procedure to choose a satisfactory clustering solution. Fourth, create a new data set, where the elements are the individuals, and for each individual, the measurement vector now consists of two categorical variables referring to the corresponding two subindividuals' classification status in the obtained solution.

3.2. Age-Invariant Cluster Structure

In merging the data from age 10 and age 13, we demanded that only individuals that were represented in both data sets be present in the new data set. The new data set, comprised of 904 subindividuals, was submitted to a residue analysis resulting in one residue case. The new data set minus the residue was then input to cluster analysis using Ward's method. A nine-clusters solution was selected with a percentage explained ESS of 64.71; some of the characteristics of this solution are shown in Table 9.8. The clusters (states) that replicated on a random half are depicted graphically in Figure 9.20 and their numerical names in the figure are prefixed by "I."

3.3. Structural Stability and Change

Part of the output from the ISOA module in SLEIPNER is shown in Fig. 9.17. As shown in the figure, the percentage distributions for each age across the different states (the clusters in the 9-clusters solution) are not markedly different between ages. In this restricted sense there is structural stability.

TABLE 9.8
The Nine-Clusters Solution for the Data Set Comprised of Subindividuals in the ISOA Analysis*

Cluster Name	Aggression		Motor Restlessness		Timidity		Disharmony		Lack of Concentration		Low School Motivation		N	HC
	M	SD	M	SD	M	SD	M	SD	M	SD	M	SD		
I1	3.4	1.0	3.4	.99	3.6	1.2	3.4	.83	2.8	.98	3.3	.94	115	2.05
I3	3.9	.76	4.4	.70	3.7	.78	4.0	.73	4.2	.59	3.9	.77	157	1.06
I6	1.9	.83	2.0	.93	4.5	1.0	2.1	.96	2.3	1.0	2.0	.72	83	1.74
I9	3.6	.84	3.9	.67	5.5	.87	4.2	.70	4.7	.95	4.3	.75	90	1.30
I19	5.4	1.2	5.8	1.0	4.0	1.3	5.5	.98	6.0	.97	5.6	1.0	182	2.45
I23	1.8	1.2	1.4	.52	2.4	1.0	1.9	1.1	1.5	.76	1.6	.83	72	1.83
I24	3.0	.89	1.8	.75	5.9	.87	4.0	1.1	3.2	1.2	3.8	.74	74	1.84
I25	2.0	.88	4.3	1.0	1.8	.75	2.0	.79	3.4	1.0	2.6	.95	40	1.75
I33	5.1	.98	5.7	.79	2.0	.84	4.3	1.1	4.4	1.1	3.9	1.0	90	2.03

*The means and the standard deviations of the variables in each cluster are given together with the homogeneity coefficient (Hc) and the number of subindividuals (N) in the cluster. The explained error sum of squares is 64.71%.

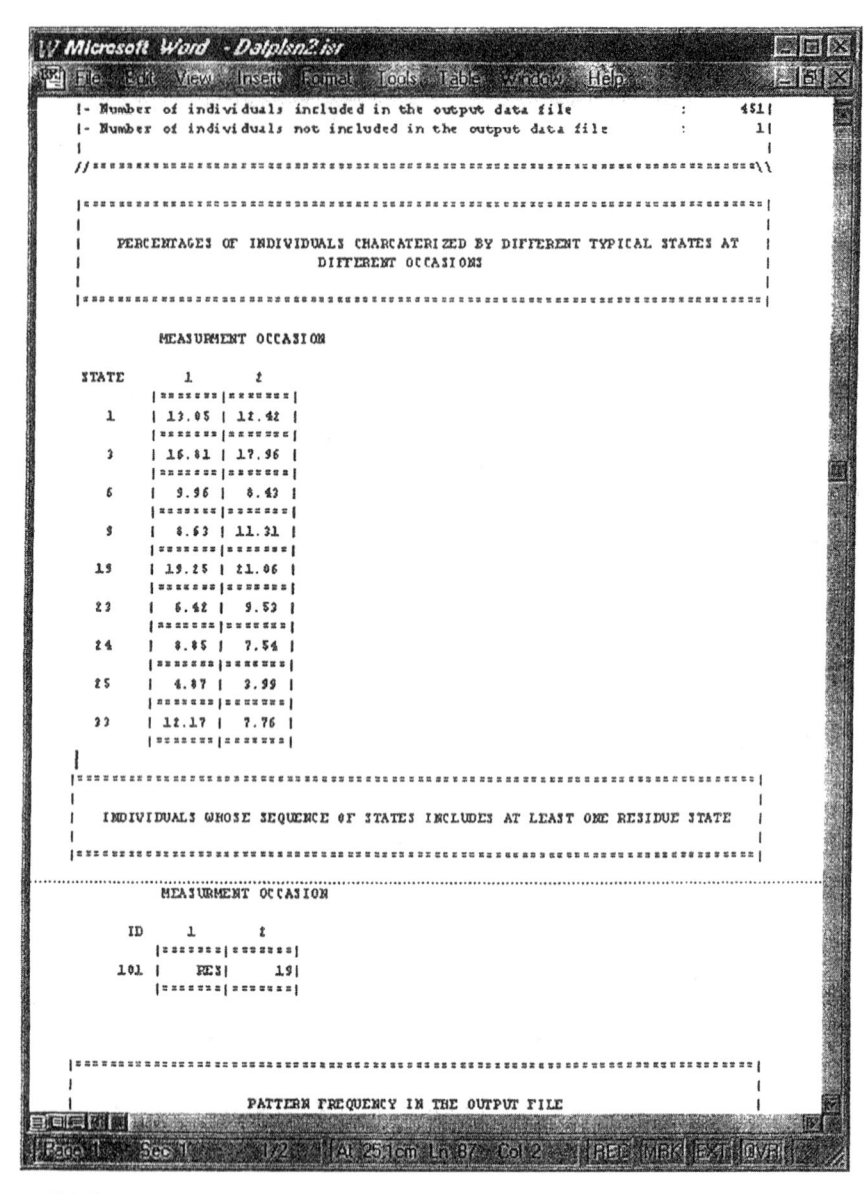

```
┌─ W Microsoft Word - Dstplsn2.isr ─────────────────────┐
│ File  Edit  View  Insert  Format  Tools  Table  Window  Help │
│                                                                │
│ |- Number of individuals included in the output data file  :  451|
│ |- Number of individuals not included in the output data file :  1|
│ |                                                              |
│ //==========================================================\\
│
│ |==============================================================|
│ |                                                              |
│ |     PERCENTAGES OF INDIVIDUALS CHARCATERIZED BY DIFFERENT TYPICAL STATES AT |
│ |                          DIFFERENT OCCASIONS                 |
│ |                                                              |
│ |==============================================================|
│
│              MEASURMENT OCCASION
│
│      STATE      1       2
│              |=======|=======|
│        1     | 13.05 | 12.42 |
│              |=======|=======|
│        3     | 16.41 | 17.96 |
│              |=======|=======|
│        6     |  9.96 |  8.43 |
│              |=======|=======|
│        9     |  8.63 | 11.31 |
│              |=======|=======|
│       15     | 19.25 | 21.06 |
│              |=======|=======|
│       23     |  6.42 |  9.53 |
│              |=======|=======|
│       24     |  8.85 |  7.54 |
│              |=======|=======|
│       25     |  4.87 |  3.99 |
│              |=======|=======|
│       33     | 12.17 |  7.76 |
│              |=======|=======|
│
│ |==============================================================|
│ |                                                              |
│ |   INDIVIDUALS WHOSE SEQUENCE OF STATES INCLUDES AT LEAST ONE RESIDUE STATE  |
│ |                                                              |
│ |==============================================================|
│
│              MEASURMENT OCCASION
│
│          ID      1       2
│              |=======|=======|
│         101 |   RES |    19 |
│              |=======|=======|
│
│
│ |==============================================================|
│ |                                                              |
│ |                 PATTERN FREQUENCY IN THE OUTPUT FILE         |
└────────────────────────────────────────────────────────────────┘
```

FIG. 9.17. Part of the output from ISOA showing the percentages of individuals characterized by different typical states at different occasions. The numbers under the heading, State, are state (= cluster) names They are referred to in the text by preceding each name with the letter "I," for example, State I1, State I3, State I6, and so forth, instead of State 1, State 3, State 6, and so forth.

For convenience, we refer to these states by preceding the original name that appears in the Ward solution and in Fig. 9.17 with the prefix I. Thus, the state called "1" in Figure 9.17 is referred to as I1, the state called 3 will be referred to as I3, and so on.

3.4. Individual Stability and Change

Now to the issue of individual stability and change. If for each individual the specific state (cluster) to which he or she belongs at time 1 is cross-tabulated against the states at time 2, then the results can be analyzed in a contingency table with the help of EXACON. We do this and test for types and antitypes in much the same way we tested individual stability when applying the LICUR methodology.

The question we first want to answer is if there are any specific states that individuals tend to stay in more frequently than would be expected by chance alone, that is, whether or not there is individual stability. We also would like to explore the table in search of movement between states that cannot be ascribed to chance fluctuations, that is, typical individual change. With regard to the first question, it turns out that eight out of nine tested cells, those corresponding to individuals having the same typical state across the two occasions, show significant types. Five of these eight cells do this with probabilities less than .0001, two cells with probabilities less than .01, and one cell with a probability less than .05. That is, eight out of nine states exhibit individual stability.

The one cell that did not show a significant type corresponds to state I1 illustrated in Fig. 9.18. This state is characterized by average levels of values in all the variables and it is very similar to the largest clusters in the LICUR analyses, namely A3L1 and A6L1 and whose linkage across time actually showed a type. An inspection of the remaining clusters in Fig. 9.20, however, reveals a second state I3 with similar shape to I1 but somewhat more elevated. The largest movement from state I1 actually occurs to I3. However, after correction for mass significance, it falls short of being significant.

3.5. Comparing ISOA States to LICUR Clusters

It is instructive at this point to compare the seven centroids at age 10 and the nine centroids at age 13, which formed the basis for the LICUR study, to the nine centroids defining the states in the ISOA analysis. Using CENTROID, we obtain a good match for the first comparison, with a range of ASEDs between .02 and .388, and a mean of .278. The best matching centroids were A3L12 and I23, which correspond to not having any problems, and A3L10 and I19, which correspond to being high on all problems except *timidity*, which was average. An almost perfect match was also found for A3L17 and I33, which had a similar shape to that of I19 but less extreme, that is, above average on most variables except for *timidity*, which here was low. Fig. 9.18 depicts graphically the result of this matching procedure for the seven centroids at age 10, and seven out of nine centroids found in the ISOA analysis.

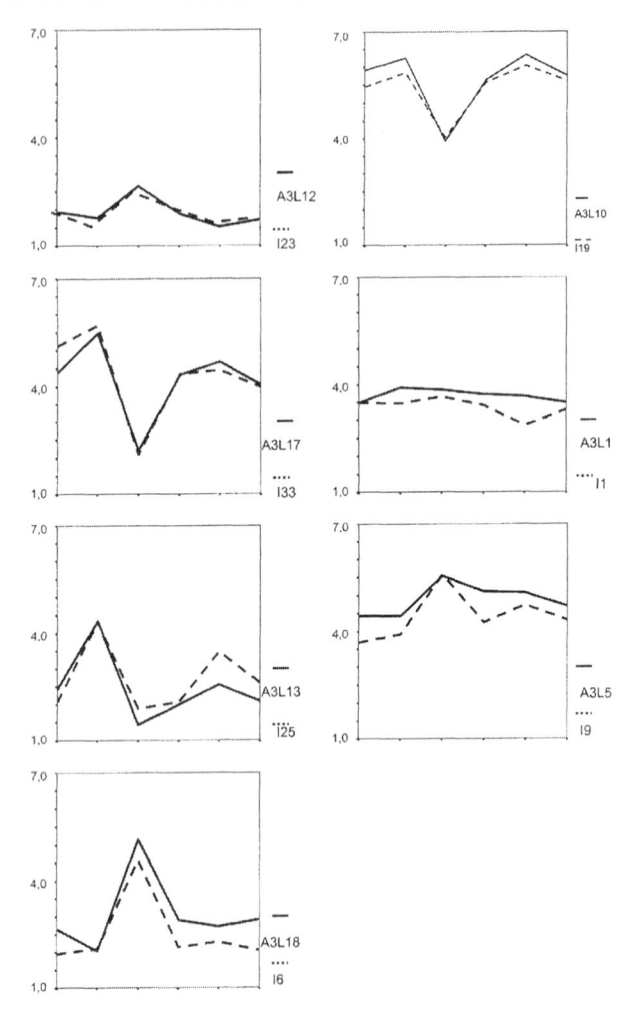

FIG. 9.18. The seven-clusters solution from age 10 LICUR analysis (A3L1–A3L18) matched to seven out of nine clusters in the nine-clusters solution from ISOA analysis (I3 and I24 did not match).

A similar comparison of the nine states in ISOA to the nine-clusters solution at age 13 was made. The range of the ASEDs was between .082 and 12.128. Fig. 9.19 depicts graphically the result of this matching procedure. It should be noted that the upper bound on the ASEDs reflects a mismatch due to the fact that the degrees of freedom are reduced as the matching proceeds, such that the last two centroids are just coupled together as leftovers. Having said that, a nice matching appears in this analysis for seven out of nine pairs. It turns out that in this case, the first and the third

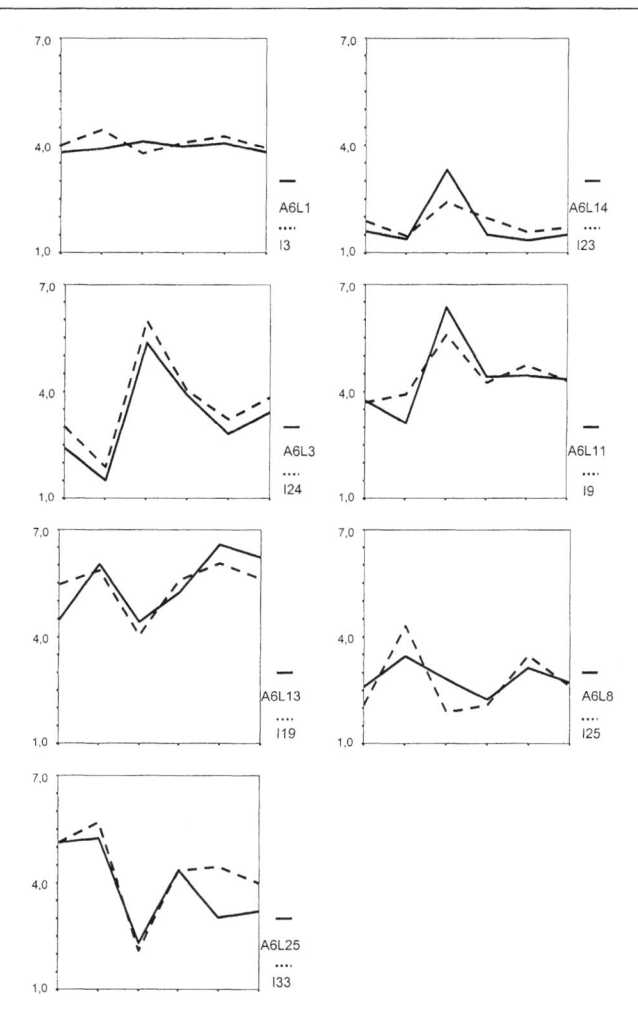

FIG. 9.19. The seven good matches when the nine-cluster solution from age 13 is matched to the nine-cluster solution from the ISOA analysis.

match correspond to the two ISOA states that did not appear in the previous matching at age 10. In other words, the seven-clusters solution at age 10 did not include two states from the nine-clusters solution in the ISOA analysis, but these two states were matched strongly in the comparison with the nine-clusters solution at age 13. That these states were not found at age 10 may reflect a successful fine-tuning of the states in ISOA, which takes into consideration information from both ages. Notice that one of these states is I3, with a profile corresponding to average on all problems, and the other is I24, which corresponds to being average on all variables except *motor restlessness,* which is low, and *timidity,* which is high.

3.6. Exploring the Remaining Cells

We now turn back to the ISOA analyses proper. In section 3.4, individual stability was studied by investigating those cells that correspond to individuals having the same typical state at both age 10 and at age 13. Exploring the remaining cells and adjusting for mass significance results in the identification of a significant antitype originating in I19, which is characterized as average on *timidity* and high on all other variables. Significantly fewer ($p < .01$) than would be expected changed state to I24, which is high on *timidity,* low on *motor restlessness,* and below average on the other variables.

In summary, the clusters that emerge in the ISOA analysis seem largely to coincide with those provided by the LICUR methodology. Less state migration was found in the ISOA analysis than in the LICUR analysis. State stability was confirmed for all states except one, but state changes did not occur frequently.

3.7. Replicating Results on a Random Half

We repeated the ISOA analysis for a random half of the original data set. Nine typical states were extracted for the random half and they were matched to the nine typical states that were found for the complete data set. Table 9.9 shows the results from that match in which the typical states are arranged in order of increasing dissimilarity as indicated by the ASEDs. As depicted in Fig. 9.20, good matching was achieved for seven out of the nine centroid pairs involved. Also shown in Table 9.9, both for the complete data set and for the random half, are the percentages of individuals at each age who were characterized by a certain state. However, percentages in the seven comparable states varied considerably between the complete data set and the random half. When state stability for the seven good matches was tested for types in the random half, five showed significant types and one showed a strong tendency.

4. ANALYZING ALL POSSIBLE PATTERNS OF SCHOOL ADJUSTMENT AND ALL POSSIBLE PATTERNS OF CHANGE

4.1. Introduction

In a multidimensional space defined by categorical variables, we can analyze the frequency of occurrence of certain patterns relative to all possible patterns that can occur in that space. Significantly overrepresented patterns, called *types,* as well as underrepresented patterns, called *antitypes,* highlight special relations between the categories that define each of those patterns. A type may then be characterized as a "significant cluster" of similar cases, densely occupying the region of space where the corresponding pattern is located. In contrast, antitypes indicate remarkably sparsely populated regions in the multidimensional space. To accomplish this kind

STABILITY AND CHANGE   173

TABLE 9.9
The Percentages of Individuals Characterized by Different Typical States at Different Occasions Both for the Complete Data Set and for One Randomly Chosen Half Set*

	The Complete Data Set			A Randomly Chosen Half Set: H1		
State Name	Age 10	Age 13	ASED	Age 10	Age 13	State Name
I3	16.81	17.96	.037	22.22	24.89	IH4
I19	19.25	21.06	.090	11.56	13.33	IH1
I9	8.63	11.31	.138	9.78	8.00	IH2
I6	9.96	8.43	.163	13.33	15.11	IH24
I25	4.87	3.99	.199	8.44	7.11	IH23
I24	8.85	7.54	.222	13.33	9.33	IH11
I33	12.17	7.76	.561	4.89	7.56	IH32
I1	13.05	12.42	2.936	12.44	11.11	IH8
I23	6.42	9.53	19.299	4.00	3.56	IH13
	100%	100%		100%	100%	

*The ASEDs between typical states' centroids are also given.

of analysis, configural frequency analysis (CFA), initiated by Gustaf Lienert, can be used as previously discussed in chapter 5 (see Krauth & Lienert, 1982, and von Eye, 1990a, for overviews).

The notion of a type in CFA can be compared, in a restricted sense, to the notion of cluster in cluster analysis. Both the type and the cluster represent agglomerations of cases that have procedural differences in the way they are formed. They share some but not all of their characteristics.[7]

In the intended analysis for our data set, we wanted to be able to do the following: (a) To locate the "dense" patterns (types), (b) to locate the "white spots" (antitypes), (c) to link the results from (a) and from (b) longitudinally, and (d) to analyze change scores directly so that typical as well as atypical change patterns can be identified.

4.2. CFA of Patterns of School Adjustment

We looked for types and antitypes directly in each age group. To do this, each variable was first dichotomized to reflect the presence or absence of a school adjust-

---

[7]For instance, in cluster analysis, we simply cluster what we observe. In CFA, it is actually the discrepancy between what we observe and what we expect that is the focus, and it is the probability of such a discrepancy that underlies the definition of types and antitypes. Also, the two notions differ in the way they cover cases. In cluster analysis, each case belongs to a definite cluster, that is, the clusters cover all the cases. In CFA, a limited number of cases belong to different types (or antitypes); the rest are neither types nor antitypes.

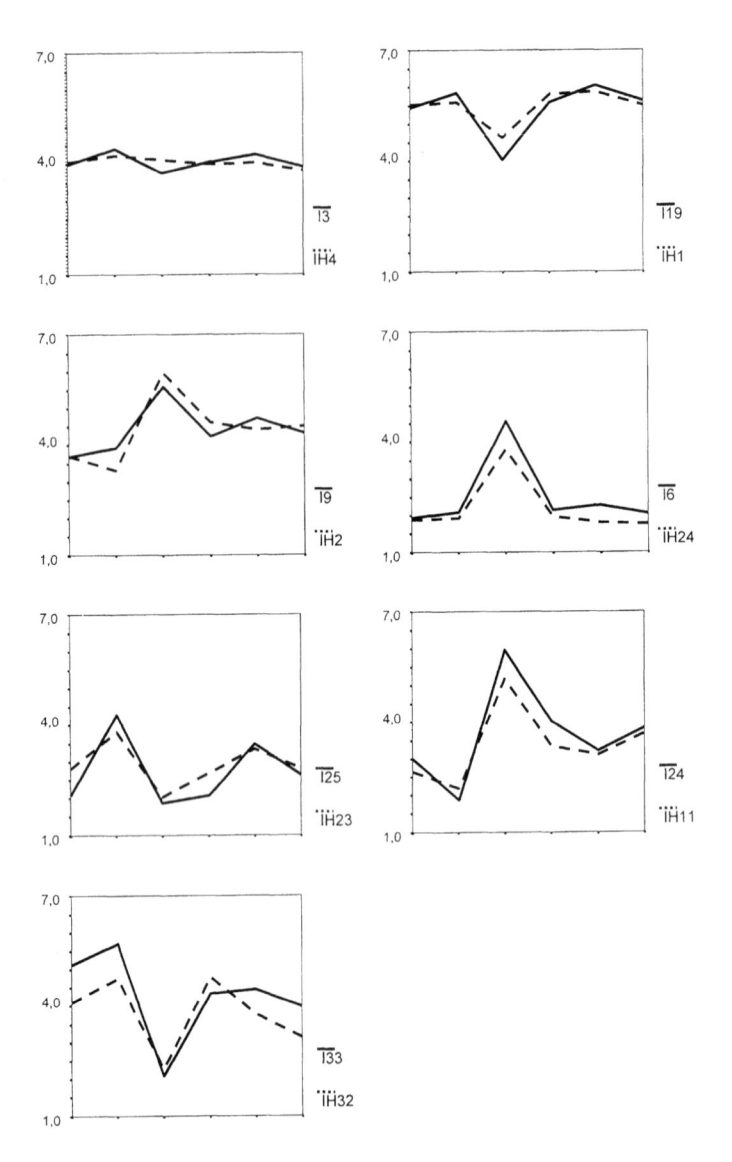

FIG. 9.20. The nine-cluster ISOA solution from the complete data set matched against the nine-cluster solution from a randomly selected half set. Only the best seven matches are shown here.

ment problem. After careful consideration, it was decided that values between one and five on the original scale of each variable were to be collapsed into one category, category "1," representing the absence of an adjustment problem in that regard. The two remaining values, six and seven, were to be collapsed to another category, category "2," representing the presence of an adjustment problem. Thus, the pattern 111111 denotes no pronounced adjustment problems on any of the variables, whereas 112211 denotes problems with regard to *timidity* and *disharmony*, but not the rest of the variables, and so on. The number and the percentage of individuals falling into one of the two categories for each variable at each point in time are shown in Table 9.10.

4.2.1. Configurations at Age 10. We performed CFA on the data set at age 10 using the CFA module in SLEIPNER. Table 9.11 summarizes the results for those patterns for which adjusted probabilities[8] fell below .10 (i.e., significant types and antitypes after correction for the mass significance problem; see chap. 5). Adjusting also for the fact that 2 kinds of tests were made, that is, one for types and one for antitypes, 13 patterns were found, of which 12 had an adjusted probability be-

TABLE 9.10

The Frequency and the Percentage of Individuals Falling Into One of the Categories 1 or 2 for All the Variables at Age 10 and at Age 13

	Absence of Problems 1		Presence of Problems 2	
	N	Percent	N	Percent
Age 10				
Aggression	368	(71,46)	147	(28,54)
Motor Restlessness	313	(60,78)	202	(39,22)
Timidity	338	(65,63)	177	(34,37)
Disharmony	352	(68,35)	163	(31,65)
Lack of Concentration	331	(64,27)	184	(35,73)
Low School Motivation	380	(73,79)	135	(26,21)
Age 13				
Aggression	363	(67,22)	177	(32,78)
Motor Restlessness	337	(62,41)	203	(37,59)
Timidity	375	(68,44)	165	(30,56)
Disharmony	370	(68,52)	170	(31,48)
Lack of Concentration	344	(63,70)	196	(36,30)
Low School Motivation	374	(69,26)	166	(30,74)

[8]The adjusted probabilities in Table 9.11 are given for only one kind of test (either a test for types or a test for antitypes). We adjust for the fact that we are doing two kinds of tests by multiplying the probabilities in Table 9.11 by two.

TABLE 9.11
Seven Types and Six Antitypes Resulting From a CFA at Age 10*

Pattern	Type/ Antitype	Observed	Expected	Chi-Square	Binomial Probability	Adjusted Probability
111111	T	138	44.93	192.78	.0000	.0000
112111	T	58	22.54	55.78	.0000	.0000
221221	T	11	2.44	30.07	.0000	.0029
221122	T	9	1.98	24.90	.0002	.0134
121222	T	9	2.30	19.47	.0006	.0397
221222	T	30	.87	976.43	.0000	.0000
222222	T	13	.44	362.05	.0000	.0000
122111	AT	1	13.87	11.94	.0000	.0007
111121	AT	7	23.92	11.97	.0000	.0023
211121	AT	0	9.03	9.03	.0001	.0070
111221	AT	0	10.50	10.50	.0000	.0015
111112	AT	2	16.02	12.27	.0000	.0008
121112	AT	0	9.85	9.85	.0000	.0030

*The order of the variables in the patterns is as follows: Aggression, Motor Restlessness, Timidity, Disharmony, Lack of Concentration, and Lack of School Motivation.

low .05 and one pattern (121222) had an adjusted probability below .1. Of these 13 patterns, seven were types and six were antitypes.

The pattern denoting problems on all variables, 222222, and the pattern denoting no problems on any of the variables, 111111, both emerged as strong types. Similar patterns in which the status of *timidity* alone is reversed, 221222 and 112111, were also revealed as types. Of the 196 individuals who, excluding *timidity*, had no problems on any of the other variables, 58 had adjustment problems on *timidity*. Of the 43 individuals who, excluding *timidity*, had problems on all the remaining variables, only 13 individuals had also a problem on *timidity*.

Interestingly, of 140 individuals who, excluding *low school motivation*, had no problems, only two individuals had problems on *low school motivation*. The corresponding pattern, 111112, came out as an antitype. Similarly, the pattern, 111121, which reflected adjustment problems only on *lack of concentration*, came out as an antitype. Of 145 individuals who, excluding *lack of concentration*, had no problems, only seven were high on *lack of concentration*.

No individuals had problems on only *aggression* and *lack of concentration*, 211121, or on only *disharmony* and *lack of concentration*, 111221, or on only *motor restlessness* and *low school motivation*, 121112. Only one individual had a joint problem on *timidity* and *motor restlessness*, 122111. All of these patterns came out as antitypes.

STABILITY AND CHANGE 177

Timidity was low in five of the seven emerging types, and high in the pattern denoting adjustment problems on all the other variables, and high in the pattern denoting no adjustment problems on all the other variables. But *motor restlessness* and *lack of concentration* were high in concert in five of the emerging types and low in concert in two.

Multiproblems except for *timidity* and *low school motivation,* that is, 221221, came out as a type, as well as multiproblems except for *timidity* and *disharmony,* 221122, and multiproblems except for *timidity* and *aggression,* 121222, which also came out as types.

4.2.2. Configurations at Age 13. The result from CFA on the data set at age 13 is summarized in Table 9.12. Only the patterns for which adjusted probabilities[9] were below .10 are shown. In all, 13 patterns were found of which five were types and eight were antitypes. Of these 13 patterns, 12 patterns have an adjusted probability below .05 and one pattern, 111211, has a probability below .1.

All the types identified in this analysis matched types that emerged at age 10. Similar to the results shown for age 10, the pattern denoting problems on all variables, 222222, and the pattern denoting no problems on any of the variables, 111111, both emerged as types. In addition, when the status of *timidity* alone is reversed, both patterns 221222 and 112111 also emerged as types. Another pattern denoting multiproblems on all variables except for *timidity* and *disharmony,* 221122, also emerged as a type.

Four of the antitypes that emerged at age 10 reemerged at age 13. Only one individual had problems on only *disharmony* and *lack of concentration,* 111221, and none on only *motor restlessness* and *low school motivation,* 121112. Only one individual had a joint problem on *timidity* and *motor restlessness,* 122111. Four individuals had problems only on *lack of concentration.*

No individuals were found having problems only on *low school motivation* and either of *aggression* or *disharmony,* the corresponding antitype patterns being 211112 and 111212 respectively. Only one individual had problems on *motor restlessness* and *disharmony,* 121211, and one individual had problems on *lack of concentration* and *low school motivation,* 111122.

4.3. Developmental Types and Antitypes

The majority of the patterns that emerged at age 10 as types or antitypes re-emerged at age 13 also as types or antitypes. As discussed in 4.2.2, all the five types emerging at age 13 had also been found as types at age 10, and four of the eight antitypes at age 13 had also been found at age 10. In all, this result indicates good structural stability in the data.

---

[9]The adjusted probabilities in Table 9.12 are given for only one kind of test (either a test for types or a test for antitypes). We adjust for the fact that we are doing two kinds of tests by multiplying the probabilities in Table 9.12 by two.

TABLE 9.12
Five Types and Eight Antitypes Resulting From a CFA at Age 13*

Pattern	Type/ Antitype	Observed	Expected	Chi-Square	Binomial Probability	Adjusted Probability
111111	T	123	36.48	205.22	.0000	.0000
112111	T	62	16.70	122.89	.0000	.0000
221122	T	21	3.29	95.15	.0000	.0000
221222	T	45	1.51	1254.17	.0000	.0000
222222	T	16	.69	339.47	.0000	.0000
122111	AT	1	10.77	8.86	.0002	.0143
121211	AT	1	10.77	8.86	.0002	.0143
111121	AT	4	22.02	14.74	.0000	.0001
111221	AT	1	10.08	8.18	.0004	.0271
211112	AT	0	8.47	8.47	.0002	.0124
121112	AT	0	10.99	10.99	.0000	.0009
111212	AT	0	7.80	7.80	.0004	.0244
111122	AT	1	10.29	8.39	.0003	.0223

*The order of the variables in the patterns is as follows: Aggression, Motor Restlessness, Timidity, Disharmony, Lack of Concentration, and Lack of School Motivation.

To study individual stability, we linked resulting types at age 10 and the resulting types at age 13 by way of a two-way contingency table using EXACON. The common patterns were included along with the five remaining nonshared patterns at age 10 and four nonshared patterns at age 13. The rest of the patterns at each age were merged into one *other* category.

Because the patterns corresponding to antitypes are sometimes empty, the resulting table had 11 rows and 11 columns corresponding to 11 patterns at age 10 and 11 patterns at age 13. In the following, we are only interested in the developmental types that emerged. Seven nonempty patterns, common to both ages, were represented in the table, five of which were types, 111111, 112111, 221122, 221222, and 222222. The corresponding cells were tested for individual stability and the results showing significant stability are presented in Fig. 9.21. Four individual stabilities were significant. The one type that didn't show individual stability was 221122. In this case, no individual having this pattern at age 10 had the same pattern at age 13.

4.4. Analyzing All Patterns of Change

We also analyzed change patterns obtained by creating for each individual a change pattern comprised of six new change variables, each corresponding to one of the original variables. Thus, for the *aggression* variable the corresponding change vari-

STABILITY AND CHANGE 179

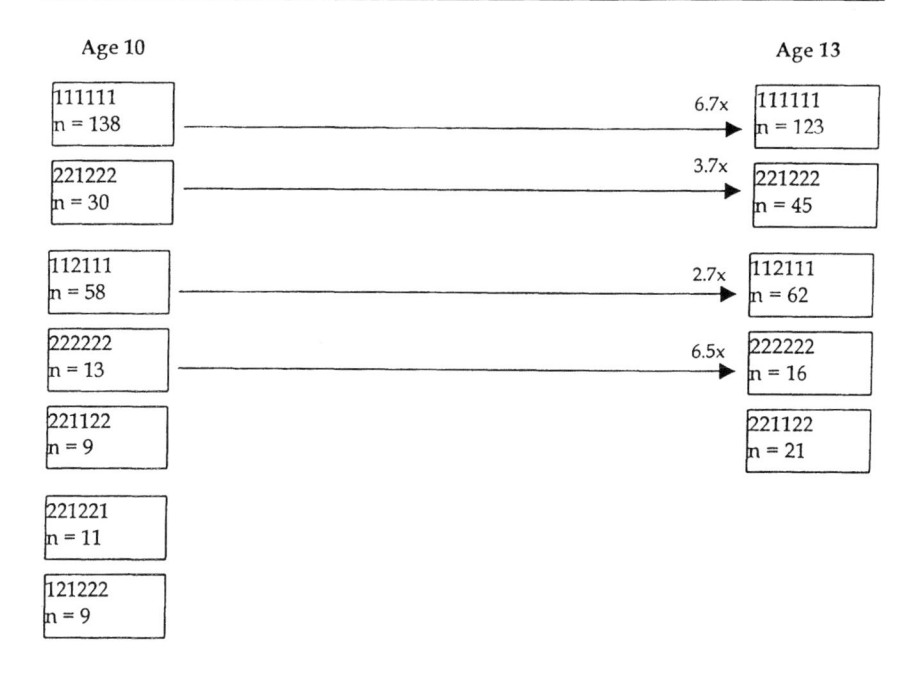

Age 10		Age 13
111111 n = 138	—— 6.7x ——▶	111111 n = 123
221222 n = 30	—— 3.7x ——▶	221222 n = 45
112111 n = 58	—— 2.7x ——▶	112111 n = 62
222222 n = 13	—— 6.5x ——▶	222222 n = 16
221122 n = 9		221122 n = 21
221221 n = 11		
121222 n = 9		

FIG. 9.21. Longitudinal streams of individuals between established types at age 10 (seven types) and at age 13 (five types). Solid arrows depict frequencies significantly higher than would be expected by chance alone. Figures attached to arrows indicate how many more times the movement was observed as compared to what would be expected from chance alone. An exact 1-tailed hypergeometric test was used. *$p < .01$, **$p < .001$, and ***$p < .0001$.

able, *change in aggression,* could be coded as having one of three possible values: 1, 2, or 3, depending on whether, for a specific individual, his or her value on *aggression* increased, remained the same, or decreased from age 10 to age 13. The same applied for the remaining change variables, *change in motor restlessness, change in timidity, change in disharmony, change in lack of concentration,* and *change in low school motivation.* For example, the change pattern, "331233," denotes an increase in the *timidity* variable from age 10 to age 13, no change in the *disharmony* variable, and decrease in all the remaining variables.

The results[10] from a CFA on the data set created in this way are summarized in Table 9.13. All of the patterns depicted are developmental types and they show for all of the variables, except Timidity, either an increase from age 10 to age 13, or a decrease.

---

[10]In these analyses, the antitypes were not studied.

TABLE 9.13
Six Developmental Types Resulting From a CFA of Change Patterns From Age 10 to Age 13

Pattern	Observed	Expected	Chi-Square	Binomial Probability	Adjusted Probability
111111	19	1.25	252.48	.0000	.0000
112111	7	.82	46.74	.0000	.0167
113111	12	1.15	101.84	.0000	.0000
331333	10	.63	139.57	.0000	.0000
332333	6	.41	75.75	.0000	.0034
333333	7	.58	70.75	.0000	.0019

This is a surprisingly clear-cut result, demonstrating the developmental coherence of generalized maladjustment, with the exception of *timidity,* which stands out on its own.

5. SUMMARY AND DISCUSSION OF EMPIRICAL FINDINGS

5.1. Summary of the Results of the Cross-Sectional Classification Analysis With Linking

In this chapter, results concerning stability and change in patterns of school adjustment were presented. A variety of person-oriented methods were used: LICUR, ISOA, and CFA. The significance of the results was tested against a model of no relationships and a random half of the data set was analyzed in the same manner as the complete data set to provide indication of the sensitivity of the results to sampling variation. This was conducted both with regard to the cluster centroids and with regard to the complete classification (i.e., individual class memberships), as well as with regard to developmental types. Not surprisingly, the results indicate that individual class membership is more sensitive to sampling variation than cluster centroids.

Broadly speaking, consistent results were obtained that provide some support for the generalizability of the results over the method–sample space studied here. This is clearer for cluster structure than for individual class membership. Considering the long time period between the two measurements (3 years), it seems reasonable to begin by presenting an overview of the results from the LICUR method, which itself is also applicable in situations when fundamental structural changes have taken place between the measurement occasions. However, as was already pointed out, similar results were obtained using the ISOA method, in which one is required to make stronger assumptions about structural invariance. The results of the LICUR analyses are summarized verbally in Fig. 9.22 (based on Fig. 9.11).

Age 10				Age 13

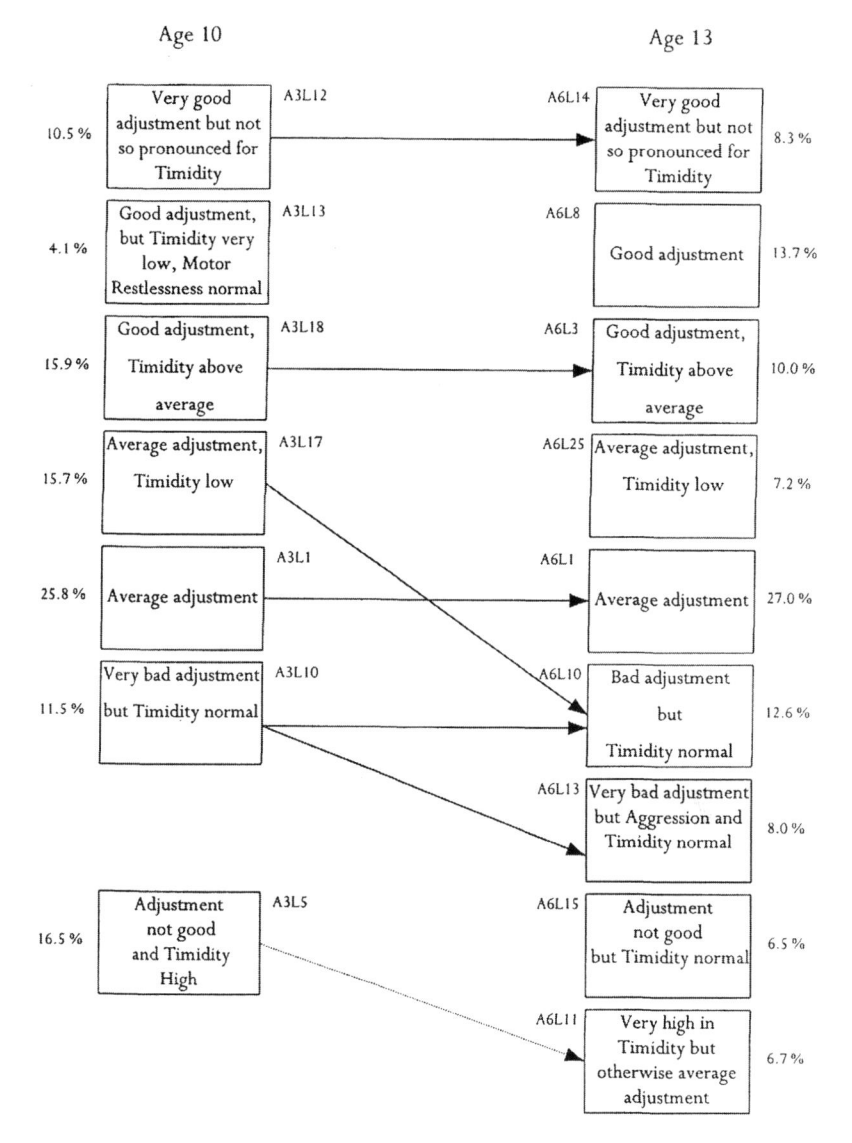

10.5%	Very good adjustment but not so pronounced for Timidity	A3L12 → A6L14	Very good adjustment but not so pronounced for Timidity	8.3%
4.1%	Good adjustment, but Timidity very low, Motor Restlessness normal	A3L13 → A6L8	Good adjustment	13.7%
15.9%	Good adjustment, Timidity above average	A3L18 → A6L3	Good adjustment, Timidity above average	10.0%
15.7%	Average adjustment, Timidity low	A3L17 → A6L25	Average adjustment, Timidity low	7.2%
25.8%	Average adjustment	A3L1 → A6L1	Average adjustment	27.0%
11.5%	Very bad adjustment but Timidity normal	A3L10 → A6L10	Bad adjustment but Timidity normal	12.6%
		A6L13	Very bad adjustment but Aggression and Timidity normal	8.0%
16.5%	Adjustment not good and Timidity High	A3L5 → A6L15	Adjustment not good but Timidity normal	6.5%
		A6L11	Very high in Timidity but otherwise average adjustment	6.7%

FIG. 9.22. Verbal summary of the results of the cross-sectional cluster analyses followed by linking. Arrows between clusters indicate significant developmental streams. The percentages indicate the cluster size relative to the total sample size.

As shown in Fig. 9.22, there are seven typical patterns that describe school adjustment at age 10. Three of these indicate an almost generalized pattern of good adjustment with the exception that, for one of them, *timidity* is high. Similar clusters to these three were also found at age 13. The typical pattern with truly generalized good adjustment (A3L12/A6L14), and the typical pattern with generalized good adjustment except for high *timidity* (A3L18/A6L3), both show significant individual stability. Two typical patterns indicate average adjustment at both age 10 and age 13, of which only one shows a significant individual stability (A3L1/A6L1). The other one, characterized by low in *timidity* (A3L17), shows significant individual change into a typical pattern characterized by generalized bad adjustment, with the exception that *timidity* is below average (A6L10). There is one typical pattern at age 10, which is characterized by very bad adjustment on all dimensions except *timidity*, which is normal (A3L10). Judging by the individual stability and change observed, it can be depicted as evolving into two different typical patterns at age 13, both characterized by generalized maladjustment, except that in one of them, *timidity*, is below average (A6L10), whereas in the other pattern, *timidity* and *aggression* are in the normal range (A6L13). Finally, there is a typical pattern in which adjustment is not good on any dimension and *timidity* is high (A3L5). It can be described as evolving into a cluster at age 13 characterized by improved adjustment, which is now about average except for *timidity*, which is very high (A6L11).

The amount of information contained in the results from the type of analysis just summarized is enormous and by necessity, an overview like the one given must be superficial. We now turn to more detailed discussions of a variety of aspects.

5.2. Structural Stability and Change

There is considerable structural stability in typical patterns of school adjustment. The only exceptions are that one of the two typical patterns found at age 10 indicating bad adjustment can be depicted as differentiating into two "specialized" typical patterns at age 13, each with different levels of *timidity* as well as general level difference in the degree of bad adjustment. The other exception is that the other pattern indicating bad adjustment and high *timidity* can be depicted as evolving into a pattern in which bad adjustment is now moderated, but *timidity* is very high. Except for *timidity*, which sometimes exhibits large differences with the other dimensions in a typical profile, the clusters are usually not very uneven and the values on the different dimensions stay largely within the "good" or "bad" adjustment region. These typical patterns of good and bad adjustment warrant separate discussions which are now provided.

In accordance with the problem gravitation hypothesis discussed by Bergman and Magnusson (1997), we see here that the percentage of boys characterized by patterns indicating average adjustment has diminished (from 41.5% to 34.2%) and, correspondingly, the percentage of boys characterized by patterns indicating good or bad adjustment has increased. The main idea of this hypothesis, which was formulated within the area of adjustment problems, is that, from a dynamic systems perspective, it is expected that maladjustment in isolated dimensions (partly corresponding to "average" adjustment) is an unstable phenomenon, which will often evolve into either a total absence of adjustment problems or into generalized adjustment problems. This hypothesis has found some support also within other areas (see, e.g., Rönkä and Pulkkinen, 1995, on "problem accumulation" and Stattin and Magnusson, 1996, on evidence of problem gravitation when studying antisocial development). Here, we find only a tendency of the occurrence of this phenomenon, but this might depend on the fact that the whole adjustment spectrum was studied, not only the negative side. Focusing just on bad adjustment, we see the strongest structural change in the direction of the hypothesis.

5.3. Individual Stability and Change

As shown in Fig. 9.22, there are four typical patterns at age 10, which exhibit significant individual stability, two characterized by, broadly speaking, good adjustment, one by average adjustment, and one by bad adjustment. There are three significant movements or changes: (1) one from average adjustment to bad adjustment, except for *timidity*, which is low at both occasions; (2) one between fairly similar clusters within the very bad adjustment region; and (3) one for those who remain high in *timidity* but overall adjustment improves. The four stable streams also appear in the CFA analysis. The following significant developmental types were found with the same value configuration at both time points: No problems at all, all problems except *timidity, timidity* as the only problem, and all problems. It is interesting to note that the three age 10 clusters that did not exhibit individual stability were also the three clusters that had the worst matches to the age 13 clusters, that is, they were the typical patterns that were the least structurally stable.

5.4. Syndromes of Bad School Adjustment

At age 10, two syndromes with generalized bad adjustment emerged. The first one could be described as having pronounced conduct problems and *disharmony*, but being within the normal range with regard to *timidity* (A3L10). This cluster is related to two typical profiles at age 13 both with regard to structure and with regard to individual streams, specifically: (a) a cluster containing children with indications of conduct problems and *disharmony* but being below average with regard to *timidity* (A6L10); and (b) a cluster characterized by children with pronounced conduct problems but in the normal range with regard to *timidity* and *aggression* (A6L13).

The *timidity* dimension is rather like the inhibition–uninhibition dimension as discussed by Kagan (1994). He also proposed that inhibition might function as a protection against externalizing problems because inhibited children would be prone to show more guilt and anxiety when breaking against the rules of society (cf. also Achenbach, 1995). From this standpoint, the results just discussed can be regarded as a consequence of the fact that a trait of "uninhibition" provides no protection in the context of unfavorable circumstances and dispositions resulting in generalized externalizing adjustment problems. It should be noted that those who are high in *timidity* never developed severe adjustment problems at age 13, as discussed in the next paragraph.

The other syndrome with below-average adjustment at age 10 (A3L5) shows indications of conduct problems and *disharmony* and is fairly high in *timidity*. It relates to one typical profile at age 13, specifically the one cluster in which the adjustment is normal but *timidity* is very high (A6L11). Again, the results provide some support for the incompatibility of inhibition with generalized externalizing problems of the type studied here. This is consistent with the finding that the significant developmental stream from average adjustment to bad adjustment concerns a cluster that is low in *timidity* (A3L17).

A slightly different view of the special role of *timidity* was obtained by analyzing the frequency of the different possible maximum and minimum combinations of the profiles, following the earlier described MAMIN rationale (see chap. 3). Because the variables are not continuous there are ties that, for a given individual, can lead to more than one maximum–minimum combination. We chose to count all combinations. As such, the results of the significance tests must be interpreted with caution. The following maximum–minimum combinations emerged most frequently at both ages and were significant types ($p < .05$ after Bonferroni correction): *timidity* minimum and either *motor restlessness* or *lack of concentration* maximum, and *timidity* maximum and *motor restlessness* or *aggression* minimum. Thus, it seems that there is a strong profile form contrast between *timidity* on one hand and *motor restlessness, lack of concentration,* and *aggression* on the other hand. These results are consistent with those reported and also support an interpretation of a possible disjunctive relation between the inhibition dimension and conduct problems. Please note that although we talk here about pairs of variables, it is still in the context of the whole profile. The product moment correlations between these variables do not reveal this subtle information as witnessed by the fact that they are low and even slightly positive between *timidity* and *lack of concentration*.

The results just discussed suggest the possibility that inhibition in boys serves a protective role against the development of generalized, externalizing, school adjustment problems. In the profile studied here, two indicators of what is usually described as internalizing problems were used, *timidity* (which just has been discussed), and *disharmony*. It is interesting to note that *disharmony* emerges as a component in the externalizing problem syndrome and does not appear together with *timidity* any more than do conduct problems. However, it should be pointed out that although the first criterion for being coded as high in *disharmony* is unhappiness, the definition also includes that "they are often in restrained or in open conflict with their surroundings or themselves." For the subgroup of children with *disharmony* where the second criterion applies, we would expect a relation to severe conduct problems, which tend to lead to conflicts with others.

With regard to the internalizing–externalizing problem distinction, we see a complex picture emerging. For the limited set of indicators studied here, we see evidence that one indicator of internalizing problems (i.e., *disharmony* or unhappiness) tends to appear together with conduct problems, consistent with the theory of multiple dysfunction (Zoccolillo, 1992), whereas the other indicator of internalizing problems (i.e., *timidity*) relates to conduct problems in a totally different way in the individual value patterns.

The results reported here indicate that severe externalizing problems of the type we studied appear together to the extent that it is almost meaningless to talk about them as isolated problems. In fact, the CFA analysis not only supports the typical profiles discussed here but also points to single externalizing problems being antitypes, occurring more rarely than under a model of independence. The CFA change analysis also shows that all the problems studied, except *timidity,* have a strong tendency to change in the same way: they all increase or all decrease, supporting the previously discussed phenomenon of problem gravitation. Because good adjustment is also included in the analyses, the phenomenon could instead be coined here as *polarization.*

Naturally one must be very careful not to generalize these findings beyond the realm of school adjustment. There are also, of course, important aspects of the internalizing–externalizing domains that have not been studied here (like depression and peer relations). For a discussion of this issue from a pattern perspective, the reader is referred to Bergman and Magnusson (1991) who studied the same sample of boys studied here in other respects, focusing on patterns of bad adjustment and to Wångby, Bergman, and Magnusson (1999) who studied girls' internalizing and externalizing problems from a developmental perspective.

So far the primary focus has been on one of the two indicators of internalizing problems, *timidity,* in relation to externalizing problems. However, the other indicator of internalizing problems, *disharmony,* is highly interesting as it can be regarded as an indicator of the general well-being of the child in the school environment. We have seen previously that a high level of *disharmony* tends to be linked strongly to generalized, externalizing adjustment problems.

We propose that *disharmony* can be regarded as the child's experience of the outcome of his or her adjustment process. Hence, we expect the strong coupling indicated earlier. *Disharmony* is seen as a necessary consequence of the other problems. It is expected to be very rare with boys having generalized conduct problems but feeling content in school (i.e., being low in *disharmony*). But we go even further: We would also expect that it is almost impossible for a child who has truly generalized good adjustment to be high in *disharmony.* Hence, we expect value combinations indicative of this phenomenon to be rare, or "white spots" in the terminology introduced in chapter 3. To test these hypotheses, we used the RESIDAN methodology described earlier and investigated whether the patterns, 666266 and 222622, were "odd." To do this, we identified the dissimilarity value thresholds that, as closely as possible, split the data set into the 5% most deviant cases and the rest. This threshold value is .67 for both ages and it provided residues of 4% and 3.7% at age 10 and 13, respectively. We then added the pattern, 222622, to the data set exclusive of the residue and noted if it came out in the residue. We then repeated this last step for pattern 666266. At both ages, pattern 222622 came out in the residue as expected but only at age 13 did the pattern 666266 come out in the residue. To support the notion that it is the contrast between *disharmony* and the others that is the crucial component, we also tested, in the same way, the patterns, 666466 and 222422, both of which are similar to the two patterns originally tested, but with a smaller contrast between *disharmony* and the other variables in the patterns. We expected that they would not come out in the residue. These hypotheses were confirmed for both ages.

Although the information provided by these simple tests should not be overestimated, they give some support to an interpretation of *disharmony* as a consequence of the child's general adjustment situation. Of course, the causality could be bidirectional; what the results just discussed show is that the coupling between *disharmony* and the other factors is essential.

5.5. Typical Patterns of Good Adjustment

In the beginning of this chapter, we pointed out that, broadly speaking, considerably less attention has been given to studying good adjustment than to studying bad adjustment. Furthermore, when good adjustment is studied, it is often operationalized as the "absence of bad adjustment," which can be a problematic approach (see, e.g., Jahoda, 1958). Here we have the advantage of having each indicator measuring the full range of adjustment from bad to good. For some indicators, this advantage is bought at the price of a possible bipolarity (different ends of the scale may not fully measure along the same dimension). This issue is discussed in the next section. There seems to be a dearth of studies focusing on patterns of good school adjustment and we have treated our results here from the standpoint of reporting briefly of a *terra incognita*.

The first observation we want to make is that, with the exception of *timidity*, good school adjustment seems to be separated from bad adjustment in a general sense, with no typical patterns containing elements from both spheres. This supports our decision to discuss these two domains separately. We find three typical patterns with generalized good adjustment but with varying levels of *timidity* at age 10. The pattern most strongly indicating good adjustment is also characterized by being low on *timidity*, and the typical pattern with the second highest general level of good adjustment is also characterized by low *timidity*. The third and largest pattern indicating fairly good adjustment is above average in *timidity*. Hence it seems as if in these data *timidity* can be regarded as a "protective" factor, not only against severe conduct problems, but also against very good adjustment.

As was found with regard to bad adjustment, and again making an exception for *timidity*, we also find when reviewing the typical patterns indicating some form of good adjustment, that good adjustment strongly tends to occur in all indicators simultaneously; we see no evidence of "specialization." There are some reasons to believe that this picture will generalize less well than it will when studying the negative side (Magnusson & Mahoney, 2002; Mahoney & Bergman, 2002), but a further analysis and discussion of the issue is deferred to another publication. Then CFA analyses should also be added that dichotomize the data into "good–not good adjustment" for each indicator instead of "bad–not bad adjustment," which was used in the analyses reported here.

6. SOME METHODOLOGICAL CONSIDERATIONS

It was mentioned earlier that the picture that emerged, when analyzing the present data set, was similar regardless of what method was used, and the main results were replicated on a random half. The question can then be raised as to why when interpreting the empirical findings we did not lean primarily on the results from the ISOA analysis. This method may be the most powerful one because a common classificatory grid is created that enables the researcher to undertake fine-grained analyses of the underlying pattern structure and to study changing frequencies and individual change within this structure. Here the assumptions underlying ISOA must be discussed. It is not necessary (as it is sometimes claimed) that all typical patterns are common to both occasions. On the contrary, the method allows for such differences in structure in that a typical pattern unique to one occasion will be first identified as a cluster in the initial cluster analysis, and then in the subsequent analysis, it will frequently be observed on that occasion in which it is unique and much less so at the other occasion. However, in order to interpret these findings, one has to assume that the variables in the profiles have the same meaning at both occasions. We judge the present situation as a borderline case in this regard. On one hand, it is attempted to measure exactly the same variables with the same instructions to the teachers, and so forth. On the other hand, some of the variables change their meaning to some extent. For instance, *motor restlessness* is more likely to be tolerated by teachers in children at lower ages ("small boys with ants in their pants"). Thus the same score at age 13 as at age 10 may mean a lower degree of the behavior at the higher age. For this reason, we focused primarily on the findings from LICUR and CFA, which are more robust methods, although it probably would have been defensible to make more use of the ISOA findings.

We have briefly mentioned the potential complications caused by the fact that some of the indicators may not completely measure in the same dimension when going from one extreme to the other. If this is taken in conjunction with the results obtained when dividing the obtained clusters into groups representing either generalized good, average, or bad adjustment (excluding *timidity*), it then supports the contention reached by Bergman and Magnusson (1987) that, when studying adjustment problems, it can be useful to only discriminate in the negative end of each indicator to ensure they are unidimensional. The same line of reasoning could be applied when studying positive adjustment. The quasiabsolute scaling suggested by Bergman and Magnusson (1987) may be a useful method. Nevertheless, we believe that as a first overview of an adjustment area, the strategy followed here is reasonable. It is, however, incomplete and should be followed up by separate analyses within the positive and negative adjustment areas.

Let us come back to the issue of whether one should or should not simultaneously study good and bad adjustment. We could have extended our study and included, for instance, a CFA analysis of the positive side similar to our analysis of the negative side. Now only the other three types of analyses cover the whole adjustment spectrum. We consider this additional CFA analysis as the next step of a more thorough analysis of positive adjustment. What we could have done, but did not do for practical reasons, would be to modify the CFA analysis to include the positive side by making each variable trichotomous, measuring good, normal, or bad adjustment. In this way there would have been three to the power of six (= 729) different patterns to study. For such an analysis the sample is too small, highlighting a limitation of CFA (cf. also von Eye, 1990b). Broadly speaking, we think the findings reported here support our contention that, after an initial bird's-eye study of patterns relating to the whole adjustment spectrum in the dimensions under study, it is normally most useful to concentrate on either good or bad adjustment to achieve a greater depth in the analyses and avoid problems of the type discussed.

To stay on our main track, we have not complemented the person-oriented analyses with variable-oriented analyses except for computing the correlations between the variables. Without denying the potential usefulness of more sophisticated, variable-oriented analysis within the area studied, we point out that it does not seem easy to capture the essence of the results reported here without studying the value patterns. For instance, the correlations indicate that to some extent, *timidity* is positively related to *low school motivation* and *disharmony,* negatively related to *motor restlessness,* and, broadly speaking, has weak or no relationship to the other indicators. From a pattern perspective, this result is misleading and does not point in the direction of the typical patterns that were obtained and in which *timidity* often stood out as the crucial component. In our opinion, variable-based, dimensional analyses in the adjustment problem area usually provide only limited information about how the problems are organized within the individual. The so-called co-morbidity issue may demand that pattern-oriented analyses be carried out if syndromes like those we found are to have the chance of being detected.

Chapter 10
DISCUSSION AND DIRECTIONS

In this book, a person-oriented perspective was presented and a tool chest of basic methods for carrying out research within this framework was described and exemplified with empirical research. Taking this theoretical framework seriously has far-reaching implications for how empirical research is carried out. However, as pointed out before, it is important not to confuse the person approach with the methods commonly used to carry it out, for example, cluster analysis, and so forth. Indeed, a wide range of methods is possible for use within the person approach and the choice should always be made in such a way so that the method matches the specific problem. For reasons that should be clear to the reader by now, in the most common types of situations, it is desirable that the method used captures, as much as possible, the system as a functioning whole. This point is now elaborated.

It is important to recognize that a person approach normally has consequences for the type of measurements for which one should strive. It often implies that a multivariate measurement procedure is implemented, ensuring that the different components of the profile are comparable; this point was elaborated in chapter 3.

1. STUDYING PROCESSES

It has been said again and again that it is of crucial importance that the methods used for studying a developmental phenomenon should have an affinity to the process under study; there must be a match between the problem and the method (Magnusson, Bergman, Rudinger, & Törestad, 1991). From this perspective, it is worrisome that many of the statistical methods used today for studying developmental processes are too indirect for this purpose. For instance, a static statistical model of the data is used frequently to make inferences about a process, which, from the researcher's theoretical perspective, is regarded as dynamic with continuous, ongoing interactions. In this case, there is a high risk that the essential properties of the process of interest are not mirrored by the method used for its study (Bergman, 2002).

Examples of this mismatch of problem and method abound and, without pointing out any one in particular, the point is illustrated by the following generic example. Data are available from n individuals at t points in time concerning k variables. The linear relationships over time for the different variables are modeled and (a) the fit of the model to data is studied, and (b) the size of various parameters is examined that are believed to "explain" the relationships. Without denying the usefulness of such an approach for providing basic information about the data set and the generic relationships the results indicate, it must be pointed out that from the perspective of understanding the process of interest, such an analysis might not be very informative.

The first reason for the mismatch in this case is that usually, when carrying out such a test, higher order interactions and nonlinearities in the data are ignored (i.e., the analysis is based on the variance–covariance matrix). The researcher might not even know this is a mistake as model fit is often measured as the model's ability to reproduce the variance–covariance matrix.

The second reason is that it might not be reasonable to believe that the model of the data in any way mirrors the process, as it is understood. For instance, a linear regression coefficient of size β between latent (or manifest) variable 1 and variable 2 implies that a change of one unit in variable 1 would lead to a change of β in variable 2 for each individual. But what does this mean? Is it reasonable to believe that the same simple law applies to all persons studied? And that the process contains no interactions and it is possible to conceptualize that one variable can be changed without affecting or reconfiguring the whole system?

Considerations like these lead one into the labyrinth of causal inferences in nonexperimental research and inevitably brings into focus the need for a more realistic model of the process under study. To obtain a first idea of how the k variables under study are related within and between the t time points, a standard variable-oriented approach can be useful, but as a means of understanding the dynamics that decide how the variables evolve in interaction over time, such an approach seems, more often than not, almost useless. This viewpoint has been expressed by several researchers, for instance, Bergman (2002), Bailey (1994), and Sörensen (1998). Sörensen (1998) says

> The failure to consider mechanism of change and to try to formulate them in models of the processes we investigate, however primitive the result may be, has important consequences for the state of sociological research. The almost universal use of statistical models and specifications has two sets of important implications. First, we are constrained by the statistical models to not consider whether or not we actually obtain, from our research, a greater understanding of the processes we investigate. In other words, the statistical models give us theoretical blinders.... Second, we may actually produce results that, on closer consideration seem theoretically unfounded and very likely misleading. (pp. 14–15)

It should be recognized that the limitations of standard variable-oriented methods in the context discussed here do not generalize to all variable-oriented methods. It is encouraging that new developments within the field of p technique and time-series analysis (Nesselroade & Ghisletta, 2000; Schmitz, 1987) come part of the way toward mirroring the single individual's development. New methods for latent growth curve modeling allow an individualization of developmental trajectories within the context of the powerful SEM framework. Still, in the opinion of the present writers, these statistical methods cannot normally be expected to provide more than a partial adjustment to the need for explaining the mechanism of change. There remains the need for an approach closer to the process; an approach that aims at explaining the nonlinear dynamics of change.

Within the natural sciences, it is now acknowledged that many phenomena are best described by dynamic systems that are nonlinear. The study of such systems is given here the acronym NOLIDS. Such systems began to be studied about a century ago, first as a branch of mathematics (Poincaré, 1946). The analytical problems in solving the differential equations of change tend to be very difficult and only by using modern computers can a larger class of problems now be "solved." Using NOLIDS, it has been shown in a number of situations that a simple nonlinear deterministic change model can explain very complex behavior involving even seemingly random behavior in the form of deterministic chaos (see e.g., Gleick, 1987, Jackson, 1989, and Smith & Thelen, 1993). A good example of the potential of this approach is given by Kelso and his co-workers in their research on the dynamics of motor coordination (Kelso, 1995).

Bergman (2002) summarized certain aspects of NOLIDS in the following way:

1. The frequent existence of sudden changes in the behavior of a system, which could be described as qualitative change in quantitative systems, and the importance of studying these phenomena in order to understand the system (Kelso, 2000). This is the antithesis of linear modeling.
2. The importance of obtaining a global, qualitative understanding of the character of the systems dynamics. This was pointed out already by Poincaré, the "father of NOLIDS," almost 100 years ago.
3. The difficulties in identifying/choosing relevant system properties for carrying out NOLIDS modeling (including defining time scales, relevant collective variables, and the level of analysis).

So if NOLIDS holds such promise, why is it not used more frequently? The reasons for this are partly given in number 3, just mentioned. In fact, successful applications of NOLIDS within the behavioral sciences seem to fall within the area of experimental research and to be concerned with more molecular behavior in situations in which one can achieve sufficient control and adequate measurements of the system under study. This seems to be a necessary prerequisite for the complex task of mapping out the behavior of the system and the mechanisms for its change (see Kelso, 2000, for an even more pessimistic view of these possibilities). Nevertheless, NOLIDS holds great promise for the future and the growing interface between it and statistical science will probably lead to improved methods for parameter estimation and model identification (see, e.g., Berliner, 1992, and Chatterjee & Yilmaz, 1992). It is also true that the introduction of powerful concepts taken from NOLIDS like attractors, bifurcation, multistability, chaos, and so forth, into developmental science and psychology in general, will enrich our thinking of processes even though, in a first step, no actual NOLIDS modeling is undertaken.

So where do the person-oriented methods we presented in this volume come in with regard to the process perspective just presented? First, it might be argued that, similar to standard statistical methods, they are static approaches in the specific sense that they picture states at different discrete points in time. The multivariate densities and white spots of the k variables from the t time points are studied. The results of the analyses do not mirror a change process in continuous time. However, as discussed in chapter 2 and chapter 3, the person-oriented approach we present does take interactions and aspects of the system as a functioning whole into account to a greater degree than conventional approaches. One important aspect from a NOLIDS perspective is the attractor, which can be regarded as a "functional" system state at which the system tends to stabilize. It is characterized by a specific pattern of values in the variables describing the system. Here it seems reasonable to assume that the concentration within the person approach on typical configurations offers the possibility of detecting such attractors. Nevertheless, the importance of devising new person-oriented methods of a more process-oriented nature should be emphasized.

2. THEORY-TESTING AND EXPLORATION

A criticism sometimes launched against the person-oriented approach is that it is atheoretical as no statistical model is formulated and tested. This criticism is unfounded. The following three considerations are relevant.

1. As was discussed above, when conducting research within a holistic interactionistic framework and when studying processes within the contexts discussed, it is normally very difficult to construct a statistical model of the process of such a quality that it can be said to bridge the gulf between theory and method. The statistical model can be useful for other purposes but it is rarely a good model of the *process* as we understand it. We claim that the information generated by the approach we suggest can in many situations be more relevant for purposes of theory construction and testing than conventional approaches.
2. The importance of careful observation and description in contrast to premature formal model building should be recognized. This applies in particular to the initial stages in a complex field in which careful observation and description

of the phenomena under study is a necessary first step. Theories can provide directions as to what to look for but if they are prematurely transformed into statistical models, they can become "blinders." They may actually prevent the researcher from seeing what is to be seen. This point has been made by, among others, Cronbach (1975), Greenwald, Pratkanis, Lieppe, & Baumgardner (1986), and Magnusson (1992). We propose that the type of research contexts we are discussing in this volume are highly complex fields, which are just opening up, and that the admonition given previously applies especially to them.

3. It is a misunderstanding that a sound scientific approach, in which theories are formulated and tested, should in any way be synonymous with an approach in which a statistical model of data is constructed and used as a means of testing one's theory (Magnusson, 2001). It is true that the SEM approach can be highly useful for testing theories and represents a major step forward when it is appropriately applied. Nevertheless, we have argued in this volume that in the situations we are discussing, this is normally not the case. However, such a model-testing approach is in no way necessary to conducting theory-driven research. What is necessary is that (a) the results of the analyses are relevant to understanding the process under study, and (b) that the theory lead to predictions (preferably contrasting empirical predictions between contrasting theories) that can be tested. This is the case with the person approach presented here.

3. ACCURATE PREDICTION VERSUS IDENTIFICATION OF PRINCIPLES AND MECHANISMS AS THE SCIENTIFIC GOAL IN DEVELOPMENTAL RESEARCH

James Watson (1913) formulated the goal for scientific psychology as to predict and control behavior. Watson purposely used his formulation to motivate psychology as a natural science.

In general terms, the role of science is to arrive at and formulate overriding scientific "laws" for the regulation of phenomena and processes. In the natural sciences, the criterion for the establishment of a scientific law is normally its predictive power. Thus, in his ambition to make psychology a natural science, it was only natural that Watson, in his formulation of the goal of psychology, referred to prediction of psychological phenomena as an overriding goal. The view that accurate prediction is the criterion of scientific success is still, implicitly or explicitly, strong and influential in psychological research. Because it has a strong impact on theorizing, research strategies, and methodology in developmental research, the following question calls for some elaboration: Are the phenomena being studied in developmental research of a character that makes accurate prediction the appropriate criterion of scientific success? The answer to that question has implications for the issues discussed in this volume. With reference to the holistic view on developmental processes, presented and discussed in chapter 2, a few comments are pertinent here.

The frequent use of the concept of prediction suffers from a lack of distinction between (a) statistical prediction in an experimental design, and (b) prediction over time of the life course of individuals. The concept of *prediction* is also applicable in numerous practical situations to which psychological methods are being applied; for example, in personnel selection or decision making. In such situations, the certainty with which predictions are made, that is, the probability that certain events will occur, is of basic interest. In these examples, statistical prediction is a useful tool for estimating the certainty of a certain outcome.

The problem arises when high statistical prediction is confused with prediction over time, across the life course of individuals, and with the overriding criterion of the discipline's scientific status. Fostered by the development and application of technically sophisticated statistical tools, prediction has survived as a central goal for research on individual development, even in areas in which it is not very appropriate. The psychological significance of single variables or composites of variables for the processes of individual development is often directly interpreted from how well data, that are supposed to reflect these processes, predict data for later outcomes in statistical terms.

The role of prediction and the scientific goal for research in life sciences was discussed by Crick (1988), the Nobel laureate who was one of the discoverers of the genetic code. His own experiences from research in physics and molecular biology led him to the conclusion that lawfulness in biological processes can never be expressed in precise laws validated by high prediction in statistical designs, as in physics, but instead should be expressed in mechanisms and principles underlying and guiding the processes. Crick's conclusion is equally valid for research on individual developmental processes. Given the complex, often nonlinear interplay of mental, biological, and behavioral subsystems within the individual, and the complex interplay between the individual and an environment operating in a probabilistic manner, it is unrealistic to hope for accurate prediction over the life course for single individuals. Nowadays most developmentalists agree that the overriding scientific goal for developmental research is to contribute to the understanding of developmental processes at the level of the individual by identifying operating mechanisms and guiding principles. To achieve that goal, the final analysis of data in an empirical study of a specific problem has often to be made with reference to a person approach. The purpose of this volume has been to present a number of methods for this type of analysis.

Research on the weather offers a metaphor that demonstrates the necessity for the distinction between accurate statistical prediction, using a variable approach on the one hand, and understanding the underlying processes, on the other (Magnusson, 1985). The fact that it is possible to predict the average summer, autumn, winter, and spring temperatures in Sweden years beforehand does not help our understanding of the meteorological processes. But by applying strict scientific modeling, meteorologists now have a good understanding of the nature of the processes and underlying principles and mechanisms without being able to make accurate weather forecasts over a longer time period.

3.1. Understanding the Constraints of Development

Robert Cairns often talked about the correlated constraints in development (e.g., Cairns, Gariepy, & Hood, 1990). By this he meant that embedded in the inherent structure of a functional developmental system is the notion that, as the parts at the different levels become organized, some developmental paths will be excluded while other factors emerge together. We believe that the methods presented here are relevant for the study of development according to this perspective. However, we have focused primarily on issues relating to finding the typical developmental paths. The other side of the coin—that constraints also imply a prescription for what will not occur—has been mentioned when introducing the concept of *white spots*.

The search for typical patterns should be complemented by a search for white spots, the patterns that seldom or never occur. This could be done cross-sectionally or longitudinally, looking for pathways of pattern development that for some reason are not traveled. Different ways of doing this cross-sectionally were presented (searching for antitypes, identification of a residue, etc.). Within the limitations of what is theoretically possible, the patterns that occur often and those that occur seldom or not at all together map out the empirical terrain being studied. A search for the boundaries of areas containing nonoccurring developmental patterns is rarely undertaken. And yet, one can often make theoretical predictions about white spots that are testable. As mentioned in chapter 3, boundary conditions were discussed by Lewin (1933) in terms of "region of freedom of movement" (p. 598) and Valsiner (1984) pointed out that the observed variability of a person is only a fraction of his or her possible range of variability. A complementary perspective on this point is offered by Kagan et al.'s (1998) emphasis on studying the extreme cases as being not only quantitatively but also qualitatively different from the rest of the sample and teaching us important things about the constraints of the system.

In our opinion, the serious study of constraints in the form of boundaries and white spots is a rare instance of a promising approach to understanding the empirical world that has been left almost unattended. Methods for studying such constraints are underdeveloped and devising improved methods must be given a high priority.

3.2. Searching for Types

It was pointed out in chapter 3 that the word "type" has been given many meanings and that the concept exists far beyond the area of classification. We also noted that it has often come to imply something that is fixed or innate and that this is not the interpretation we employ. We are strongly opposed to a revival of typological thinking in which persons are seen as belonging to unalterable, permanent classes. A number of ways of looking at types, both conceptually and methodologically, have been presented in this book. Let us dwell here a moment on one specific perspective. A type can sometimes be regarded as an expression of an attractor in a dynamic system. Thus, the type needs not be part of a complete typology applying to all or even to most people. It is just an "important" co-occurrence of values in the variables relating to the system under study. Such a low-key approach in which one or a few types are found, together not covering the whole sample, can sometimes be more realistic than aiming at a complete typology (Bergman & El-Khouri, 2001). It can also form a road to new studies directed toward explaining the type(s) found and relating the results to those already known about pairwise relationships between the variables. In this way, it can also form a bridge to a variable-oriented approach.

4. SOME GUIDELINES FOR FUTURE RESEARCH

At the basis of all successful quantitative empirical research is, of course, sound measurement. Nowhere is this more true than when patterns are the focus of interest. As discussed in chapter 3, not only must each variable in itself be well measured, they must all have a comparative meaning that enables the researcher to form individual profiles of values that are interpretable. It is important to consider procedures for constructing multivariate measurements. For instance, in the context of studying adjustment problems, we argued that quasiabsolute scaling could be useful (Bergman & Magnusson, 1991). We then suggested that it is important to obtain a multivariate measurement procedure reflecting both varying prevalences of different problems and varying prevalences for the same problem over time. This issue of achieving comparable measures seems to be one that is too often dodged and sometimes unsuccessfully circumvented by basing the analyses on standardized scores. The limitations of many pattern-oriented methods in handling errors of measurement also highlight the importance of reliability issues with regard to the variables involved.

But, as previously discussed, the most important issue concerning measurement in a pattern-oriented perspective is that the variables in the profile together provide a reasonable representation of a meaningful (sub)whole with good correspondence to the system under study. Variables cannot just be "thrown in" as is sometimes done in, for instance, factor analysis. They must be carefully considered and their inclusion must be theoretically motivated. In fact, it is precisely the type of "throw in" exploratory approach in cluster analysis that has contributed to the undeservedly bad reputation of this type of method. The old saying, "garbage in, garbage out," is relevant here.

To all researchers, the questions of trustworthiness and generalizability of the results are at the forefront. It has been argued in previous chapters that pattern-oriented methods produce trustworthy results if applied with good judgment on sound data. As discussed in chapter 7, the issue of generalizability of the results has many aspects with the first one being *what* is to be generalized (individual class memberships, centroids, relative frequencies of centroids, only major centroids, etc.). The other main aspect has to do with *to which universe* the generalization is directed (from a random sample to a population, from one population to another class of populations, from one set of variables to another set of variables, etc.). These issues deserve more attention than they usually have been given. The need for replication of findings, which is generally underemphasized (Rutter & Pickles, 1990), must be taken even more seriously when using person-oriented methodology where, in many cases, no proper modeling of measurement or sampling error is possible. But in most situations, the results from replications are more informative than the results of statistical deliberations on one particular sample.

In this book we have advocated the usefulness of person-oriented methodology within a person-oriented theoretical framework. We have also briefly discussed limitations inherent in the use of many standard variable-oriented methods in the contexts we highlighted. It must not be interpreted that we pass judgment on certain methods as being "good" or "bad." Of course, a standard variable-oriented method can be highly useful if applied in an appropriate situation. To reiterate: It is the match between the problem and the method that is of importance. We believe it often is highly productive to mix the two types of approaches, or rather alternate between them. To obtain a preliminary understanding of a new area, it is frequently useful to apply variable-oriented methods (e.g., by computing correlations, performing factor analysis, comparing means) in order to obtain a provisory understanding of which factors are involved in individual processes. Based on this and good theory it might be possible to construct reliable and valid scales measuring central concepts and to form relevant profiles mirroring the system under study. A person-oriented methodology can then be used to find/test for typical (developmental) configurations. Sometimes, after such an approach has been carried out, it might be possible to formulate a nonlinear SEM model in which important interactions that have been previously identified are incorporated. This might lead to new theoretical formulations that can be empirically tested, most frequently by a person-oriented methodology; and so on. Having said this we must also point out that, in our experience, the variable and the person perspectives are not easy to reconcile. Finding ways to integrate these two perspectives is a challenge we should continue to work toward.

REFERENCES

Achenbach, T. M. (1995). Developmental issues in assessment, taxonomy, and diagnosis of child and adolescent psychopathology. In D. Cicchetti & D. J. Cohen (Eds.), *Developmental psychopathology: Theory and methods* (Vol. 1, pp. 57–80). New York: Wiley.
Ahn, W., & Medin, D. L. (1992). A two-stage model of category construction. *Cognitive Science, 16,* 81–121.
Allport, G. W. (1961). *Pattern and growth in personality.* New York: Holt, Rinehart & Winston.
American Psychological Association (APA). (1983). *Diagnostic and Statistical Manual of Mental Disorders* (3rd ed.) (DSM-III). Washington, DC: Author. American Psychological Association.
Anastasi, A. (1968). *Differential psychology.* New York: Macmillan.
Anderberg, M. R. (1973). *Cluster analysis for applications.* New York: Academic Press.
Andersson, T. (1988). *Alkoholvanor i ett utvecklingsperspektiv* [Drinking habits in a developmental perspective]. Unpublished doctoral dissertation, Department of Psychology, University of Stockholm.
Andrews, D. F. (1972). Plots of high-dimensional data. *Biometrics, 28,* 125–135.
Arabie, P., & Hubert, L. J. (1996). An overview of combinatorial data analysis. In P. Arabie, L. J. Hubert, & G. De Soete (Eds.), *Clustering and classification* (pp. 5–63). Singapore: World Scientific Publishing.
Asendorpf, J. B. (2000). A person-centered approach to personality and social relationships: Findings from the Berlin Relationship Study. In L. R. Bergman, R. B. Cairns, L.-G. Nilsson, & L. Nystedt (Eds.), *Developmental science and the holistic approach* (pp. 281–298). Mahwah, NJ: Lawrence Erlbaum Associates.
Backteman, G., & Magnusson, D. (1981). Longitudinal stability of personality characteristics. *Journal of Personality, 4,* 689–703.
Bailey, K. D. (1994). *Typologies and taxonomies.* An introduction to classification techniques. New York: SAGE.
Baltes, P. B. (1979). Life-span developmental psychology: Some converging observations on history and theory. In P. B. Baltes & O. G. Brim (Eds.), *Life-span development and behavior* (Vol. 2, pp. 255–279). New York: Academic Press.

Baltes, P. B., Lindenberger, U., & Staudinger, U. M. (1998). Life-span theory in developmental psychology. In R. M. Lerner (Vol. Ed.) & W. Damon (Ed.-in-Chief), *Handbook of child psychology. Theoretical models of human development* (Vol. 1, pp. 1029–1143). New York: Wiley.

Barton, S. (1994). Chaos, self-organization, and psychology. *American Psychologist, 49,* 5–15.

Bateson, P. P. G. (1978). How does behavior develop? In P. P. G. Bateson & P. H. Klopfer (Eds.), *Perspectives in ecology, Vol. 3: Social behavior.* New York: Plenum Press.

Bereiter, C. (1963). Some persistent dilemmas in the measurement of change. In C. Harris (Ed.), *Problems in measuring change* (pp. 3–20). Madison, WI: University of Wisconsin Press.

Bergman, L. R. (1972). Change as the dependent variable. *Reports from the Psychological Laboratories,* University of Stockholm (Suppl. 14).

Bergman, L. R. (1973). Parent's education and mean change in intelligence. *Scandinavian Journal of Psychology, 23,* 425–441.

Bergman, L. R. (1988a). Modeling reality: Some comments. In M. Rutter (Ed.), *Studies of psychosocial risk* (pp. 354–366). Cambridge, England: Cambridge University Press.

Bergman, L. R. (1988b). You can't classify all of the people all of the time. *Multivariate Behavioral Research, 23,* 425–441.

Bergman, L. R. (1993). Some methodological issues in longitudinal research: Looking ahead. In D. Magnusson & P. Casaer (Eds.), *Longitudinal research on individual development: Present status and future perspectives* (pp. 217–241). Cambridge, England: Cambridge University Press.

Bergman, L. R. (1995). Describing individual development using i-states as objects analysis (ISOA). *Reports from the Department of Psychology,* Stockholm University (No. 806).

Bergman, L. R. (1998). A pattern-oriented approach to studying individual development: Snapshots and processes. In R. B. Cairns, L. R. Bergman, & J. Kagan (Eds.), *Methods and models for studying the individual* (pp. 83–121). Thousand Oaks, CA: Sage.

Bergman, L. R. (2000). The application of a person-oriented approach: Types and clusters. In L. R. Bergman, R. B. Cairns, L.-G. Nilsson, & L. Nystedt (Eds.), *Developmental science and the holistic approach* (pp. 137–154). Mahwah, NJ: Lawrence Erlbaum Associates.

Bergman, L. R. (2002). Studying processes: Some methodological considerations. In L. Pulkkinen & A. Caspi (Eds.), *Paths to successful development. Personality in the life course* (pp. 177–199). Cambridge, England: Cambridge University Press.

Bergman, L. R. (in press). Studying individual patterns of development using i-state sequence analysis (ISSA).

Bergman, L. R., Eklund, G., & Magnusson, D. (1991). Studying individual development: Problems and methods. In D. Magnusson, L. R. Bergman, G. Rudinger, & B. Törestad (Eds.), *Matching problems and methods in longitudinal research: Stability and change* (pp. 1–27). Cambridge, England: Cambridge University Press.

Bergman, L. R., & El-Khouri, B. M. (1986). On the preparatory analysis of multivariate data before (longitudinal) cluster analysis: Some theoretical considerations and a data program. *Reports from the Department of Psychology,* Stockholm University (No. 651).

Bergman, L. R., & El Khouri, B. M. (1987). EXACON—a Fortran 77 program for the exact analysis of single cells in a contingency table. *Educational and Psychological Measurement, 47,* 155–161.

Bergman, L. R., & El Khouri, B. M. (1999). Studying individual patterns of development using i-states as objects analysis (ISOA). *Biometrical Journal, 41,* 753–770.

Bergman, L. R., & El Khouri, B. M. (2001). Developmental processes and the modern typological perspective. *European Psychologist, 6,* 177–186.

Bergman, L. R., & El Khouri, B. M. (in press). Rater-based classification methods.
Bergman, L. R., & Magnusson, D. (1983). The development of patterns of maladjustment. *Report from the project Individual Development and Environment*, Psychological Department, Stockholm University (No. 50).
Bergman, L. R., & Magnusson, D. (1984a). Patterns of adjustment problems at age 10: An empirical and methodological study. *Reports from the Department of Psychology*, University of Stockholm (No. 615).
Bergman, L. R., & Magnusson, D. (1984b). Patterns of adjustment problems at age 13: An empirical and methodological study. *Reports from the Department of Psychology*, University of Stockholm (No. 620).
Bergman, L. R., & Magnusson, D. (1986). Type A behavior. A longitudinal study from childhood to adulthood. *Psychosomatic Medicine, 48,* 134–142.
Bergman, L. R., & Magnusson, D. (1987). A person approach to the study of the development of adjustment problems: An empirical example and some research considerations. In D. Magnusson & A. Öhman (Eds.), *Psychopathology: An interactional perspective* (pp. 383–401). New York: Academic Press.
Bergman, L. R., & Magnusson, D. (1990). General issues about data quality in longitudinal research. In D. Magnusson & L. R. Bergman (Eds.), *Data quality in longitudinal research* (pp. 1–31). Cambridge, England: Cambridge University Press.
Bergman, L. R., & Magnusson, D. (1991). Stability and change in patterns of extrinsic adjustment problems. In D. Magnusson, L. R. Bergman, G. Rudinger, & B. Törestad (Eds.), *Problems and methods in longitudinal research: Stability and change* (pp. 323–346). Cambridge, England: Cambridge University Press.
Bergman, L. R., & Magnusson, D. (1997). A person-oriented approach in research on developmental psychopathology. *Development and Psychopathology, 9,* 291–319.
Bergman, L. R., & Eye, A. von (1987). Normal approximations of exact tests in configural frequency analysis. *Biometric Journal, 29,* 849–855.
Berliner, L. M. (1992). Statistics, probability and chaos. *Statistical Science, 7,* 69–90.
Bishop, Y. M. M., Feinberg, S. E., & Holland, P. W. (1975). *Discrete multivariate analysis: Theory and practice.* Cambridge, MA: MIT Press.
Blashfield, R. K. (1980). The growth of cluster analysis: Tryon, Ward and Johnson. *Multivariate Behavioral Research, 15,* 439–458.
Blashfield, R. K., & Aldenderfer, M. S. (1988). The methods and problems of cluster analysis. In J. R. Nesselroade & R. B. Cattell (Eds.), *Handbook of multivariate experimental psychology* (2nd ed., pp. 447–473). New York: Plenum.
Block, J. (1971). *Lives through time.* Berkeley, CA: Bancroft Books.
Breckenridge, J. N. (1989). Replicating cluster analysis: Method, consistency and validity. *Multivariate Behavioral Research, 24,* 147–161.
Cairns, R. B. (1979). *Social development: The origins and plasticity of interchanges.* San Francisco: W. H. Freeman & Co.
Cairns, R. B. (1986). Phenomena lost: Issues in the study of development. In J. Valsiner (Ed.), *The individual subject and scientific psychology* (pp. 79–112). New York: Plenum Press.
Cairns, R. B. (2000). Developmental science: Three audacious implications. In L. R. Bergman, R. B. Cairns, L.-G. Nilsson, & L. Nystedt (Eds.), *Developmental science and the holistic approach* (pp. 49–62). Mahwah, NJ: Lawrence Erlbaum Associates.
Cairns, R. B., & Cairns, B. D. (1994). *Lifelines and risks. Pathways of youth in our time.* New York: Cambridge University Press.
Cairns, R. B., Elder, G. H., Jr., & Costello, E. J. (Eds.) (1996). *Developmental Science.* New York: Cambridge University Press.

Cairns, R. B., & Gariepy, J.-L., & Hood, K. E. (1990). Development, microevolution, and social behavior. *Psychological Review, 97,* 49–65.

Cairns, R. B., & Rodkin, P. C. (1998). Phenomena regained: From configurations to pathways. In R. B. Cairns, L. R. Bergman, & J. Kagan (Eds.), *Methods and models for studying the individual* (pp. 245–263). Thousand Oaks, CA: Sage.

Carmichael, J. W., & Sneath, P. H. A. (1969). Taxometric maps. *Systematic Zoology, 18,* 402–415.

Casti, J. L. (1989). *Alternate realities. Mathematical models of nature and man.* New York: Wiley.

Cattell, R. B. (1957). *Personality and motivation structure and measurement.* New York: World Book.

Cattell, R. B., & Coulter, M. A. (1966). Principles of behavioural taxonomy and the mathematical basis of the taxonom computer program. *British Journal of Mathematical and Statistical Psychology, 19,* 237–269.

Chatterjee, S., & Yilmaz, M. R. (1992). Chaos, fractals and statistics. *Statistical Science, 7,* 49–68.

Cicchetti, D. (1996). Child maltreatment: Implications for developmental theory and research. *Human Development, 39,* 18–39.

Clogg, C. C. (1979). Some latent structure models for the analysis of Likert-type data. *Social Science Research, 8,* 237–269.

Clogg, C. C. (1981a). Latent structure models of mobility. *American Journal of Sociology, 86,* 836–868.

Clogg, C. C. (1981b). New developments in latent structure analysis. In D. M. Jackson & E. F. Borgatta (Eds.), *Factor analysis and measurement* (pp. 215–246). Beverly Hills, CA: Sage.

Clogg, C. C., Eliason, S. R., & Grego, J. M. (1990). Models for the analysis of change in discrete variables. In A. von Eye (Ed.), *Statistical methods in longitudinal research, Vol. II: Time series and categorical longitudinal data* (pp. 409–441). New York: Academic Press.

Coie, J. D., Watt, N. F., West, S. G., Hawkins, J. D., Asarnow, J. R., Markman, H. J., Ramey, S. L., Shure, M. B., & Long, B. (1993). The science of prevention. A conceptual framework and some directions for a national research program. *American Psychologist, 48,* 1013–1022.

Colinvaux, P. (1980). *Why big fierce animals are rare.* Princeton, NJ: Princeton University Press.

Collins, L. M., & Wugalter, S. E. (1992). Latent class models for stage-sequential dynamic latent variables. *Multivariate Behavioral Research, 27,* 131–157.

Cormack, R. M. (1971). A review of classification. *Journal of the Royal Statistical Society, 134,* 321–367.

Cowen, E. L. (1991). In pursuit of wellness. *American Psychologist, 46,* 404–408.

Cox, A., Rutter, M., Yule, B., & Quinton, D. (1977). Bias resulting from missing information: Some epidemiological findings. *British Journal of Preventive Social Medicine, 31,* 131–136.

Crick, F. (1988). *What mad pursuit: A personal view of scientific discovery.* New York: Basic Books.

Cronbach, L. J. (1975). Beyond the two disciplines of scientific psychology. *American Psychologist, 30,* 116–127.

Cronbach, L. J., & Gleser, G. C. (1953). Assessing similarity between profiles. *Psychological Bulletin, 50,* 456–473.

Cronbach, L. J., Gleser, G. C., Nanda, H., & Rajaratnam, N. (1971). *The dependability of behavioral measurements: Multifacet studies of generalizability.* New York: Wiley.

Cudeck, R., Du Troit, S., & Sörbom, D. (Eds.). (2001). *Structural equation modeling: Present and future—A Festschrift in honor of Karl G. Jöreskog*. Chicago: Scientific Software International.

Curran, P. J., & Bollen, K. A. (2001). The best of both worlds: Combining autoregressive and latent curve models. In L. M. Collins & A. G. Sayer (Eds.), *New methods for the analysis of change* (pp. 105–136). Washington, DC: American Psychological Association.

DeNeve, K. M., & Cooper, H. (1998). The happy personality: A meta-analysis of 137 personality traits and subjective well-being. *Psychological Bulletin, 124*, 197–229.

De Soete, G. (1993). Using latent classification analysis in categorization research. In I. Van Mechelen, J. Hampton, R. S. Michalski, & P. Theuns (Eds.), *Categories and concepts* (pp. 309–330). San Diego: Academic Press.

De Soete, G., & DeSarbo, W. S. (1991). A latent class probit model for analyzing pick any/N data. *Journal of Classification, 4*, 155–173.

Diday, E., & Simon, J. C. (1976). Clustering analysis. In K. S. Fu (Ed.), *Communication and cybernetics 10* (pp. 47–94). Berlin: Springer Verlag.

Diener, E., Suh, E. M., Lucas, R. E., & Smith, H. L. (1999). Subjective well-being: Three decades of progress. *Psychological Bulletin, 125*, 276–302.

Dubes, R., & Jain, A. K. (1979). Validity studies in clustering methodologies. *Pattern Recognition, 11*, 235–254.

Durlak, J. A. (1997). *Successful prevention programs for children and adolescents*. New York: Plenum Press.

Edelbrock, C. (1979). Mixture model tests of hierarchical clustering algorithms. The problem of classifying everybody. *Multivariate Behavioral Research, 14*, 367–384.

Ekman, G. (1951). On typological and dimensional systems of reference in describing personality. *Acta Psychologica, 8*, 1–24.

Ekman, G. (1952). *Differentiell psykologi* [Differential psychology]. Uppsala, Sweden: Almqvist & Wiksell.

El-Khouri, B. M., & Bergman, L. R. (1992). M-PREP: A Fortran 77 program for the preparatory analysis of multivariate data. *Reports from the Department of Psychology*, Stockholm University (No. 751).

Everitt, B. (1974). *Cluster analysis*. New York: Wiley.

Eysenck, H. J. (1953). *The structure of human personality*. New York: Wiley & Sons.

Fortier, J. J., & Solomon, H. (1966). Clustering procedures. In P. R. Krishnaiah (Ed.), *Multivariate analysis* (pp. 493–506). New York: Academic Press.

Frank, O., & Harary, F. (1982). Cluster inference by using transitivity indices in empirical graphs. *Journal of the American Statistical Association, 77*, 835–840.

Gangestad, S., & Snyder, M. (1985). To carve nature at its joints: On the existence of discrete classes in personality. *Psychological Review, 92*, 317–349.

Gleick, J. (1987). *Chaos: Making a new science*. New York: Viking Press.

Gordon, A. D. (1981). *Classification: Methods for the exploratory analysis of multivariate data*. London: Chapman & Hall.

Gordon, A. D. (1996). Hierarchical classification. In P. Arabie, L. J. Hubert, & G. De Soete (Eds.), *Clustering and classification* (pp. 65–121). Singapore: World Scientific Publishing.

Gordon, A. D., & Hendersson, J. T. (1977). An algorithm for Euclidean sum of squares. *Biometrics, 33*, 355.

Greenwald, A. G., Pratkanis, A. R., Lieppe, M. R., & Baumgardner, M. H. (1986). Under what conditions does theory obstruct research progress? *Psychological Review, 93*, 216–229.

Gregson, R. A. M. (1975). *Psychometrics of similarity*. New York: Academic Press.

Groves, R. M. (1989). *Survey errors and survey costs*. New York: John Wiley.

Gustafson, S. B., & Ritzer, D. R. (1995). The dark side of normal: A psychopathy-linked pattern called aberrant self-promotion. *European Journal of Personality, 9,* 147–183.

Haberman, S. J. (1973). The analysis of residuals in cross-classified tables. *Biometrics, 29,* 205–220.

Harré, R. (2000). Acts of living. *Science, 289,* 1303–1304.

Harris, C. W. (1963). *Problems in measuring change.* Madison, WI: University of Wisconsin Press.

Hartigan, J. A. (1975). *Clustering algorithms.* New York: Wiley.

Hellvik, O. (1988). *Introduction to causal analysis. Exploring survey data by crosstabulation.* Oslo: Norwegian University Press.

Hildebrand, D. K., Laing, J. D., & Rosenthal, H. (1977). *Prediction analysis of cross-classifications.* New York: Wiley.

Holm, S. (1979). A simple sequentially rejective multiple test procedure. *Scandinavian Journal of Statistics, 6,* 65–70.

Hubert, L. J., & Arabie, P. (1985). Comparing partitions. *Journal of Classification, 2,* 193–218.

Jackson, A. E. (1989). *Perspectives on nonlinear dynamics* (Vol. 1). Cambridge, England: Cambridge University Press.

Jahoda, M. (1958). *Current concepts of positive mental health.* New York: Basic Books.

Jardine, N., & Sibson, R. (1968a). A model of taxonomy. *Mathematical Biosciences, 2,* 465–482.

Jardine, N., & Sibson, R. (1968b). The construction of hierarchic and non-hierarchic classification. *Computer Journal, 11,* 177–184.

Johnson, S. C. (1967). Hierarchical clustering schemes. *Psychometrika, 32,* 241.

Jones, C. J., & Nesselroade, J. R. (1990). Multivariate, replicated, single-subject designs and P-technique factor analysis: A selective review of the literature. *Experimental Aging Research, 16,* 171–183.

Kagan, J. (1994). *Galen's prophecy. Temperament in human nature.* New York: Basic Books.

Kagan, J. (2000). The modern synthesis in psychological development. In L. R. Bergman, R. B. Cairns, L.-G. Nilsson, & L. Nystedt (Eds.), *Developmental science and the holistic approach* (pp. 65–80). Mahwah, NJ: Lawrence Erlbaum Associates.

Kagan, J., Snidman, N., & Arcus, D. (1998). The value of extreme groups. In R. B. Cairns, L. R. Bergman, & J. Kagan (Eds.), *Methods and models for studying the individual* (pp. 65–80). Thousand Oaks, CA: Sage.

Kelso, J. A. S. (1995). *Dynamic patterns: The self-organization of brain and behavior.* Cambridge, MA: MIT Press.

Kelso, J. A. S. (2000). Principles of dynamic pattern formation and change for a science of human behavior. In L. R. Bergman, R. B. Cairns, L.-G. Nilsson, & L. Nystedt (Eds.), *Developmental science and the holistic approach* (pp. 63–83). Mahwah, NJ: Lawrence Erlbaum Associates.

Kitchener, R. F. (1982). Holism and the organismic model of developmental psychology. *Human Development, 25,* 233–249.

Krauth, J. (1993). *Einführung in die Konfigurationsfrequenzanalyse (KFA)* [Introduction to configuration frequency analysis—CFA]. Weinheim, Basel: Beltz, Psychologie-Verlag-Union.

Krauth, J. (1985). Typological personality research by configural frequency analysis. *Personality and Individual Differences, 6,* 161–168.

Krauth, J., & Lienert, G. A. (1973). *KFA. Die Konfigurationsfrequenzanalyse und ihre Anwendung in Psychologie und Medizin* [CFA configuration frequency analysis and its application in psychology and medicine]. Freiburg, Germany: Alber.

Krauth, J., & Lienert, G. A. (1982). Fundamentals and modifications of configural frequency analysis (CFA). *Interdisciplinaria, 3,* 1.

Lambert, J. M., & Williams, W. T. (1966). Multivariate methods in plant ecology VI. Comparison of information-analysis and association-analysis. *Journal of Ecology, 54,* 634–664.

Lance, G. N., & Williams, W. T. (1966). Computer programs for hierarchical polythetic classification ("similarity analyses"). *Computer Journal, 9,* 60–64.

Lazarsfeld, P. F., & Henry, N. W. (1968). *Latent structure analysis.* New York: Houghton Mifflin Company.

Lehmacher, W. (1981). A more powerful simultaneous test procedure in configural frequency analysis. *Biometrical Journal, 23,* 429–436.

Lerman, I., & Peter, P. (1985). Élaboration et logiciel d'un indice de similarité entre objects d'un type quelconque: Application au problem de concencus en classification [Development and software of an index of similarity between objects of arbitrary types: Application of the problem of consensus in classification]. *Rapports de Recherche, No. 434.* Rennes: Institut Nationale de Recherche en Informatique et en Automatique.

Lerner, R. M. (1984). *On the nature of human plasticity.* New York: Cambridge University Press.

Lerner, R. M. (1991). Changing organism-context relations as the basis of development: A developmental contextual perspective. *Developmental Psychology, 27,* 27–32.

Lewin, K. (1933). Environmental forces in child behavior and development. In C. Murchison (Ed.), *A handbook of child psychology* (2nd ed., pp. 590–625). Worcester, MA: Clark University Press.

Lienert, G. A., & Bergman, L. R. (1985). Longisectional interaction structure analysis (LISA) in psychopharmacology and developmental psychopathology. *Neuropsychobiology, 14,* 27–34.

Lienert, G. A., & zur Oeveste, H. (1985). CFA as a statistical tool for developmental research. *Educational & Psychological Measurement, 45,* 301–307.

Ling, R. F. (1973). A probability theory of cluster analysis. *Journal of the American Statistical Association, 68,* 159–164.

Lord, F. M. (1963). Elementary models for measuring change. In C. W. Harris, *Problems in measuring change* (pp. 21–38). Madison, WI: The University of Wisconsin Press.

Lorr, M., & Radhakrishnan, B. (1967). A comparison of two methods of cluster analysis. *Educational and Psychological Measurement, 27,* 47–53.

Luthar, S. S. (1993). Annotation: Methodological and conceptual issues in research on childhood resilience. *Journal of Child Psychology and Psychiatry, 34,* 441–453.

Macnaughton-Smith, P., Williams, W. T., Dale, M. B., & Mockett, L. G. (1964). Dissimilarity analysis: A new technique of hierarchical sub-division. *Nature, 202,* 1034–1035.

MacQueen, J. (1967). Some methods for classification and analysis of multivariate observations. In L. M. Le Cam & J. Neyman (Eds.), *Proceedings of the Fifth Berkeley Symposium on Mathematical Statistics and Probability* (Vol. 1, pp. 281–297). Berkeley: University of California Press.

Magnusson, D. (1976). The person and the situation in an interactional model of behavior. *Scandinavian Journal of Psychology, 17,* 253–271.

Magnusson, D. (1985). Implications of an interactional paradigm for research on human development. *International Journal of Behavioral Development, 8,* 115–137.

Magnusson, D. (1988). Individual development from an interactional perspective. In D. Magnusson (Series Ed.), *Paths through life* (Vol. 1). Hillsdale, NJ: Lawrence Erlbaum Associates.

Magnusson, D. (1990). Personality development from an interactional perspective. In L. Pervin (Ed.), *Handbook of personality* (pp. 193–222). New York: Guilford Press.

Magnusson, D. (1992). Back to the phenomena: Theory, methods and statistics in psychological research. *European Journal of Personality, 6,* 1–14.

Magnusson, D. (1993). Human ontogeny: A longitudinal perspective. In D. Magnusson & P. Casaer (Eds.), *Longitudinal research on individual development. Present status and future perspectives* (pp. 1–25). Cambridge, England: Cambridge University Press.

Magnusson, D. (1995). Individual development: A holistic integrated model. In P. Moen, G. H. Elder, & K. Lüscher (Eds.), *Linking lives and contexts: Perspectives on the ecology of human development* (pp. 19–60). Washington, DC: APA Books.

Magnusson, D. (1996). Towards a developmental science. In D. Magnusson (Ed.), *The life-span development of individuals: Behavioral, neurobiological and psychosocial perspectives* (pp. XV–XVII). Cambridge, MA: Cambridge University Press.

Magnusson, D. (1998a). The logic and implications of a person approach. In R. B. Cairns, L. R. Bergman, & J. Kagan (Eds.), *Methods and models for studying the individual* (pp. 33–63). Thousand Oaks, CA: Sage.

Magnusson, D. (1998b). The person in developmental research. In J. G. Adair, D. Bélanger, & K. L. Dion (Eds.), *Advances in psychological sciences* (Vol. 1, pp. 495–511). Hove, England: Psychology Press.

Magnusson, D. (1999a). Holistic interactionism: A perspective for research on personality development. In L. Pervin & O. John (Eds.), *Handbook of personality* (pp. 219–247). New York: Guilford.

Magnusson, D. (1999b). On the individual: A person approach to developmental research. *European Psychologist, 4,* 205–218.

Magnusson, D. (2000). The individual as the organizing principle in psychological inquiry: A holistic approach. In L. R. Bergman, R. B. Cairns, L.-G. Nilsson, & L. Nystedt (Eds.), *Developmental science and the holistic approach* (pp. 33–47). Mahwah, NJ: Lawrence Erlbaum Associates.

Magnusson, D. (2001). The holistic-interactionistic paradigm: Some directions for empirical developmental research. *European Psychologist, 6,* 153–162.

Magnusson, D., & Allen, V. L. (1983a). Implications and applications of an interactional perspective for human development. In D. Magnusson & V. L. Allen (Eds.), *Human development: An interactional perspective* (pp. 369–387). New York: Academic Press.

Magnusson, D., & Allen, V. L. (1983b). An interactional perspective for human development. In D. Magnusson & V. L. Allen (Eds.), *Human development: An interactional perspective* (pp. 3–31). New York: Academic Press.

Magnusson, D., Andersson, T., & Törestad, B. (1993). Methodological implications of a peephole perspective on personality. In D. C. Funder, R. D. Parke, C. Tomlinson-Keasey, & K. Wideman (Eds.), *Studying lives through time. Personality and development* (pp. 207–220). Washington, DC: American Psychological Association.

Magnusson, D., & Bergman, L. R. (1988). Individual and variable-based approaches to longitudinal research on early risk factors. In M. Rutter (Ed.), *Studies of psychosocial risk: The power of longitudinal data* (pp. 45–61). Cambridge, England: Cambridge University Press.

Magnusson, D., & Bergman, L. R. (1990). A pattern approach to the study of pathways from childhood to adulthood. In L. N. Robins & M. Rutter (Eds.), *Straight and devious pathways from childhood to adulthood* (pp. 101–115). Cambridge, England: Cambridge University Press.

Magnusson, D., Bergman, L. R., Rudinger, G., & Törestad, B. (1991). *Problems and methods in longitudinal research. Stability and change.* Cambridge, England: Cambridge University Press.

Magnusson, D., & Cairns, R. B. (1996). Developmental science: Toward a unified framework. In R. B. Cairns, G. H. Elder, Jr., E. J. Costello, & A. McGuire (Eds.), *Developmental science* (pp. 7–30). New York: Cambridge University Press.

Magnusson, D., Dunér, A., & Zetterblom, G. (1975). *Adjustment: A longitudinal study.* Stockholm: Almqvist & Wiksell.

Magnusson, D., & Mahoney, J. L. (2002). A holistic person approach for research on positive development. In L. G. Aspenwill & U. M. Staudinger (Eds.), *Human strengths.* Washington, DC: APA Books.

Magnusson, D., & Stattin, H. (1998). Person-context interaction theories. In R. M. Lerner (Vol. Ed.) & W. Damon (Ed.-in-Chief), *Handbook of child psychology. Theoretical models of human development* (Vol. 1., pp. 685–759). New York: Wiley.

Magnusson, D., Stattin, H., & Allen, V. L. (1986). Differential maturation among girls and its relation to social adjustment: A longitudinal perspective. In P. Baltes, D. Featherman, & R. Lerner (Eds.), *Life span development* (Vol. 7, pp. 134–172). New York, Academic Press.

Mahoney, J. L., & Bergman, L. R. (2002.). *Toward a developmental perspective to the study of positive adaptation.* Manuscript in preparation.

Mayr, E. (1997). *This is biology.* Cambridge, MA: The Belknap Press of Harvard University Press.

McArdle, J. J., & Epstein, D. B. (1987). Latent growth curves within developmental structural equation models. *Child Development, 58,* 110–133.

McQuitty, L. L. (1956). Agreement analysis: Classifying persons by predominant patterns of responses. *British Journal of Statistical Psychology, 9,* 5–16.

McQuitty, L. L. (1964). Capabilities and improvements of linkage analysis as a clustering method. *Educational and Psychological Measurement, 24,* 441–456.

McQuitty, L. L. (1966). Similarity analysis by reciprocal pairs for discrete and continuous data. *Educational and Psychological Measurement, 26,* 825–831.

Meehl, P. E. (1992). Factors and taxa, traits and types, differences of degree and differences in kind. *Journal of Personality, 60,* 117–174.

Meehl, P. E., & Yonce, L. J. (1992). Taxometric analysis by the method of coherent cut kinetics [Tech. Rep.]. Minneapolis, MN: University of Minnesota Psychology Department.

Miller, K. F. (1987). Geometric methods in developmental research. In J. Bisanz, C. J. Brainerd, & R. Kail (Eds.), *Formal methods in developmental psychology* (pp. 216–262). New York: Springer Verlag.

Milligan, G. W. (1996). Clustering validation: Results and implications for applied analyses. In P. Arabie, L. Hubert, & G. De Soete (Eds.), *Clustering and classification* (pp. 341–375). River Edge, NJ: World Scientific Press Publishers Co.

Milligan, G. W. (1980). An examination of the effect of six types of error perturbation on fifteen clustering algorithms. *Psychometrika, 45,* 325–342.

Milligan, G. W. (1981a). A Monte Carlo study of thirty internal criterion measures for cluster analyses. *Psykometrika, 46,* 187–199.

Milligan, G. W. (1981b). A review of Monte Carlo tests of cluster analysis. *Multivariate Behavioral Research, 16,* 379–407.

Milligan, G. W., & Cooper, M. C. (1985). An examination of procedures for determining the number of clusters in a data set. *Psykometrika, 50,* 159–179.

Misiak, H., & Sexton, V. (1966). *History of psychology.* New York: Grune & Stratton.
Miyamoto, S. (1990). *Fuzzy sets in information retrieval and cluster analysis.* Dordrecht, The Netherlands: Kluwer Academic Press.
Morey, L. C., Blashfield, R. K., & Skinner, H. A. (1983). A comparison of cluster analysis techniques within a sequential validation framework. *Multivariate Behavioral Research, 18,* 309–329.
Mumford, M. D., & Owens, W. A. (1984). Individuality in a developmental context: Some empirical and theoretical considerations. *Human Development 27,* 84–108.
Muthén, B., & Muthén, L. (2000). Integrating person-centered and variable-centered analyses: Growth mixture modeling with latent trajectory classes. *Alcoholism: Clinical and Experimental Research, 24,* 882–891.
Nesselroade, J. R., & Baltes, P. B. (1984). Sequential strategies and the role of cohort effects in behavioral development: Adolescent personality (1070–72) as a sample case. In S. A. Mednick, M. Harway, & K. M. Finello (Eds.), *Handbook of longitudinal research* (Vol. 1, pp. 55–87). New York: Praeger.
Nesselroade, J. R., & Ford, D. H. (1985). P-technique comes of age: Multivariate, replicated, single-subject designs for research on older adults. *Research on Aging, 7,* 46–80.
Nesselroade, J. R., & Ghisletta, P. (2000). Beyond statistic concepts in modeling behavior. In L. R. Bergman, R. B. Cairns, L.-G. Nilsson, & L. Nystedt (Eds.), *Developmental science and the holistic approach* (pp. 121–135). Mahwah, NJ: Lawrence Erlbaum Associates.
Nesselroade, J. R., & Reese, H. W. (1973). *Life-span developmental psychology. Methodological issues.* New York: Academic Press.
Olweus, D. (1979). Stability of aggressive reaction patterns in males: A review. *Psychological Bulletin, 86,* 852–857.
Pierzchala, M. (1990). A review of the state of the art in automated data editing and imputation. *Journal of Official Statistics, 6,* 1.
Poincaré, H. (1946). *The foundations of science.* Lancaster, England: The Science Press.
Pulkkinen, L., Männikö, K., & Nurmi, J.-E. (2000). Self-description and personality styles. In L. R. Bergman, R. B. Cairns, L.-G. Nilsson, & L. Nystedt (Eds.), *Developmental science and the holistic approach* (pp. 265–280). Mahwah, NJ: Lawrence Erlbaum Associates.
Raudenbush, S. W. (2001). Toward a coherent framework for comparing trajectories of individual change. In L. M. Collins, & A. G. Sayer (Eds.), *New methods for the analysis of change* (pp. 35–64). Washington, DC: American Psychological Association.
Robins, R. W., John, O. P., & Caspi, A. (1998). The typological approach to studying personality. In R. B. Cairns, L. R. Bergman, & J. Kagan (Eds.), *Methods and models for studying the individual* (pp. 135–158). New York: Sage.
Rogosa, D., & Willett, J. B. (1985). Understanding correlates of change by modeling individual differences in growth. *Psychometrika, 50,* 203–228.
Rohlf, F. J. (1970). Adaptive hierarchical clustering schemes. *Systematic Zoology, 19,* 58–82.
Rönkä, A., & Pulkkinen, L. (1995). Accumulation of problems in social functioning in young adulthood: A developmental approach. *Journal of Personality and Social Psychology, 69,* 381–391.
Ross, G. J. S. (1969). Algorithm As15. Single linkage cluster analysis. *Applied Statistics, 18,* 106–110.
Rutter, M. (1989). Age as an ambiguous variable in developmental research: Some epidemiological considerations from developmental psychopathology. *International Journal of Behavioral Development, 12,* 1–34.
Rutter, M. (1994). Family discord and conduct disorder: Cause, consequence, or correlate? *Journal of Family Psychology, 8,* 170–186.

Rutter, M., & Pickles, A. (1990). Improving the quality of psychiatric data: classification, cause, and course. In D. Magnusson & L. R. Bergman (Eds.), *Data quality in longitudinal research* (pp. 32–57). Cambridge, England: Cambridge University Press.

Ryff, C. D., & Singer, B. (1998). The contours of human health. *Psychological Inquiry, 9,* 1–28.

Schaie, K. W. (1965). A general model for the study of developmental problems. *Psychological Bulletin, 64,* 92–107.

Schmitz, B. (1987). *Zeitreihenanalyse in der Psychologie. Verfahren zur Veränderungsmessung und Prozessdiagnostik.* Weinheim and Basel, Germany: Deutscher Studien Verlag.

Seligman, M. E. P. (1998). Message from the President of APA. Internetmeddelande inför den 106:e årliga APA kongressen [Internet message at the prospect of the 106th annual APA congress] available at http://www.apa.org/convention98/program/message.html (99-02-26).

Shepard, R. N. (1988). George Miller's data and the development of methods for representing cognitive structures. In W. Hirst (Ed.), *The making of cognitive science: Essays in honor of George A. Miller* (pp. 45–70). New York: Cambridge University Press.

Shepard, R. N., & Arabie, P. (1979). Additive clustering: Representation of similarities of discrete overlapping properties. *Psychological Review, 80,* 87–123.

Smith, L. B., & Thelen, E. (1993). *A dynamic systems approach to development. Applications.* Cambridge, MA: MIT Press.

Sokal, R. R., & Michener, C. D. (1958). A statistical method for evaluating systematic relationships. *University of Kansas Science Bulletin, 38,* 1409–1438.

Sörensen, A. B. (1998, October). *Statistical models and mechanisms of social processes.* Paper presented at the conference on Statistical Issues in the Social Sciences, Royal Swedish Academy of Sciences, Stockholm, Sweden.

Stattin, H., & Magnusson, D. (1990). Pubertal maturation in female development. In D. Magnusson (Series Ed.), *Paths through life* (Vol. 2). Hillsdale, NJ: Lawrence Erlbaum Associates.

Stattin, H., & Magnusson, D. (1996). Antisocial behavior—a holistic approach. *Development and Psychopathology, 8,* 617–645.

Stevens, S. S. (1946). On the theory of scales of measurement. *Science, 103,* 677–680.

Thelen, E. (1989). Self-organization in developmental processes: Can systems approaches work? In M. R. Gunnar & E. Thelen (Eds.), *Systems theory and development* (pp. 77–117). Hillsdale, NJ: Lawrence Erlbaum Associates.

Thelen, E., & Smith, L. B. (1998). Dynamic systems theory. In R. M. Lerner (Vol. Ed.) & W. Damon (Ed.-in-Chief), *Handbook of child psychology. Theoretical models of human development* (Vol. 1, pp. 563–634). New York: Wiley.

Thomae, H. (1979). The concept of development and life-span developmental psychology. In P. B. Baltes & J. O. G. Brim (Eds.), *Life-span development and behavior* (Vol. 2, pp. 281–312). New York: Academic Press.

Townsend, J. T., & Ashby, F. G. (1984). Measurement scales and statistics: The misconception misconceived. *Psychological Bulletin, 96,* 394–401.

Udy, S., Jr. (1959). 'Bureaucracy' and 'rationality' in Weber's organization theory: An empirical study. *American Sociological Review, 24,* 791–795.

Urban, H. B. (1979). The concept of development from a systems perspective. In P. B. Baltes & O. G. Brim (Eds.), *Life-span development and behavior* (Vol. 2, pp. 45–83). New York: Academic Press.

Vaillant, G. E. (1977). *Adaptation to life.* Boston: Little, Brown & Co.

Vallacher, R. B., & Nowak, A. (1994). *Dynamical systems in social psychology.* San Diego, CA: Academic Press.
Valsiner, J. (1984). Two alternative epistemological frameworks in psychology: The typological and variational modes of thinking. *The Journal of Mind and Behavior, 5,* 449–470.
Valsiner, J. (1986). *The individual subject and scientific psychology.* New York: Plenum.
Vargha, A. (2001). Kísérleti helyzetek és csoportok összehasonlítása új statisztikai módszerekkel. [Comparison of experimental conditions and groups by means of new *alkotás (Learning, initiatives, and creation)*]. Budapest: ELTE Eötvös Kiadó, 371–386.
Velleman, P. F., & Wilkinson, L. (1993). Nominal, ordinal, interval, and ratio typologies are misleading. *The American Statistician, 47,* 65–72.
von Eye, A. (1987). *BASIC programs for configural frequency analysis.* Unpublished computer program.
von Eye, A. (1990a). Configural frequency analysis of longitudinal multivariate responses. In A. von Eye (Ed.), *Statistical methods in longitudinal research* (Vol. 2, pp. 545–570). New York: Academic Press.
von Eye, A. (1990b). *Introduction to configural frequency analysis. The search for types and antitypes in cross-classifications.* Cambridge, England: Cambridge University Press.
von Eye, A., & Bergman, L. R. (1986). A note on numerical approximations of the binomial test in configural frequency analysis. *EDV in Medizin und Biologie, 17,* 108–111.
von Eye, A., & Clogg, C. C. (1994). *Latent variables analysis. Applications for developmental research.* London: Sage Publications.
von Eye, A., Spiel, C., & Wood, P. (1996). Configural frequency analysis in applied psychological research. *Applied Psychology: An International Review, 45,* 301–327.
Waller, N. G., & Meehl, P. E. (1998). *Multivariate taxometric procedures. Distinguishing types from continua.* Thousand Oaks, CA: Sage.
Wångby, M., Bergman, L. R., & Magnusson, D. (1999). Development of adjustment problems in girls: What syndromes emerge? *Child Development, 70,* 678–699.
Ward, J. H. (1963). Hierarchical grouping to optimize an objective function. *Journal of the American Statistical Association, 58,* 236–244.
Watson, J. B. (1913). Psychology as the behaviorist views it. *Psychological Review, 20,* 158–177.
Weber, M. (1947). *Theory of social and economic organization.* Translated by A. R. Henderson & T. Parsons, edited by T. Parsons. Glencoe, IL: Free Press.
Werts, C. E., & Linn, R. L. (1970). A general linear model for studying growth. *Psychological Bulletin, 73,* 17–22.
Wiener-Ehrlich, W. K. (1981). Hierarchical vs. generally overlapping models in psychiatric classification. *Multivariate Behavioral Research, 16,* 455–482.
Wikman, A. (1991). Att utveckla sociala indikatorer [To develop social indicators]. *Urval, No. 21.* Stockholm: Stockholm Statistiska Centralbyrån.
Wishart, D. (1969). An algorithm for hierarchical classification. *Biometrics, 25,* 165–170.
Wishart, D. (1987). *CLUSTAN* [User manual]. Cluster analysis software (pp. 4–10). Scotland: Computing Laboratory, University of St. Andrews.
Wohlwill, J. F. (1970). The age variable in psychological research. *Psychological Review, 77,* 49–64.
Wood, P. (1990). Applications of scaling to developmental research. In A. von Eye (Ed.), *Statistical methods in longitudinal research* (Vol. 1, pp. 225–256). New York: Academic Press.
Zoccollillo, M. (1992). Co-occurrence of conduct disorder and its adult outcomes with depressive and anxiety disorders: A review. *Journal of the American Academy of Child and Adolescent Psychiatry, 31,* 547–556.
Zubin, J. (1937). The determination of response patterns in personality adjustment inventories. *Journal of Educational Psychology, 28,* 401–413.

AUTHOR INDEX

A

Achenbach, T. M., 183
Ahn, W., 72
Aldenderfer, M. S., 54, 113
Allen, V. L., 6, 14, 26
Allport, G. W., 135
Anastasi, A., 35
Anderberg, M. R., 54, 56
Andersson, T., 21, 22
Andrews, D. F., 63
Arabie, P., 54, 63, 98, 113, 129, 163
Arcus, D., 13, 50, 195
Asarnow, J. R., 134
Asendorpf, J. B., 36
Ashby, F. G., 37

B

Backteman, G., 136
Bailey, K. D., 32, 35, 190
Baltes, P. B., 8, 16, 17
Barton, S., 30, 92
Bateson, P. P. G., 14
Baumgardner, M. H., 193
Bereiter, C., 42
Bergman, L. R., 6, 13, 19, 20, 23, 25, 26, 29, 31, 32, 36, 38, 39, 41, 42, 43, 44, 47, 48, 50, 53, 58, 59, 60, 67, 72, 79, 85, 87, 88, 90, 92, 94, 95, 101, 119, 134, 135, 136, 139, 156, 166, 182, 185, 187, 188, 189, 190, 196
Berliner, L. M., 192
Bishop, Y. M. M., 44, 81, 85
Blashfield, R. K., 32, 54, 68, 97, 101, 113
Block, J., 18, 31, 36, 87, 88
Bollen, K. A., 30
Breckenridge, J. N., 101

C

Cairns, B. D., 94
Cairns, R. B., 6, 8, 11, 50, 94, 195
Carmichael, J. W., 63
Caspi, A., 36
Casti, J. L., 31, 92
Cattell, R. B., 32, 63
Chatterjee, S., 192
Cicchetti, D., 13
Clogg, C. C., 20, 44, 70
Coie, J. D., 134
Colinvaux, P., 31
Collins, L. M., 44, 81, 85.
Cooper, H., 135
Cooper, M., 68, 90, 150
Cormack, R. M., 56
Costello, E. J., 11
Coulter, M. A., 63
Cowen, E. L, 135
Cox, A., 43
Crick, F., 194

Cronbach, L. J., 51, 57, 96, 193
Cudeck, R., 29
Curran, P. J., 30

D

Dale, M. B., 62
De Soete, G., 61
DeNeve, K. M, 135
DeSarbo, W. S., 61
Diday, E., 56
Diener, E., 135
Du Troit, S., 29
Dubes, R., 97
Dunér, A., 27, 134, 137
Durlak, J. A., 135

E

Edelbrock, C., 50, 53, 58
Eklund, G., 6
Ekman, G., 35,
Elder, G. H., 11
Eliason, S. R., 44
El-Khouri, B. M., 44, 47, 72, 90, 92, 119, 139, 156, 166, 196,
Epstein, D. B, 30
Everitt, B., 54, 56
Eysenck, H. J., 36

F

Feinberg, S. E., 44, 81, 85
Ford, D. H., 29
Fortier, J. J., 63
Frank, O., 61

G

Gangestad, S., 13, 31
Gariépy, J. L., 195
Ghisletta, P., 29, 84, 191
Gleick, J., 191
Gleser, G. C., 57, 96
Gordon, A. D., 54, 61, 63, 68
Greenwald, A. G., 193
Grego, J. M., 44
Gregson, R. A. M., 54
Groves, R. M., 44, 101
Gustafson, S. B., 36

H

Haberman, S. J., 48
Harary, F., 61
Harré, R., 5, 6
Harris, C. W., 42
Hartigan, J. A., 54
Hawkins, J., 134
Hellvik, O., 20
Hendersson, J. T., 63
Henry, N. W., 61, 81
Hildebrand, D. K., 95
Holland, P. W., 44, 81, 85
Holm, S., 78
Hood, K. E., 195
Hubert, L. J., 54, 98, 113, 129, 163

J

Jackson, A. E., 191
Jahoda, M., 186
Jain, A. K., 97
Jardine, N., 63
John, O. P., 36
Johnson, S. C., 62
Jones, C. J., 84

K

Kagan, J., 13, 50, 183, 195
Kelso, J. A. S., 30, 191, 192
Kitchener, R. F., 8
Krauth, J., 34, 36, 46, 74, 75, 79, 80, 158, 173

L

Laing, J., D., 95
Lambert, J. M., 62
Lance, G. N., 62, 57, 67
Lazarsfeld, P. F., 61, 81
Lehmacher, W., 79
Lerman, I., 56
Lerner, R. M., 8, 10
Lewin, K., 50, 195
Lienert, G. A., 46, 74, 75, 80, 94, 95, 158, 173
Lieppe, M. R., 193
Lindenberger, U., 8
Ling, R. F., 63
Linn, R. L., 42

Long, B., 134
Lord, F. M., 42
Lorr, M., 59
Lucas, R. E., 135
Luthar, S. S, 134

M

Macnaughton-Smith, P., 62
MacQueen, J., 63
Magnusson, D., 4, 5, 6, 7, 8, 9, 10, 11, 12, 13, 14, 15, 18, 19, 20, 21, 22, 23, 25, 26, 27, 29, 32, 38, 39, 41, 43, 44, 50, 87, 92, 94, 134, 135, 136, 137, 182, 183, 185, 187, 188, 189, 193, 194
Mahoney, J. L., 8, 135, 187
Männikö, K., 36
Markman, H. J., 134
Mayr, E., 9
McArdle, J. J., 30
McQuitty, L. L., 62
Meehl, P. E., 32, 46, 70, 71
Michener, C. D., 62
Miller, K. F., 54
Milligan, G. W., 59, 60, 68, 90, 96, 98, 101, 102, 121, 129, 150
Misiak, H., 36
Miyamoto, S., 67
Mockett, L. G., 62
Morey, L. C., 68, 97, 101
Mumford, M. D., 86
Muthén, B., 30
Muthén, L., 30

N

Nanda, H., 96
Nesselroade, J. R., 17, 29, 84, 101, 191
Nowak, A., 30
Nurmi, J. E., 36

O

Olweus, D., 134
Owens, W. A., 86

P

Peter, P., 56
Pickles, A., 197

Pierzchala, M., 44
Poincaré, H., 191
Pratkanis, A. R., 193
Pulkkinen, L., 36, 183

Q

Quinton, D., 43

R

Radhakrishnan, B., 59
Rajaratnam, N., 96
Ramey, S. L., 134
Raudenbush, S. W., 30
Reese, H. W., 101
Ritzer, D. R., 36
Robins, R. W., 36
Rodkin, P. C., 6, 50
Rogosa, D., 43
Rohlf, F. J., 63
Rönkä, A., 183
Rosenthal, H., 95
Ross, G. J. S., 63
Rudinger, G., 189
Rutter, M., 16, 43, 134, 197
Ryff, C. D., 135

S

Schaie, K. W., 17
Schmitz, B., 29, 191
Seligman, M. E. P., 135
Sexton, V., 36
Shepard, R. N., 54, 63
Shure, M. B., 134
Sibson, R., 63
Simon, J. C., 56
Singer, B., 135
Skinner, H. A., 68, 97, 101
Smith, H. L., 135
Smith, L. B., 7, 30, 92, 191
Sneath, P. H. A., 63
Snidman, N., 13, 50, 195
Snyder, M., 13, 31
Sokal, R. R., 62
Solomon, H., 63
Sörbom, D., 29
Sörensen, A. B., 6, 190
Spiel, C., 75, 94
Stattin, H., 6, 14, 10, 134, 136, 183

Staudinger, U. M., 8
Stevens, S. S., 37
Suh, E. M., 135

T

Thelen, E., 7, 12, 30, 92, 191
Thomae, H., 9
Törestad, B., 21, 22, 189
Townsend, J. T., 37

U

Udy, S., Jr., 35
Urban, H. B., 7

V

Vaillant, G. E., 135
Vallacher, R. B., 30
Valsiner, J., 13, 31, 84, 195
Velleman, P. F., 37
von Eye, A., 20, 46, 47, 75, 76, 79, 90, 94, 158, 173, 188

W

Waller, N. G., 32, 71

Wångby, M., 185
Ward, J. H., 62
Watson, J. B, 193
Watt, N. F., 134
Weber, M., 35
Werts, C. E., 42
West, S. G., 134
Wiener-Ehrlich, W. K., 32, 46
Wikman, A., 43
Wilkinson, L., 37
Willett, J. B., 43
Williams, W. T., 62, 57, 67
Wishart, D., 59, 63
Wohlwill, J. F., 16
Wood, P., 45, 75, 85, 94
Wugalter, S. E., 44, 81, 85

Y

Yilmaz, M. R., 192
Yonce, L. J., 46, 70
Yule, B., 43

Z

Zetterblom, G., 27, 134, 137
Zoccolillo, M., 185
Zubin, J., 74
zur Oeveste, H., 94

SUBJECT INDEX

A

Adaptive, 8, 9, 12, 18, 20, 23, 25
Adaptive ability, 8, 9
Adjustment, 3, 24, 25, 33, 38, 41, 136, 181, 182, 186, 187
Adjustment problems, 25, 33, 38, 39, 41, 175, 177
Agglomerative methods, 62, 63, 68, 113
Aggression, 25, 32, 136, 137, 140, 154, 156, 158, 175–179, 181–183
Algorithm, 64
Anti-classes, 50
Antitype(s), 48–50, 75–80, 90, 117, 161, 169, 172, 173, 175–178
ASED, *see* Euclidean distance

B

Binominal test, 79
Biological maturation, 10, 14–16
Bonferroni correction, 78

C

CENTROID, 104, 105, 123, 125, 126, 152, 153, 161, 169
Centroid (methods), 32, 33, 66, 98, 99, 101, 102, 150, 152, 154, 162–164, 169, 170
CFA, configural frequency analysis, 2, 34, 46–48, 50, 74–80, 82, 83, 85, 94, 95, 104, 105, 117–120, 128, 173, 175, 177, 179, 187, 188
Chi-square component, 76, 125
Chronological age, 14–16
Classifier, 72–73
Classification, 28, 31–38, 41, 44, 46, 47, 52, 55, 60, 61, 68, 69, 71, 72, 74, 81, 86–89, 90–92, 94–101, 113, 129, 195
Classification phase, 60
Classificatory system, 93
CLUSTER, 104, 114–116, 140, 148
Cluster analysis, 2, 32–34, 36–38, 58–61, 67, 74, 81, 82, 86, 87, 89, 90, 97, 102, 113, 114, 138, 139, 148, 150, 173, 187, 189
Cluster centroids, 32, 33, 102,
Clustering, 45, 96, 97, 100, 102, 113
Conditional probability, 69
Conduct problems, 32, 33, 147, 183, 184
Confirmatory set, 79
Contingency tables, 46, 81, 90
Correlation, 14, 19, 21, 22, 24, 37, 38, 41, 49, 98
Cross-sectional, 1, 2, 14, 15, 24, 36, 46, 88, 94, 95, 117, 138, 147, 161–162, 180, 195
Cross-sectional matrix, 15
Cross-tabulation, 2, 80, 90, 95, 98, 157

215

CWRITE, 104, 128

D

Data description, 106
Data pre-processing, 106
DENSE, 104, 129, 130
Density seeking, 63
DESCRIBE, 104, 107, 108, 140–142
Descriptive methods, 45, 85
Development track, 46, 92
Developmental process, 16, 17, 21, 23, 25, 27, 29, 46, 86, 189, 194
Developmental research, 6, 4, 9–12, 16–20, 23, 85, 193
Developmental science, 6, 11, 17, 192
Dichotomized, 21, 75–78, 95, 173, 187
Dichotomy, 117
Disharmony, 21, 22, 136, 137, 140, 146, 147, 154–156, 175–177, 179, 183–186, 188
Dissimilarity, 2, 32, 36, 37, 54–58, 59, 63, 64, 65–67, 93, 97–99, 146, 158, 172
Dissimilarity matrix, 37, 59, 97, 98, 158
Divisive methods, 62
Dynamic interaction, 8, 9
Dynamic system, 1, 13, 30, 92, 183, 191

E

Environmental factors, 17, 23
Euclidean distance, 37, 56–58, 66, 93, 98, 99, 107, 109, 123, 125, 140, 154, 162
EV error sum of squares, 99
EVALUATE, 104, 105, 129, 131
EXACON, 81, 90, 98, 104, 105, 125, 127, 128, 156, 169, 178
Exact cell-wise tests, 2
Expected frequency, 34, 49, 75, 80, 117, 125, 156, 166
Explained error sum of squares ESS, 66, 89, 99, 114, 115, 117, 129, 150, 162, 164, 166
Exploratory set, 79
Externalizing (adjustment) problems, 184, 185

G

Generalizability, 38, 97–101
Gestalt, 1, 31, 101
Good adjustment, 154
Goodness-of-fit, 129

H

Hierachical agglomerative methods, 113
Hierachical methods, 61
HLM, 30
Holistic, 1, 6, 8–11, 13, 17, 18, 22, 25, 26, 28
Holistic framework, 31
Holistic interactionistic paradigm, 1, 11, 17–28, 31
Holistic model, 7, 11, 17
Holistic view, 7–10, 12, 16, 193
Holistic-interactionistic, 6, 8, 9, 13, 17, 18, 22, 26, 27, 192
Holm-procedure, 79
Homogeneity, 55, 150

I

IDA program, 6, 14, 21
Identification phase, 59
Idiographic, 7
Imputation , 39, 44, 51, 107, 138, 140
IMPUTE, 104–111, 119, 140
Individual change, 47, 93, 125, 152, 156, 169, 178
Individual differences, 7, 12, 14–16, 30
Individual level, 22
Individual stability, 47, 125, 150, 152, 156, 169, 172, 178, 182, 183
Individual value pattern, 36, 37
Inhibiton, 183, 184
Integrated organism, 7, 13, 16
Integrated person-environment system, 7–9
Interaction structure analysis, ISA, 80
Interactional paradigm, 1
Interindividual differences, 11, 14, 31, 40, 84, 86, 88
Internalizing (adjustment) problems, 184, 185
Ipsative stability, 88
I-State as Objects Analysis, ISOA, 2, 47, 91–93, 104, 105, 119, 121, 122, 132, 166, 168–172, 174, 187

SUBJECT INDEX

I–State Sequency Analysis, ISSA, 47

L

Lack of concentration, 32, 136, 137, 140, 146, 147, 154–156, 175–177, 179, 184
Latent class, 46, 81, 85
Latent class analysis, 44, 85, 69, 70
Latent class probability, 69
Latent profile analysis, 69
Latent structure analysis, 2, 69, 81
Latent trait analysis, 69
Latent transition analysis, LTA, 2, 44, 85
LICUR, 2, 21, 47, 68, 88, 89, 91, 95, 114, 132, 138, 139, 164, 169, 172, 180, 187
Linear models, 19, 23, 44
Linear regression models, 20, 25
LISA, 95
LOGLIN, 2, 46, 81
Log-linear modeling, 2, 46, 81, 85
Longitudinal design, 16, 17
Longitudinal perspective, 46
Longitudinal typology, 36, 88
Low school motivation, 32, 136, 137, 140, 146, 147, 154–156, 175–177, 179, 188

M

Mahalanobis distance, 57
Maladjustment, 24, 76, 80, 82, 180, 182, 183
MAMIN, 48, 49, 184
Mass significance problem, 78, 90, 158, 169, 175
Measurement model(s), 18, 19
Minkowski, 57, 58
Missing data (values), 12, 43, 44, 107, 109, 138, 140, 143
Mode seeking, 63
Model-based methods, 2, 44, 81, 85
Motor restlessnes, 21, 22, 32, 136, 137, 140, 154–156, 158, 172, 175–177, 179, 181, 184, 187, 188
Multidetermined, 7, 8
Multidimensional scaling, 45, 85, 162, 163
Multidimensional data, 74

Multiple time–series, 29
Multiproblems, 177
Multivariate space, 172

N

Negative adjustment, 134, 135, 188
NOLIDS nonlinear dynamic systems, 30, 31, 191, 192
Nomothetic, 7, 20, 23
Nonlinear models, 19

O

Observed frequency, 34, 48, 49, 75–79, 117, 25, 156
Ontogenesis, 13
Optimization–partitioning techniques, 62
Outliers, 2, 50, 58, 60

P

Pattern, 1–3, 12, 13, , 27, 31, 34, 36, 37, 47, 85, 86, 94, 172, 173, 175–179, 182, 183, 186, 195
Pattern analysis, 13, 26, 27, 37, 38, 51
Pattern development, 50, 84–86, 94, 195
Pattern-oriented analysis, 51, 103, 105
Personality types, 13, 87
Person-oriented approach, 1, 18, 26, 38, 44, 135, 189, 192
Point-biseral correlation, 98, 99
Positive adaption, 135
Power, 79, 81, 85
Profile, 2, 31, 32, 34, 38, 43, 47, 48, 74, 85, 87, 88, 97, 101, 119, 147, 166, 171, 196
Protective factors, 134, 135
Proximity, 55, 69, 107, 109, 113
P-technique, 29, 30, 191

Q

Q-factor analysis, 53, 63, 87
Q-sort, 87
Q-sort methology, 87
Quasi-absolute scaling, 41, 42, 196

R

RAND index, 129, 163,

RANDOM, 104, 105, 128
Random half, 161–164, 166, 172, 187
Random samples, 91, 101, 128
Rank order stability, 16
Relocate, 90
RELOCATE, 59, 104, 105, 115, 117, 118, 128
RESIDAN, 2, 50, 58, 59, 89, 93
Residue, 50, 59, 88, 89, 100, 109, 146, 161, 166
RESIDUE, 104, 111, 112, 119, 140, 144, 145

S

School adjustment, 134, 135, 138, 147, 173, 180, 182, 186
School performance, 147
SHAKE, 104, 105, 128
Short-term development, 54–57, 92
Similarity, 2, 27, 33, 34, 37, 38, 45, 52, 54–57, 87, 88, 94, 96, 97, 123
Similarity matrix, 37
SIMULATE, 100, 104, 105, 121, 123, 124, 128
Simulation analysis, 121
SLEIPNER, 3, 44, 51, 58, 79, 91, 94, 98, 100, 101, 103–105, 107, 115, 128, 132, 136, 138, 145, 147, 150, 152, 156, 157, 166, 175
Snapshot-and-linking approach, 88
States, 3, 13, 31, 92, 93, 129
Stochastic process, 7, 8
Stockholm Laboratory for Development Science, 103
Structural change, 93, 123, 151, 166
Structural equation modeling, SEM, 19, 29, 38

Structural stability, 93, 123, 150–152, 166, 182
SUBIND, 104, 105, 119, 132, 133
Subindividual, 129, 132
Subjective well-being, 135
Subsystem, 8, 12, 13, 17, 18

T

Taxonicity, 70, 71
Teachers ratings, 136, 137
Theory driven, 2
Time-independent, 92
Timidity, 137, 140, 146, 147, 154–156, 158, 161, 172, 175–177, 179, 180–185, 187, 188
Trichotomized, 46, 76, 78, 95
Trichotomy, 117
Twin, 44, 146
Type(s), 32, 33, 49, 80, 87, 90, 91, 95, 75, 76, 78, 117, 125, 156, 161, 172, 173, 175–178, 180, 195
Typology, 32–35, 53, 195–196

U

Ultrametricity, 61
Undivided organism, 7

V

Value profiles, 31, 33, 74, 86–89, 93, 99, 119, 146
Variable approach, 18–20, 23, 24, 31, 194
Variable-oriented approach, 26, 50

W

Ward´s method, 66–68, 89, 113, 166
White spots, 2, 13, 50, 58, 93, 173, 185, 195